Sunset over Lake Nona. Photo by Tom Hurst

Sunset Skyline from Lake Eola of Orlando, Florida. Photo by Bill Bachmann

Central Florida Visions

Expanding Orlando's Horizons

Central Florida Visions
Expanding Orlando's Horizons

Written by: Joe Lee

Stephen Hung, Publisher

Staff for *Central Florida Visions*
Art Director: Thad Pickett
Managing Editor: Julie Clark
Sales Manager: Henry Hintermeister
Associate Publisher: Tamera Nielsen
Profile Writer: Edward Schmidt, Jr.
Staff Writers: Patricia Barletta,
Barbara Bellesi, and Melissa Gentile
Photo Editor: Tom Hurst

PAGODA GROUP
PUBLISHING SOLUTIONS

Needham, Massachusetts

First Edition
ISBN: 0-9759736-1-4

CITYSCAPES
SERIES

The Lake Eola landscape in Orlando offers a visitor water, the skyline, the sky, and various birds. Photo by Lee Foster

Fireworks light up the sky on the 4th of July over Lake Eola. Photo by Tom Hurst

Table of Contents

Citrus Industry with Orange Tree Near Winter Haven, Florida. Photo by Bill Bachmann

Today's Orlando—with its sprawling theme park resort complexes, massive convention center, world renown golf communities like Isleworth, Bay Hill and Lake Nona, luxurious shopping malls with retailers like Neiman-Marcus, Bloomingdale's and Nordstrom, gleaming office and condominium buildings overlooking Lake Eola, and a downtown arena where the NBA's Orlando Magic play—is light years away from the city I first saw almost forty years ago.

My initial introduction to Orlando was in 1967. Bill Darden and I were driving from Waycross, Georgia, to Lakeland, Florida, to open the first Red Lobster restaurant. Orange groves dotted the landscape and the sweet fragrance of the orange blossoms wafted through the air. Back then, Central Florida was known more for its citrus industry, not a warm and friendly mouse named Mickey.

Bill's dream was to create a casual dining seafood restaurant. He had already made his mark in the restaurant business—he was president of the Georgia Restaurant Association and operated several successful restaurants in Georgia and Florida, including the legendary Gary's Duck Inn on Orange Blossom Trail in Orlando. It was the best-known seafood restaurant in Orlando at the time.

Bill assembled a team that shared his dream. Wally Buckley, Charlie Woodsby, Al Woods, Bill's brother Denham, Gus Gornto and I joined him to open

A phony fish statue seen in Orlando, FL. - Photo by Carl M. Purcell

a seafood restaurant with great food and service that would be positioned between fine dining and quick-serve restaurants. The concept seems like a no-brainer now, but back then lots of people wondered if it would work.

Let's just say it worked out pretty well. That simple idea evolved into a company with more than 140,000 employees—nearly one out of every 900 American workers—and is now one of only two Fortune 500 companies based in Orlando. Today, we have 7,000 employees in the Orlando area, including 1,100 at corporate headquarters in Orlando Central Park.

As Bill and I drove through Central Florida back in 1967, we talked about our plans for the new restaurant. In fact, we got so involved in the conversation that we missed the Lakeland exit and drove all the way to Tampa! We chose Lakeland because we already had the seafood restaurant in Orlando, and because we had to be close to the Gulf as a source of fresh fish, since this was in the days before refrigerated trucks.

We opened our first Red Lobster in Lakeland with sixty employees, none of us knew quite what to expect, and, frankly, we were stunned by the reaction. The restaurant was packed every night, and within two weeks we had to hire thirty more people, and even had to redesign the kitchen so we could handle higher volumes of business. It far surpassed even our most optimistic expectations!

*I*t wasn't long after the opening that Bill decided to move company headquarters across the Georgia/Florida border to Orlando. At the time our plan was to grow Red Lobster into a regional restaurant company serving the Southeast (we couldn't have imagined it would eventually evolve into a national chain), and with Walt Disney announcing plans to build Disney World, we knew the Orlando Airport would give us easy access to other cities as we expanded. Orlando would be a perfect platform for growth.

We quickly established strong business relationships in Orlando. For instance, we worked with the old First National Bank of Orlando, now SunTrust, which helped us finance our first Red Lobster. As our company grew, we knew how important that relationship with SunTrust was. For one thing, we were buying huge amounts of fish and needed to make guarantees to the fishermen. In those early days we didn't have a lot of spare cash, so Al Woods sat down with the SunTrust people and came up with the bank's first "fish loan." That's just one example of how the bank has always tried to grow the Central Florida community.

I moved with my family to Orlando in 1969 and began opening Red Lobster restaurants in Orlando and

Chihuly Glass as seen at Millenia Gallery. Photo by Tom Hurst

in other states. We first lived in the Conway area near downtown, where and my two children attended Conway Elementary. Later, we moved to a five-acre spread in Gotha, which was out in the country back then. We had a couple of cows, some horses for my daughter and motorbike trails to ride. Today, it's part of a single-family housing development in the booming southwest corridor of Orlando. Celebrities like golf greats Tiger Woods, Arnold Palmer and NBA superstar Grant Hill who reside in Windermere call this area of Orlando home. The celebrities are, no doubt, attracted to Central Florida by many of the same things all Orlandoans love about our city—a great climate, a world-class airport, a never-ending list of things to do and a strong sense of community.

The strength of Orlando's community spirit and pride comes from its variety of close knit neighborhoods such as downtown areas like Conway, Colonialtown, Lake Como, Thornton Park, Delaney Park, and Lake Highland; Winter Park, which is reminiscent of a small New England town; innovative urban villages like Avalon Park, Celebration, and Baldwin Park and master-planned golf course communities like Heathrow, MetroWest and Alaqua.

Orlando is continuing to grow at a mercurial pace. Thirty-eight years ago there were fewer than 400,000 people in the metropolitan are. Today, we are approaching 2 million people. Our new citizens—many of whom were introduced to Orlando through a theme park vacation visit—come from all over the globe including the U.S., The Caribbean, Europe, South America, and the Far East. Orlando has become a true melting pot and the influence of the various new cultures is evident whether you're sipping ale in an Irish pub in downtown, dining on Caribbean flavored delicacies at one of our Bahama Breeze restaurants or shopping at a French boutique at Millennia Mall.

One of the fastest growing housing markets in the country, Orlando is building homes at an unprecedented pace in outlying communities like Windermere, Winter Garden, Ocoee, Longwood, Altamonte Springs, Apopka, Oviedo, Winter Springs and Kissimmee. It seems there is no shortage of people in the world who want to share in the Orlando lifestyle.

With Orlando's phenomenal growth in the past four decades, it's hard to believe how small the city was back then. Our first restaurant in Orlando was on Lee Road. At

Yellow Tabebuia tree on Via Tuscany in Winter Park.
Photo by Phil Eschbach

*Lou Pearlman and Governor
Jeb Bush of Florida.*

the time, there was a Howard Johnson's restaurant there and not much else. It was actually considered to be on the outskirts of Orlando, but we figured the area would grow.

Another restaurant that seemed a long way from town at the time was a Red Lobster we built in Altamonte Springs. Altamonte Mall was just on the drawing board at that time, and we were often asked, "What if that mall doesn't get built?" Some also felt that we should stick to building restaurants closer to population centers in Winter Park and Orlando. Looking back, we feel pretty good about our decision!

The restaurant we really took a risk on was a Red Lobster on International Drive. The only thing there at the time was a motel on Kirkman Road and another motel at the other end of International Drive at Sand Lake Road.

It's amazing when I think about the remoteness of the area back then. Now Orlando's tourism infrastructure, which encompasses International Drive, is considered one of the best, if not the best, in the world. Today, Orlando has 114,000 hotel rooms, three major world renowned theme park resort complexes, a convention center with over 2 million square feet of exhibit space, upscale shopping malls, over 100 golf courses within thirty minutes of downtown, and a lengthy restaurant line-up.

While Orlando represents a vacation destination to so many people around the world, to me, my fellow citizens and my company, it is home. In fact, Orlando has been more than our corporate home, it's where we've tested and launched all of our successful concepts since Red Lobster. We opened the first Olive Garden and Bahama Breeze on International Drive, the first Smokey Bones on Colonial Drive and the first Seasons 52. We found, as other companies have, that Orlando is a great market for testing ideas, partly because we have so many visitors from around the United States, and even the world. We can do research here and find out what people in, say, Illinois think about our ideas.

Our Seasons 52 restaurant, a contemporary fine dining experience on Sand Lake Road—a three-block stretch locals call "Restaurant Row"—is part of a recent trend in Orlando to develop a world-class culinary reputation. Orlando will forever be known for its plethora of excellent, casual, affordable restaurants but the recent arrival of celebrity chefs like Norman Van Aken at the Ritz-Carlton Orlando, Melissa Kelly at the JW Marriott, Todd English at the Walt Disney World Dolphin and Emeril Lagasse at two Universal restaurants has brought an exciting sizzle to Orlando's culinary world.

The Living Seas exhibit at Epcot Center, Orlando, FL.
Photo by Carl M. Purcell

Like world class chefs, our leaders in Orlando are excited about what they love most—Orlando. The passion I see in leaders of this community is tremendous, and it has manifested itself in so many civic institutions and great businesses. We've also been fortunate to have strong political leaders. I think back on what past Mayor Bill Frederick did to help shape our city, as well as the contributions of many other mayors before and since. Bill set the tone. He knew Orlando would only grow by expanding its economic base beyond agriculture, and he understood the importance of continuing to preserve the area's beauty, even as it grew. In many ways, Orlando is even more beautiful today than when Bill Darden and I first drove through in 1967.

We're just one of many corporate success stories in Orlando. The Martin Company came here to start an aerospace business, and today Lockheed-Martin leads the world in its industry. I remember going to meetings years ago with a young fellow named David Hughes. He had a family business and was determined to build it into an international company in the Fortune 500. Today Hughes Supply is Orlando's other locally-based Fortune 500 company. Orlando is also an emerging high-tech center with a growing number of companies involved in laser applications, simulation technology, and video game design.

A key component in Orlando's high-tech maturation and an integral part of the fabric of every day life in Orlando is the University of Central Florida. When Bill and I first came here it was called Florida Technological University, and it was just opening its doors. Today UCF has more than 40,000 students and is one of the largest university's in the nation, with top notch engineering and business departments and one of the finest hospitality schools in the nation—the Rosen School of Hospitality Management.

The emergence of Orlando, the modern day metropolis, of course, coincides with the arrival of our great theme parks. Starting with Walt Disney's vision to transform thousands of acres of palmetto-dotted Central Florida land into Walt Disney World, the new Orlando was born. Later, SeaWorld and Universal arrived on the scene and the theme parks eventually expanded into full-fledge resort destinations with nighttime entertainment complexes, lavish, themed hotels, golf courses, and restaurants. More importantly, they created thousands of

Top Left: Beautiful Sunrise at Orange County Convention Center in Orlando, Florida. Photo by Bill Bachmann

jobs for Central Floridians and spawned countless ancillary businesses that have propelled Orlando's economy.

Thanks to the theme park and hospitality industry as well as other great corporate citizens, there is a superb quality of life in Orlando. From wonderful museums like the Orlando Museum of Art, Charles Hosmer Morse Museum, and Orange County Regional History Center to sports events like the Capital One Citrus Bowl game on New Year's Day, Bay Hill Invitational and Walt Disney World Classic PGA Tour golf tournaments to our beautiful parks like Lake Eola and Wekiva Springs State Park, Orlando is a wonderful place to visit and live.

Orlando is now one of the nation's major metropolitan areas. Yet, even with its phenomenal growth and change, it still retains that small, hometown feeling it had when I first moved here. Yes, you can still smell the orange blossoms when you drive around town. That's one reason I'm staying in this wonderful part of Florida when I retire as Chairman of Darden in December 2005.

Top Right: A floral sundial greets visitors at the Henry P. Leu Gardens in Orlando.
Photo by Lee Foster

The American Flag greets visitors to the Orange County Convention Center. Photo by Tom Hurst

Clarence Clemence performs at a WMMO free downtown concert.
Photo by Tom Hurst

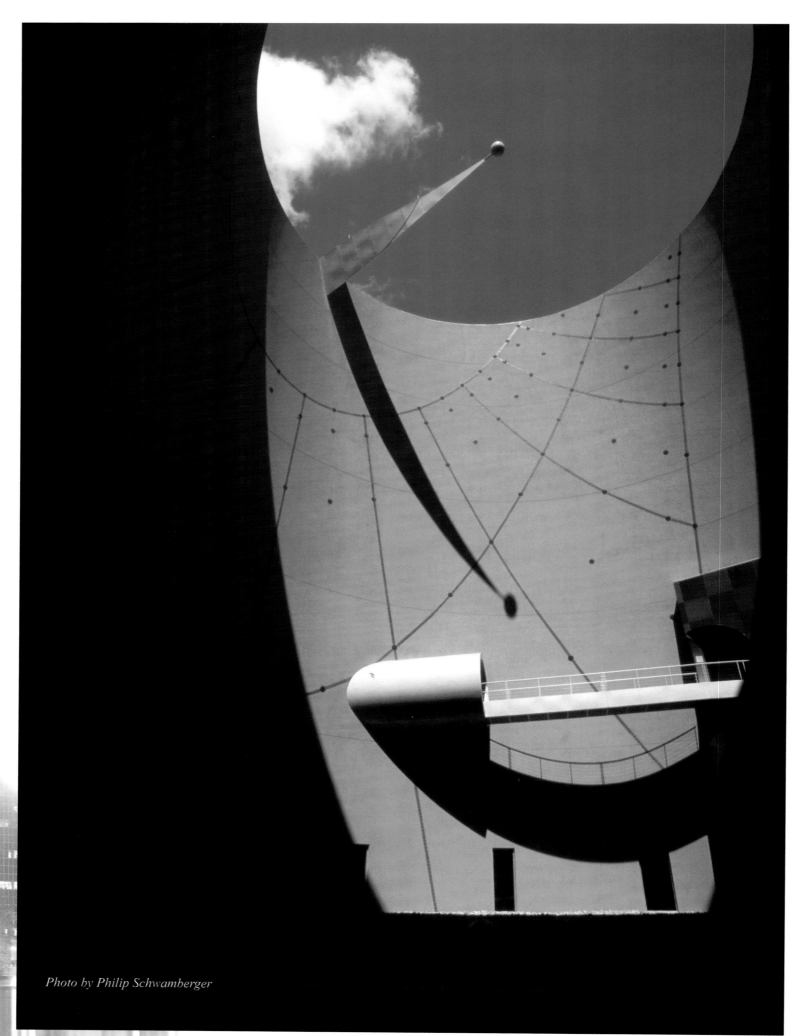

Photo by Philip Schwamberger

Children's Museum, Orlando, FL.
Photo by Carl M. Purcell

Photo by Nancy Granger

Office building, Celebration
Photo by Eric Breitenbach

A white alligator is among the
curiosities at Alligator Farm in
St. Augustine.
Photo by Lee Foster

Bergamo's Restaurant, Mercado - Photo by Michael Lowry

Theme park worker and child tourist, Orlando
Photo by Eric Breitenbach

Photo by Nancy Granger

Marina on Lake Monroe in Sanford, Florida.
Photo by Bill Bachmann

Mural painted on downtown building by artist Pablo in memory of 9-11.
Photo by Tom Hurst

Fresh orchids grace the lobby of Gaylord Palms Resort.
Photo by Tom Hurst

Aerial Skyline of Downtown and Lake Eola Orlando, Florida. Photo by Bill Bachmann

The historic El Castillo Fort protected St. Augustine from sea attacks.
Photo by Lee Foster

Clown make-up for visitors at Circus World.
Photo by Carl M. Purcell

Max's Grille, Celebration, FL
Photo by Michael Lowry

Works by Chihuly, Miro, and
Chadwick can be seen at the
Millenia Gallery.
Photo by Tom Hurst

Airboat captains are available to take riders on an exploration of the St. Johns River near Orlando. - Photo by Eric Dusenbery

Fountain and sculpture by Albin Polasek in Central Park in downtown Winter Park. Photo by Phil Eschbach

Seafood entre at Restaurant K. Photo by Michael Lowry

Skyline with City Hall of Orlando, Florida.
Photo by Bill Bachmann

Grilled local fish is a delicious meal at restaurants along the central Florida coast. Photo by Lee Foster

Painting seen in the Mennello Museum in Orlando, FL.
Photo by Carl M. Purcell

Orlando sky at sunset. Photo by Tom Husrt

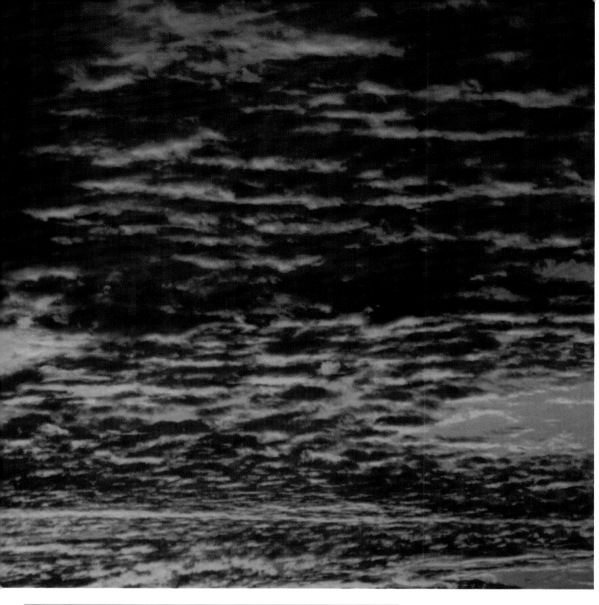

Photo by Nancy Granger

One of the oldest and grandest oak trees in the Orlando region can be seen at a public park. Photo by Lee Foster

Health Central, Winter Garden, FL
Photo by Michael Lowry

Mayor Bob Carr Performing Arts
Center in Orlando, FL.
Photo by Carl M. Purcell

Orlando's "antique row" is along North Orange Street. Photo by Lee Foster

Drive-in movie, Sanford Photo by Eric Breitenbach

Dusk at the Orlando City Hall on Orange Avenue in downtown
Orlando. Photo by Phil Eschbach

Desert at Wolfgang Duck's Restaurant. Photo by Michael Lowry

*Painted Orlando bus seen in
downtown Orlando, FL.
Photo by Ann F. Purcell*

*Patrons dine at Hue Restaurant
in the new downtown of Orlando.
Photo by Lee Foster*

Exclamation point sculpture at the Art Museum and Science Museum complex of Orlando, FL. Photo by Carl M. Purcell

Exedra in Kraft Azalea Gardens overlooking Lake Osceola in Winter Park. Photo by Phil Eschbach

Teammates pose for a shot during production of Noggin's Girls vs. Boys. Photo by Tom Hurst

The historic lighthouse in St. Augustine guided ships along the Florida coast.
Photo by Lee Foster

Photo by Philip Schwamberger

The newest addition to the downtown landscape is the new LYNX Headquarters and LYNX Central Station.
Photo by Tom Hurst

Photo by the University of Central Florida News and Information

Orlando Museum of Art at Loch Haven Park on Mills Avenue in Orlando. Photo by Phil Eschbach

Citrus industry truck full of oranges near Winter Haven, Florida.
Photo by Bill Bachmann

A CSX train worker makes a stop in Orlando.
Photo by Eric Dusenbery

Lee's Lakeside overlooking Lake Eola. Photo by Michael Lowry

Mayor Bob Carr Performing Arts Center in Orlando, FL.
Photo by Carl M. Purcell

Works by Dale Chihuly and Andy Warhol can be seen at the Millenia Gallery. Photo by Tom Hurst

View over Orlando from a hot air balloon. - Photo by Carl M. Purcell

Photo by Nancy Granger

Tourists on vacation with Pink Flamingos at Silver Springs near Ocala, Florida. Photo by Bill Bachmann

Horticultural enthusiasts will want to visit the Harry P. Leu House and Gardens in Orlando. Photo by Lee Foster

The Cherokee School was
built in 1926 and is a fine
example of Mediterranean style
historic architecture.
Photo by Eric Dusenbery

Portobello Yacht Club
Photo by Michael Lowry

Demonstrations by re-enactors about early Florida life intrigue visitors at Old St. Augustine Village in St. Augustine.
Photo by Lee Foster

Dawn of Christmas Day on newly bricked Park Avenue in Winter Park.
Photo by Phil Eschbach

Colorful architectural glass building downtown in Orlando, Florida.
Photo by Bill Bachmann

Azaleas bloom at Orlando's Dickson Azalea Park.
Photo by Tom Husrt

Curvy necks of flamingos. Photo by Carl M. Purcell

Triathlete, Lake Mary - Photo by Eric Breitenbach

Young joggers pass a fountain in Orlando, FL.
Photo by Carl M. Purcell

Front of the Mennello Museum in
Orlando, FL.
Photo by Carl M. Purcell

Night Ranger performs at a
WMMO free downtown concert.
Photo by Tom Hurst

Student at UCF learning laser technology. Photo by the University of Central Florida News and Information

Portofino Bay Resort at Universal Studios, FL Photo by Michael Lowry

Fishing is a popular pasttime at numerous lakes in Orlando.
Photo by Eric Dusenbery

Barbershop, Orlando - Photo by Eric Breitenbach

*Colorful Architecture at New Section of Park at Universal Studios
in Orlando, Florida. Photo by Bill Bachmann*

The quiet presence of an alligator is a reality in the central Florida wetlands. Photo by Lee Foster

Dawn of Christmas Day on newly bricked Park Avenue in Winter Park, corner of Morse Blvd and Park Avenue. Photo by Phil Eschbach

Contemporary Central Florida interior. Photo by Michael Lowry

4th of July in Orlando. Photo by Tom Husrt

Street scene in Orlando, FL. - Photo by Carl M. Purcell

Photo by Philip Schwamberger

Nickelodeon Studios enters the 2005 Guinness Book of World Records for simultaneously sliming the largest crowd ever of 762 people. Photo by Tom Hurst

A tower juts out at the historic El Castillo Fort in St. Augustine. Photo by Lee Foster

Welcome sign to historic downtown area of Kissimmee, Florida.
Photo by Bill Bachmann

Aerial view of Wet and Wild, Orlando, FL.
Photo by Carl M Purcell

Nickelodeon Studios enters the 2005 Guinness Book of World Records for simultaneously sliming the largest crowd ever of 762 people. Photo by Tom Hurst

Photo by Nancy Granger

The Castle Resort, Orlando
Photo by Michael Lowry

An ostrich roams through Animal Kingdom at Disney in Orlando.
Photo by Lee Foster

Co-host of Slime Time Live,
Candace Bailey (in sunglasses),
appears with some of the
mass-sliming victims.
Photo by Tom Hurst

The Atlantic Coast Line Station was built in the 1920's and is an example of Spanish Mission Revival style architecture. Photo by Eric Dusenbery

Photo by the University of Central Florida News and Information

Interior of Orange County Courthouse in downtown Orlando on Orange Avenue. Photo by Phil Eschbach

Photo by Philip Schwamberger

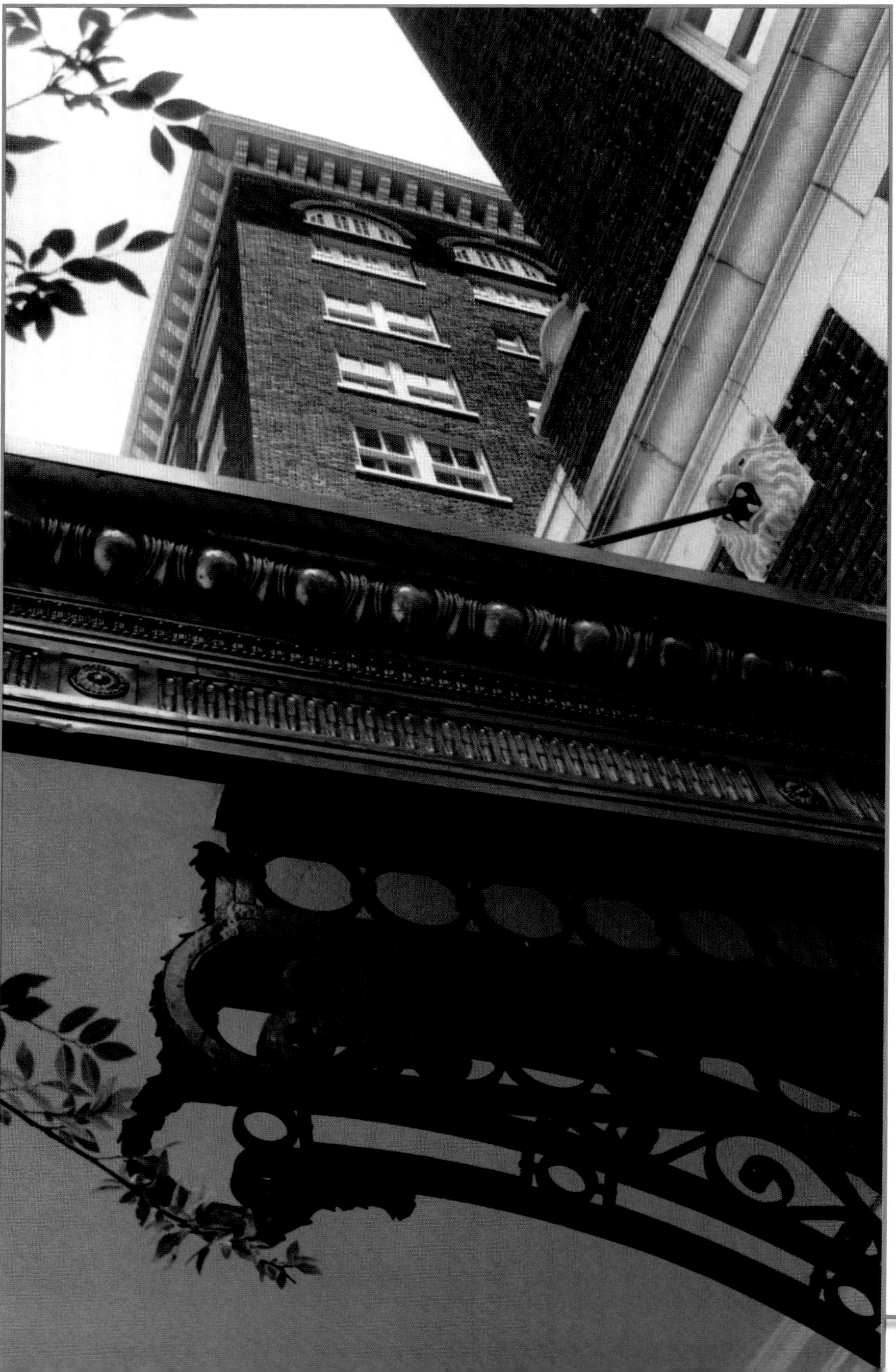

Catamaran on Lake Monroe.
Photo by Tom Hurst

1890's Donnelly House in Mount Dora, Florida.
Photo by Bill Bachmann

Monorail at Epcot Center, Orlando, FL. - Photo by Carl M. Purcell

Late afternoon skyline of downtown Orlando. Photo by Tom Hurst

Harvey's Bistro, Downtwon Orlando
Photo by Michael Lowry

The historic Maitland Art Center is a collection of distinctive buildings, courtyards, and sculptures.
Photo by Eric Dusenbery

Suntrust Bank Building across Lake Eola in downtown Orlando.
Photo by Phil Eschbach

The beautiful campus at UCF. Photo by the University of Central Florida News and Information

Triathlete stretching, Clermont
Photo by Eric Breitenbach

Helen Stairs Theater in Sanford, Florida.
Photo by Bill Bachmann

Magic Kingdom, Disney World, Orlando, FL.
Photo by Carl M. Purcell

Surfers enjoy the close proximity
Orlando has with the coast.
Photo by Tom Hurst

Festival of Trees, Orlando Museum of Art.
Photo by Tom Hurst

Storm brewing behind the Chapel at Rollins College in Winter Park.
Photo by Phil Eschbach

The Cathedral of Saint Luke is an architectural landmark in downtown Orlando. - Photo by Eric Dusenbery

Famous Mel's Diner at Universal Studios in Orlando, Florida.
Photo by Bill Bachmann

Sculpture at the entrance of Winter Park's Rachael Murrah Civic Center. Photo by Phil Eschbach

Brothers, Seminole County - Photo by Eric Breitenbach

Rainforest Cafe, Downtown Disney - Photo by Michael Lowry

Photo by the University of Central Florida News and Information

Art exhibits at Orlando City Hall.
Photo by Michael Lowry

Wachovia Bank Building on Magnolia Avenue in downtown Orlando.
Photo Phil Eschbach

Early morning, Orlando
Photo by Eric Breitenbach

Christmas parade, Sanford - Photo by Eric Breitenbach

Scene on International Drive, downtown Orlando, FL.
Photo by Carl M. Purcell

Weekend athletes, Orlando - Photo by Eric Breitenbach

*Gator Entrance at Gatorland Jungle in Kissimmee, Florida.
Photo by Bill Bachmann*

*Tourists and natives alike enjoy touring central Florida lakes via
canals that connect several lakes in and around Winter Park on the
Scenic Boat Tour. Photo by Phil Eschbach*

Plenty of SLIME flows on the set of SPLAT! Photo by Tom Hurst

Tropical flowers on the grounds of The Delta Orlando Resort.
Photo by Tom Hurst

A Lady receiving a kiss from a killer whale at Sea World in Orlando, FL.
Photo by Carl M. Purcell

Children romp on the central
Florida beaches, such as
Anastasia State Beach in
St. Augustine.
Photo by Lee Foster

City View combines retail and
residence in a new downtown
building. Photo by Tom Hurst

Brother and sister during
physical education at Peaceforce
Christian. Photo by Tom Hurst

Nesting flamingos
Photo by Carl M. Purcell

Photo by the University of
Central Florida News and
Information

Central Florida's first lady of jazz and blues, Miss Jacqueline Junes.
Photo by Tom Hurst

The historic cathedral in St. Augustine shows Spanish architectural motifs.
Photo by Lee Foster

Skyline from Brand-New Walkway by Lake Eola in Orlando, Florida.
Photo by Bill Bachmann

Re-enactors demonstrate early agriculture at historic restorations on St. George Street in St. Augustine.
Photo by Lee Foster

Child playing, Oak Hill - Photo by Eric Breitenbach

Rockets at Kennedy Space Center. Photo by Bill Bachmann

Pink Cake Celebration at Cinderella's Castle in Disney World in Orlando, Florida.
Photo by Bill Bachmann

International Drive in downtown Orlando, FL.
Photo by Carl M. Purcell

The "kids rule" atmosphere inspired by hotel president Terry Whaples is the reason why this resort is transforming into the first-ever Nickelodeon Family Suites by Holiday Inn. Photo by Tom Hurst

Rockets against a Florida sky at Spaceport USA, Kennedy Space Center. Photo by Tom Hurst

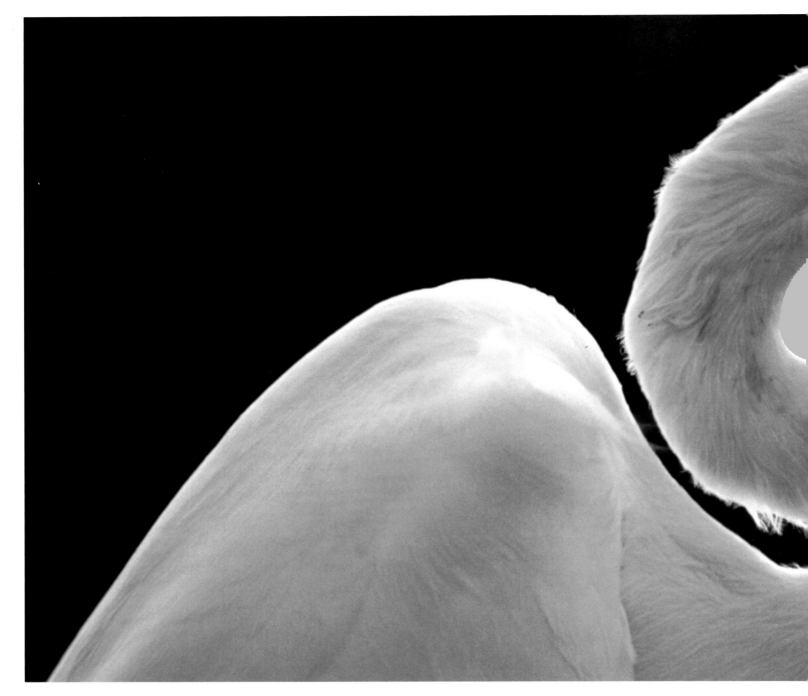

The graceful neck of an egret is part of the pleasure of the central Florida wetlands.
Photo by Lee Foster

Universal Studios Florida
Photo by Tom Hurst

The Pier at Cocoa Beach, one of Orlando's closest beaches.
Photo by Tom Hurst

History Center Museum in Orlando, FL.
Photo by Carl M. Purcell

The Orlando downtown skyline arises behind a fountain in Lake Eola.
Photo by Lee Foster

Chinese pavilion as seen during twilight at Lake Eola.
Photo by Tom Hurst

Fishing is one of Central Florida's favorite past times. Photo by Tom Hurst

*Dry Tortugas National Park, Orlando, FL.
Photo by Carl M. Purcell*

*Street art, the statue of a porpoise seen in Orlando, FL.
Photo by Carl M. Purcell*

Character Actors at Universal Studios in Orlando, Florida. Photo by Bill Bachmann

The China exhibit at Epcot at Disney in Orlando features a pond and the architecture of Beijing's Forbidden City. Photo by Lee Foster

Interior and exterior architecture is sure to amaze vistors at The Mall At Millenia. Photo by Tom Hurst

Christmas lights at Disneyworld, Orlando, FL.
Photo by Carl M. Purcell

Statue in Loch Haven Park
Orlando, Florida.
Photo by Bill Bachmann

The sky, the water, the marsh grass, and the abundant fish life attract kayakers to the intercoastal waterways of central Florida.
Photo by Lee Foster

Golfers take to the course at Reunion's Resort and Club of Orlando. Photo by Tom Hurst

Colorful Amphitheatre Band Shell on Lake Eola in Orlando, Florida. Photo by Bill Bachmann

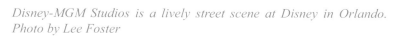

Disney-MGM Studios is a lively street scene at Disney in Orlando. Photo by Lee Foster

Artist working with glass. Photo by Tom Hurst

Anastasia State Beach near St. Augustine is typical of the many excellent beaches along the central Florida coast.
Photo by Lee Foster

Sidewalk art in downtown Orlando, FL.
Photo by Ann F. Purcell

Sister buildings at the Capitol One Plaza downtown Orlando.
Photo by Tom Hurst

Students get some exercise at Manatee Elementary School.
Photo by Tom Hurst

Family Feeding Birds at the Famous Mount Dora Lighthouse in Florida. Photo by Bill Bachmann

Paddle Boat at Disney Village, Orlando, FL. - Photo by Carl M. Purcell

Cannons at historic Fort El Castillo attest to the bellicose past in Saint Augustine.
Photo by Lee Foster

Mad Cow's production of Galileo.
Photo by Tom Hurst

Stained glass window at the Charles Hosmer Morse Foundation (Tiffany Museum) in Orlando, FL.
Photo by Ann F. Purcell

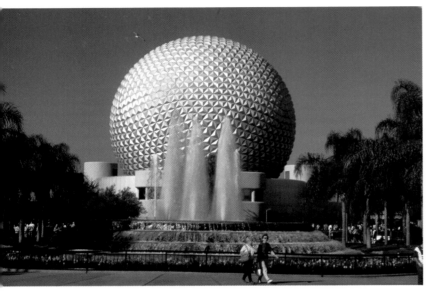

Spaceship Earth at Epcot Center, Orlando, FL.
Photo by Carl M. Purcell

Skyline from Lake Eola of
Orlando, Florida.
Photo by Bill Bachmann

Thornton Park and Hue Restaurant are part of the new, emerging downtown in Orlando. Photo by Lee Foster

Interior is part of the New Southern Home collection at Reunion Resort and Club of Orlando. Photo by Tom Hurst

Interior and exterior architecture is sure to amaze visitors at The Mall at Millenia. Photo by Tom Hurst

THE BODY SHOP

Swan Peddle Boat and Skyline from Lake Eola of Orlando, Florida.
Photo by Bill Bachmann

Windows in the Orlando Museum of Art. - Photo by Ann F. Purcell

Chef Ray Kalmus prepares fresh seafood at McCormick and Schmicks. Photo by Tom Hurst

*Park Avenue is the shopping district in trendy Winter Park.
Photo by Lee Foster*

*A couple shops for colorful
ceramics in St. Augustine.
Photo by Lee Foster*

*Duck march through the Atrium of the Peabody Hotel in Orlando, FL.
Photo by Carl M. Purcell*

*Daytona Beach from Inter-
coastal in Daytona, Florida.
Photo by Bill Bachmann*

American Jewish Ballet dancers at the Maitland Art Center, Orlando, FL. - Photo by Ann F. Purcell

Chamber of Commerce Headquarters Building of Orlando, Florida. Photo by Bill Bachmann

Entre at Roy's Restaurant. Photo by Tom Hurst

Students gather at lunch at
Teachers Hand Academy,
Orlando, Florida.
Photo by Tom Hurst

Pink Flamingos in the Wild at Sea World in Orlando, Florida. Photo by Bill Bachmann

Citrus industry with man picking oranges in orange groves near Winter Haven, Florida.
Photo by Bill Bachman

Demonstrations by re-enactors about early Florida life intrigue visitors at Old St. Augustine Village in St. Augustine.
Photo by Lee Foster

Tropical flowers on the grounds of The Delta Orlando Resort. Photo by Tom Hurst

Carvings on the Tree of Life ornament Animal Kingdom at Disney in Orlando. Photo by Lee Foster

Elephant seen at Circus World, Orlando, FL. Photo by Carl M. Purcell

*Couple Having Picnic at Lake
Eola in Orlando, Florida.
Photo by Bill Bachmann*

Old water wheel mill seen in Orlando, FL.
Photo by Ann F. Purcell

Twilight sky above the 2004 Battle of the BBQ at Lake Eola downtown Orlando.
Photo by Tom Hurst

The French Pavilion at Epcot at Disney in Orlando is particularly floral. Photo by Lee Foster

*Pink Flamingos in the Wild at
Sea World in Orlando, Florida.
Photo by Bill Bachmann*

Palms reflecting in the pool at The Delta Orlando Resort. Photo by Tom Hurst

Athletic young performers at Cypress Gardens, Orlando, FL. - Photo by Carl M. Purcell

City scene of downtown Orlando.
Photo by Tom Hurst

Orlando locals enjoy nightlife at
Pointe Orlando.
Photo by Tom Hurst

Hot air ballooning on an early Orlando morning.
Photo by Tom Hurst

FAO Schwartz Toy Store in downtown Orlando, FL.
Photo by Carl M. Purcell

Mural painted on downtown building by artist Robin Van Arsdale with assistance from students of Ferncreek Elementary School. Photo by Tom Hurst

The Grand Floridian Resort is one of the lodging options at Disney in Orlando.
Photo by Lee Foster

The pelican is widely seen in the
wetlands of central Florida.
Photo by Lee Foster

Three killer whales leaping at Sea World in Orlando, FL.
Photo by Ann F. Purcell

Riding an alligator, sidewalk art in downtown Orlando, FL.
Photo by Ann F. Purcell

Swan Peddle Boats and Skyline from Lake Eola of Orlando, Florida.
Photo by Bill Bachmann

Climb And Punishment

Orange County Courthouse. Photo by Tom Hurst

Art Museum and Science Museum complex in Orlando, FL.
Photo by Carl M. Purcell

The pink color of the flamingo comes from eating shrimp which is the staple of its diet.
Photo copyright: Ann F. Purcell

Central Florida's intercoastal waterways offer many adventures for kayakers.
Photo by Lee Foster

Jet Skiers at Lake Ivanhoe in Orlando, Florida.
Photo by Bill Bachmann

Fishing around Orlando. Photo by Tom Hurst

Dancers enliven the Magic Moments Parade at Disney in Orlando.
Photo by Lee Foster

North Bridge apartment homes provide ultra-luxury living to Orlando residents. Photo by Tom Hurst

Great American Pie Festival, Celebration, Florida. Photo by Tom Hurst

*Aerial of the Peabody Hotel in
Orlando, Florida.
Photo by Bill Bachmann*

Dry Tortugas
National Park
Fort Jefferson

Dry Tortugas National Park, Orlando, FL. - Photo by Carl M. Purcell

Orlando enjoys close proximity to Jetty Park, one of Orlando's closest beaches. Photo by Tom Hurst

There is nothing quite like stretching out on the endless sands of the central Florida beaches. Photo by Lee Foster

EPCOT alien acrobats performing in front of Spaceship Earth at Disney World in Orlando, Florida. Photo by Bill Bachmann

One of the many beautiful sculptures in Orlando, FL. Photo by Carl M. Purcell

Men's breakfast, Orlando - Photo by Eric Breitenbach

The osprey flourishes at the top of the food chain in the central Florida wetlands.
Photo by Lee Foster

Cornell Fine Arts Museum sculpture in Orlando, FL.
Photo by Carl M. Purcell

Classic downtown properties are restored on either side of Rosalind Avenue.
Photo by Tom Hurst

Futuristic design elements are part of the architecture at Epcot at Disney in Orlando. Photo by Lee Foster

Slicing up some BBQ. Photo by Tom Hurst

Swan Peddle Boats and Skyline from Lake Eola of Orlando, Florida. Photo by Bill Bachmann

The Charles Hosmer Morse Foundation (Tiffany Museum) in Orlando, FL. - Photo by Carl M. Purcell

You never know when you could end up with pie in your face in Orlando, FL. - Photo by Carl M. Purcell

Colin Hay of Men at Work performs at a WMMO downtown concert. Photos by Tom Hurst

Lake Eola is a major amenity in downtown Orlando.
Photo by Lee Foster

Upper Right: Children at the Slime Machine in Nickelodeon at Universal Studios in Orlando, Florida. Photo by Bill Bachmann

Neon street sign in Orlando, FL. Photo by Carl M. Purcell

Plane arriving at Orlando International Airport. Photo by Tom Hurst

Skyline of City Hall and Surrounding Buildings in Orlando, Florida. Photo by Bill Bachmann

The Westside "downtown" at Disney in Orlando is an adult playground. Photo by Lee Foster

EPCOT Center's annual Flower and Garden Festival. Photo by Tom Hurst

Flamingos as if posing for the camera .
Photo by Carl M. Purcell

Jet Skiers at Lake Ivanhoe in Orlando, Florida.
Photo by Bill Bachmann

Graceful neon curves of the new LYNX Central Station.
Photo by Tom Hurst

*American Jewish Ballet dancers
at the Maitland Art Center,
Orlando, FL.
Photo by Ann F. Purcell*

Lake Eola cityscape. Photo by Tom Hurst

Alligators are an enduring presence in Florida. Photo by Lee Foster

Tropical flowers on the grounds of The Delta Orlando Resort. Photo by Tom Hurst

Profiles in Excellence

*F*or some students, enrolling in Career and Technical Education is the first important step towards an exciting, dynamic career. For others, it's a chance to reinvent themselves and prepare for a second or multiple career change. Orange County Public Schools (OCPS) Career and Technical Education (CTE) offers secondary school students and adults a wide range of outstanding opportunities to prepare and train for challenging and satisfying careers in the 21st century.

"Meeting the needs of Central Florida's tourism industry"

"Supplying the demand for future health care workers"

Helping Central Florida citizens is at the core of the CTE mission that states "The Career and Technical Education Team is committed to supporting and enhancing student academic achievement through success in secondary and postsecondary programs."

With an enrollment of 45,121 students in 2003, OCPS Career and Technical Education served more students than most of the state universities. It is estimated that the cumulative earnings of OCPS Career and Technical Education graduates over a five-year period will impact the Central Florida economy in excess of $1 billion. In addition $4 million in scholarships and grants enables approximately 2,000 students to train for careers without having to repay student loans.

Positive Programs

Many Central Florida citizens are not aware of the scope of the career and technical opportunities offered by CTE or the widespread assistance provided by local corporate partners. Career and Technical Education offers more than a hundred programs for adult and secondary students, including job specific certification programs, licensure and refresher courses, dual enrollment and academic programs for high school students, Adult English Literacy (formerly ESOL), GED classes and personal enrichment classes. Last year 2,087 adults earned GEDs, 8,500 students participated in Adult English Literacy programs and more than 800 students enrolled in the PALMAS Refugee Program.

An integral part of the OCPS K-12 system, Career and Technical Education works in close partnership with Central Florida businesses and industries. More than 1,000 business partners support CTE by serving on school advisory committees as industry services partners and by providing externships, mentors and judges for leadership competitions.

High-Tech Campuses

At the heart of the Career and Technical Education success story are its four multi-faceted technical centers and thirteen Adult Community Education Centers located throughout Orange County. Offering a combination of proven, efficient, affordable, and reliable training by highly skilled instructors, the Technical Centers provide a broad range of programs in several key career fields. A brief overview of the four technical centers including one of the most technically advanced: One of the most technically advanced training centers in Florida, Mid Florida Tech, offers training in the following career clusters: Arts, Audio-Video and Communications, Business Administrative Services, Construction, Health Services, Hospitality and Tourism, Legal and Protective Services, Manufacturing, Retail/Wholesale Sales and Services, and Transportation, Distribution and Logistics Services. In partnership with Toyota, Mid Florida Tech offers a Toyota T-Ten Advanced Automotive Service Technology program that provides trained technicians for Toyota dealers throughout Florida. Mid Florida Tech is also home to the

Central Florida Fire Academy and features four centers of excellence: Electronic Technology; Computer Electronics Technology; Automotive Services Technology; and Heating, Ventilation and Air Conditioning. In addition to the 106 acres at 2900 West Oak Ridge Road in southwest Orlando, Mid Florida Tech encompasses Adult and Community Education Centers and Instructional Service Centers.

At Orlando Tech's downtown facility, learning is enhanced by a campus-wide, state-of-the-art electronic delivery system of multimedia learning resources to encourage and motivate students. Training at Orlando Tech is provided in the following career clusters: Arts, Audio-Visual Technology and Communications; Business Administrative Services; Education and Training Services, and Health Services specializing in direct patient care. Orlando Tech has a proven track record of placing highly trained students into local business and industry markets. In partnership with Orlando Regional Healthcare, Orlando Tech is a model site for the national Allied Healthcare Technology Based Training Program using both adult and pediatric Human Patient Simulators as the key components for training. In addition to state-of-the-art programs, Orlando Tech offers students a culturally diverse learning environment.

Westside Tech is a dynamic and innovative technical center that primarily serves west and northwest Orange County and adjacent Lake County. Westside offers over twenty-four full and part-time academic and technical programs, evening classes, and courses at five Adult Community Centers. Westside offers training in the following program clusters: Agricultural and Natural Resources, Business and Administrative Services, Construction, Health Services, Human Services and Information Technology Services. In order to better serve students and the Westside community, the center also offers non-traditional programs and services, such as the off-campus adult handicapped educational program. Westside Tech is a vibrant center, with a friendly, family atmosphere, serving the workforce needs of the community and its citizens.

Located in the heart of Winter Park, Winter Park Tech offers post-secondary occupational training certificate programs and academic programs. Designated as a center with emphasis on information technology training, Winter Park Tech also provides programs in the following career clusters: Business Technology, Health Sciences, Family & Consumer Sciences and Industrial Technology. In addition to these clusters, two health science programs award Applied Technology Diplomas (ATDs) to students completing Medical Records Transcription and Medical Coder/Biller programs. Graduates from these programs may matriculate to state community colleges and earn advanced credits toward two-year degrees in Office Systems Technology or Health Information Services. Students at Winter Park Tech represent many cultural and ethnic backgrounds in eighteen occupational training certificate programs, nine academic programs, continuing workforce education classes and personal enrichment courses.

All four Orange County Public Schools Career and Technical Education Centers are accredited by the Commission of the Council on Occupational Education and the Southern Association of Colleges and Schools Commission on Middle and Secondary Schools.

"Reversing the traditional role"

"Preparing for Florida's diverse economy"

Mention the Orlando Sentinel and Central Floridians are keenly aware of their hometown Pulitzer Prize-winning daily newspaper. Yet, the newspaper is only one component of Orlando Sentinel Communications, a progressive, constantly evolving multimedia company providing information via the Orlando Sentinel, El Sentinel, niche publications, Internet, radio, and television. If you want comprehensive, accurate, and entertaining information, Orlando Sentinel Communications is always within easy reach in a variety of convenient media options.

Multimedia Impact

While the *Orlando Sentinel* is the company's high-profile flagship publication, a growing number of Central Floridians retrieve news and information from additional Orlando Sentinel Communications sources. The company was one of the first in the region to address the information needs of the rapidly growing Hispanic population. In 1999, the Orlando Sentinel opened a full-time news bureau in San Juan, Puerto Rico, and expanded coverage of Central Florida's Hispanic community. In 2001, *El Sentinel*, a weekly Spanish-language newspaper, debuted.

Orlando Sentinel Communications maintains a strong online presence by hosting a diverse menu of Web sites, including OrlandoSentinel.com, an up-to-the-minute source for local breaking news, business, weather, sports, and classifieds; elSentinel.com, the online companion to El Sentinel; OrlandoWeather.com, a partnership between the Orlando Sentinel and WESH NewsChannel 2 providing Central Florida weather coverage seven days a week; OrlandoCityBeat.com, a unique Web site devoted to the

area's nightlife and social scene; and go2orlando.com, an interactive travel guide for visitors to the Central Florida area.

The company also publishes several magazines targeted to specific market segments such as home buyers, employment seekers, automobile buyers, relocation and entertainment. *Job Xtra* is a weekly guide that lists employment opportunities. *OrlandoCityBeat.com Street Edition* is a weekly publication that highlights entertainment possibilities. *Weekend Home Preview* is a weekly resale and new-home publication. *New Homes* is a monthly advertising guide showcasing new communities and homesites. *Hot Properties* is a monthly residential and commercial real estate publication. *From House to Home* is a colorful, upscale lifestyle and home furnishings magazine that publishes every quarter. *AutoFinder* is a weekly guide to new and used vehicles. *Coupon Catalogue* and *Coupon Values* are inserts distributed through the *Orlando Sentinel*. *Orlando Citybook* is a full-color annual Central Florida relocation guide.

Further enhancing its multimedia efforts, Orlando Sentinel Communications has taken to the airwaves in recent years to further diversify its product offerings. As one example, the company hosts the TV show *Orlando Sentinel Varsity Sports* in partnership with WESH NewsChannel 2. The weekly

show highlights outstanding local high school athletes and events. The company also partners with other local English- and Spanish-language television and radio stations and *Orlando Sentinel* and *El Sentinel* staff members regularly are on the air.

History

Recognized as the oldest continually operating company in Orlando, the *Orlando Sentinel* first printed its newspaper under the name *Orange County Reporter* on June 6, 1876. In 1916, the *Orange County Reporter* combined with another paper, the *Orlando Evening Star*, and became the *Reporter Star*. The Orlando *Morning Sentinel* acquired *Reporter Star* in 1931 and Martin Andersen came to Orlando to manage both. Andersen purchased the *Morning Sentinel* and the *Reporter Star* in 1945 and the newspapers moved into a new plant on North Orange Avenue in 1951. The newspapers flourished and the Orange Avenue plant more than doubled in size by 1960. Five years later, Andersen sold his newspapers to Tribune Company of Chicago and the *Sentinel* and *Star* merged in 1973 to become a single daily, *The Sentinel Star*. A massive production center was added to the original plant building in 1981. A year later the paper was named *The Orlando Sentinel* and the Sentinel Star Co. became Sentinel Communications Co. In recent years the company further expanded its production center and purchased several properties adjacent to its main plant to round out the campus.

Always at the forefront of important issues impacting Orlando and Florida, the *Orlando Sentinel* has won three Pulitzer Prizes. Its first came in 1988 for "Florida's Shame," an editorial series written by Editorial Page Editor Jane Healy on mismanaged growth in Central Florida. In 1993, the newspaper garnered its second Pulitzer Prize for investigative reporting for a series written on the unjust seizure of cash from motorists by the Volusia County sheriff's drug squad. The third Pulitzer Prize was achieved in 2000 for editorial writing by John Bersia titled "Fleeced in Florida," a year-long series that prompted lawmakers to regulate reform of cash-advance businesses that prey on people in desperate financial situations.

Legacy Of Caring

Orlando Sentinel Communications has a long history of helping improve the lives of people in the communities it reaches. To provide financial assistance to qualified non-profit organizations that serve the needs of the community, the Orlando Sentinel Family Fund, a fund of the McCormick Tribune Foundation, was created. Since 1990, the Orlando Sentinel Family Fund has distributed more than $20 million to nonprofit organizations in Central Florida. In addition, Orlando Sentinel Communications supports a wide variety of community and cultural organizations, among them Heart of Florida United Way and United Arts of Central Florida. The company sponsors more than 200 community and business events each year and more than 50 arts and cultural events.

Stetson University

Take a walk on Stetson University's historic DeLand campus and you'll know you're in a world of strong academic traditions. Florida's first private university, founded in 1883, Stetson features a campus of stately brick buildings and majestic oaks surrounding a historic fountain and an academic quad—where students and professors meet and talk, sit and read, and sometimes hold class.

Stetson University's low 12:1 student/faculty ratio fosters relationships between students and professors both in and out of the classroom.

You don't have to travel far to see some of the country's best athletic talent.
A member of the Atlantic Sun Conference, Stetson competes at the NCAA Division I level in 15 intercollegiate sports.

The core campus was designated a National Historic District in 1991, but the university does not live in the past. The DeLand campus is home to Stetson's College of Arts and Sciences, School of Business Administration and School of Music. New high-tech buildings enable the university to offer the best of the future to students as well. Stetson also offers law, graduate, and continuing education programs at its campuses in Celebration, Tampa, and Gulfport/St. Petersburg, where its College of Law is located.

Stetson's tradition of academic excellence and commitment to values is recognized by a variety of prestigious publications and organizations. Since 1985, *U.S. News & World Report* has ranked Stetson one of the South's leading universities. Stetson is one of only 270 universities to have a chapter of Phi Beta Kappa, the nation's oldest and most esteemed undergraduate organization; and *The Princeton Review* lists Stetson's School of Business Administration one of the best business schools in the country.

Commitment to Values

With more than sixty undergraduate majors and minors, Stetson offers the variety of a large university and the close personal attention of a small college. Stetson's undergraduates are as diverse as its course offerings, with more than 2,200 undergraduates representing forty-one states and forty-one foreign countries. More than 75 percent of students are Florida residents, and about 12 percent of students represent minority groups. Fifty-eight percent of students are women, while 42 percent are men.

Why do students choose Stetson University?

First, Stetson puts its focus on teaching. Small, seminar-style classes that invite personal interaction are hallmarks of a Stetson education. Stetson's low 12:1 student/faculty ratio, with an average class size of nineteen, gives students opportunities to get to know their professors. Many Stetson students also take advantage of off-campus learning experiences such as internships and study-abroad programs in Innsbruck, Austria; Madrid, Spain; Oxford, England; Avignon, France; Freiburg, Germany; Hong Kong, China; Moscow, Russia; and Guanajuato, Mexico.

Second, Stetson's location gives students easy access to major urban amenities in Orlando, as well as to the beaches of Daytona Beach. DeLand itself offers a vibrant downtown area within walking distance. Students can also take advantage of nearby natural attractions, including Blue Spring State Park, the St. Johns River, DeLeon Springs State Park, and Ocala National Forest.

Third, Stetson is fully committed to integrating academic excellence and values into its core mission. Stetson's Values Council oversees efforts to incorporate seven core values into the Stetson University experience: religious and spiritual life, ethical decision-making, diversity, gender equity, environmental responsibility, community service, and health and wellness.

Academic Excellence

A visible example of Stetson's values is the recently reconstructed Lynn Business Center. Completely rebuilt from a failed savings and loan facility, it is the first building in Florida to be certified by the U.S. Green Building Council under its Leadership in Energy and Environmental Design Green Building Rating System. The six-story brick building, with smaller structures housing an auditorium and multi-use space, combines environmentally-sensitive planning, siting, and architecture with energy-efficient building systems.

Inside the Lynn Business Center, students use the latest high-tech equipment. Unique to the business school is the Roland George Investments Program, in which students invest a real portfolio of more than $2.8 million. For four consecutive years, George students have captured top honors in the national investment competition RISE (Redefining Investment Strategy Education). Other notable programs are Stetson's Family Business Center, which offers the only Family Business major in the nation; the Prince Entrepreneurship Program for those interested in starting a business; and an innovative Executive MBA Program at the Stetson University Center at Celebration.

Elsewhere on campus, students use other first-rate facilities. Music students study in a complex that includes a digital arts lab, performance auditorium, and rehearsal rooms with acoustic features. Innovative equipment and technology abound at Sage Hall, Stetson's science center, and the equipment is actually available for under-graduates to use, often in projects done jointly with professors. The duPont-Ball Library is online, offering access to many specialized databases, and houses more than 330,000 books and periodicals as well as 245,000 federal documents.

Campus Life

When the charts, calculators and books are put away, Stetson offers a host of extracurricular activities. Students can explore varied interests and cultures in more than a hundred campus organizations, from Model Senate to Habitat for Humanity, from Future Educators to the Caribbean Club. In addition, Stetson is home to six national sororities and eight national fraternities. Stetson's internationally recognized Stewart Lecture Series has featured guest lecturers like journalist/author Bill Moyers and scientist and conservationist Jane Goodall. Its Howard Thurman Lecture Series brings several civil rights leaders to campus each semester.

On the sports scene, Stetson University is an NCAA Division I member of the Atlantic Sun Conference. Hatter athletes compete in fifteen intercollegiate sports, including baseball and softball; and men's and women's basketball, crew, cross-country, golf, soccer, tennis, and volleyball. Students can also compete in numerous intramural sports.

Students in Stetson's School of Music have access to modern facilities and receive personal attention from artist faculty members. The school also stages a number of professional performances each year, on and off campus.

Located near downtown DeLand, the university's picturesque main campus was designated a National Historic District in 1991.

Built in an environmentally sensitive manner, Stetson's state-of-the-art Lynn Business Center trains students on the latest business practices and trends.

Siemens

The greater Orlando metropolitan area in central Florida is a key growth hub for Siemens and acts as an important gateway to the global economy. In fact, Siemens has stepped up its investments in the region over the last few years in a wide variety of businesses. For Siemens, the Orlando region has become a major center of its business in the southeastern U.S. and a tangible factor in its success in the global economy—with more than 3,000 employees in the Orlando area and more than 5,500 altogether in Florida.

Siemens in the Orlando Region

The anchor of Siemens' presence in the Orlando area is Siemens Power Generation (formerly Siemens Westinghouse Power Corporation), which sits in the high-tech corridor near the University of Central Florida. Siemens Power Generation, which became part of the global electrical engineering company in 1998, is a leading power generation equipment supplier in the U.S. and worldwide.

A highly regarded Orlando corporate resident, Siemens Power Generation is just one of several major divisions of Siemens active in the Orlando area and throughout the state. Orlando also is home to Siemens Medical Solutions, Siemens Communications, Siemens Building Technologies, and Siemens Shared Services. The company's dedicated professionals from these businesses develop a wide range of important products and services that do everything from improving patient care and safety in hospitals to enabling communication networks to enhancing the comfort and security in some of the most technically advanced buildings in the world.

Siemens' influence as a business and as an infrastructure products and services provider in Orlando

An aerial photo of the Siemens complex.

mirrors the larger significance of the U.S. market for our global company.

Snapshot Overview of Siemens

Siemens is a $91.3 billion electronics company with 430,000 employees in 192 countries. The United States is one of Siemens' largest markets, generating annual revenues of $16.6 billion. Siemens dedicates 70,000 employees towards key businesses and public sectors of America's economy— Medical, Power, Automation and Control, Information and Communications, Lighting, Building Technologies, Water Technologies, and Services and Home Appliances.

Founded by the inventor of the electric dynamo nearly 160 years ago, Siemens today still maintains innovation as its lifeblood. As the sixth largest R&D investor in the world, Siemens ranks in the top 10 of U.S. patent holders and 75 percent of its sales are derived from products developed in the past five years. Siemens technologies generate a third of America's power, process 90 percent of the nation's mail, treat 30,000 cancer patients every business day, supply automotive technologies for 50 percent of the cars manufactured in the United States, provide communications for many U.S. military installations, and help secure America's 438 major commercial airports.

Siemens is number one in the U.S. in lighting, water technologies, ultrasound systems, light rail vehicles and material handling systems. Integrating technologies from its different sectors, Siemens produces smart buildings, digital hospitals, high-tech stadiums, wired campuses and safer, more efficient airports.

The Importance of the Orlando Region

In the Orlando area, Siemens develops and markets products and services that not only serve the U.S. market, but are adapted for export to markets around the globe.

Siemens Power Generation offers a full spectrum of power generating products and services, including gas and steam turbine-generator technology, process control and power management systems, operations and maintenance support, power plant modernization and upgrade equipment, wind power systems and fuel cell technology. These systems help to generate more than one-third of the nation's electricity. In the past two years, the company had delivered systems that help customers in the United States and worldwide start up more than 20 billion watts of new power generation equipment—enough to light eight million homes. In addition, high voltage systems from Siemens Power Transmission & Distribution, which also is headquartered in the SE region in North Carolina, have helped U.S. utilities increase capacity on existing transmission lines by up to 24 percent.

In Orlando, Siemens Power Generation provides jobs to nearly 3,000 people in the functions of power equipment engineering, project planning and implementation, sales and marketing and general operations. The company occupies nearly one million square feet of office and warehouse pace in central Florida.

Siemens Medical Solutions is one of the largest suppliers of

medical equipment in the world. In Orlando, a research and development office for its IT division focuses on Soarian Financials software, which helps to improve administration at hospitals across the country. The local Siemens Medical Solutions Florida customer office oversees local implementation and service for Siemens imaging software and service solutions that are designed to help hospitals streamline workflow to improve efficiencies and reduce costs.

Siemens has a strong commitment to community service and social responsibility. Through corporate donations and the company's Caring Hands employee volunteerism program Siemens demonstrates its commitment to improving the Orlando community. Throughout the city, Siemens is involved in numerous community organizations, including the Metro Orlando Economic Development Commission, Greater Orlando Chamber of Commerce, Florida Hospital, University of Central Florida, The Foundation for Seminole County Schools. In addition to local nonprofit organizations, Siemens supports national math and science education programs with the goal of inspiring and facilitating more young people to pursue studies in these areas. Siemens presented more than $1.5 million in scholarships awards in 2004, including the Siemens Westinghouse Competition in Math, Science & Technology, which encourages and awards students around the country every year providing much needed visibility and resources. Corporate citizen, infrastructure provider, community participant—these are all levels on which Siemens operates in Orlando—and together they create the backdrop for one of the company's key business strategies: invest locally and grow globally.

Siemens Medical Solutions brings together innovative diagnostic and IT solutions to help its healthcare customers achieve tangible, sustainable, clinical and financial outcomes

Combined cycle power plant in Central Florida utilizing Siemens Power Generation equipment.

In his insightful book, <u>The Great Good Place</u>, sociologist Ray Oldenburg defines "third places" as relaxing settings where communities come together. In the past, neighborhood cafes, taverns, and corner stores met those needs, but as society has grown, developed, and sprawled, neighbors now struggle to get to know each other.

The Central Florida YMCA has become just such a "Third Place," a place where young and old congregate to put aside the concerns of home and work, to enjoy each others company, and to exercise their personal commitment to their health. Through a combination of state-of-the-art facilities, well-developed programs and an atmosphere that promotes positive values, the Central Florida YMCA continues to impact thousands of lives each year—not only in Orlando, but in the surrounding Orange, Osceola, Seminole, Brevard, Lake, and Marion county communities.

At the core of the YMCA's appeal is its dedication to providing a positive, safe place for youth and their families, welcoming and celebrating different cultures, faiths, ethnicities, and giving people a sense of belonging and self-worth.

Through twenty-four well-staffed, expertly-designed and friendly Family Centers and twelve Teen Centers, the Central Florida YMCA helps families live healthier, more socially connected, spiritual lives. With a 2005 budget of $50 million and more than 2,000 employees, the Central Florida YMCA is an integral part of the everyday fabric of life in the Orlando area. Nearly 28,000 children are served through membership and outreach programs every year.

Strong Kids

Building strong families and strong communities begins with building strong kids. The Central Florida YMCA teaches character development in our youth programs, emphasizing five core values: caring, honesty, respect, responsibility, and faith. Children and teens develop into leaders through youth sports, aquatics, after-school and summer child care, and summer camp programs. A strong emphasis is placed on developing an appreciation of one's own worth, a sense of world mindedness, and faith for daily living. From basketball to soccer and several sports in between, more than 12,000 children participate in Central Florida YMCA's sports program every year. The YMCA sports philosophy is a simple one: Everyone wins and everyone plays.

The YMCA leads the nation in water safety instruction, and the Central Florida YMCA has committed tremendous resources to ensure Central Floridians are safe in and around the water. With more than twenty-six pools throughout six counties, the Central Florida YMCA provides more than 15,000 children and adults with swim instruction.

With the generous support of Dr. Phillips Charities, the Central Florida YMCA has launched "Safe Start," a ground-breaking program that teaches infants and toddlers how to survive in the water. In Florida, drowning is the number one cause of accidental death among children under the age of four, and this program's goal is that not one more child drown in this community. To date, more than 3,700 children have been taught critical survival skills.

Strong Families

The goal of the Central Florida YMCA after-school program is to make sure that no child has to stay home alone. Serving more than 5,000 children from eleven Orange County middle schools, three Osceola County middle schools, and seventeen Central Florida elementary schools, the YMCA's after-school program offers children a safe, professionally-staffed environment that helps them succeed in and out of school.

Once the school year has concluded, the Central Florida YMCA offers thirty-five day camps packed with fun, character-building activities to 3,600 kids each week. For children seeking a residential camping experience, the YMCA Wewa Outdoor Center in Apopka has provided children with an opportunity to immerse themselves in a wonderland of adventure, discovery, and exploration for more than thirty-five years. The beautiful "old Florida" environment enables campers to acquire leadership skills, build self-confidence, and enjoy the camaraderie of new friends.

The Central Florida YMCA goes to great lengths to ensure every child, no matter what their family's financial capability, has an opportunity to benefit from a wide range of sports, child care, camps, and character development programs. With the support of generous donors, subsidies, and funds set aside from dues and program fees, nearly half of all Central Florida YMCA participants—approximately 100,000 people—are able to learn to swim, attend camp, join teen leadership programs, or enjoy individual, family, or senior memberships.

Strong Communities

Assisting in Central Florida YMCA's goal to impact greater numbers of Central Floridians are more than 125 collaborative partners, ranging from governmental agencies to corporations to schools and individuals.

Among the newest partnerships are Walt Disney World and Brevard Community College, helping enhance the Central Florida YMCA's impact on the community.

The Central Florida YMCA and the Walt Disney World Resort have teamed together to launch an innovative early child care and education solution created to meet the unique demands and needs of those employed by the tourism industry. The two new Central Florida YMCA Family Centers located at the Walt Disney World Resort, are the largest child care centers in the nation, providing healthy, positive environments that enrich the lives of Central Florida children. The Cocoa YMCA Family Center at Brevard Community College is the very first YMCA on a community college campus. This new YMCA provides vital programs and services to the underserved members of the community while bringing together college and high school students with adults, children, and seniors in an enriching campus setting.

The Future

The Central Florida YMCA is continually adapting to the changing needs of the Orlando and Central Florida community. With an unwavering commitment to core values, great strides are being made in terms of strengthening children and families, establishing YMCA Family Centers in new communities, and developing new programs and partnerships to attract and serve people from all walks of life, thus ensuring that the YMCA will be Central Florida's Third Place for generations to come.

Florida Hospital

Although primarily known as the vacation capital of the world, Central Florida is even more than that—it's a community, spread from coast-to-coast, sharing the same needs as other bustling, growing areas of the country. And one of the most critical needs of its' residents is quality healthcare.

A Mission of Healing

As an established member of the community since 1908, Florida Hospital's mission has been to extend the healing ministry of Christ throughout the community with a commitment to compassionate care and excellence in medicine. Over the years, Florida Hospital has received numerous awards recognizing its high quality of care including being named one of "America's Best Hospitals" annually since 1999 by *U.S. News and World Report* and recognized as having Central Florida's "Best Doctors" by *Orlando Magazine*. Other accolades include *The Orlando Sentinel's* 2002 & 2003 - Top 25 Companies for Working Families, National Research Corporation's 1996-2003 Consumer Choice Winner and *Fit Pregnancy Magazine* - One of the top 10 hospitals in the country to have a baby in 2002.

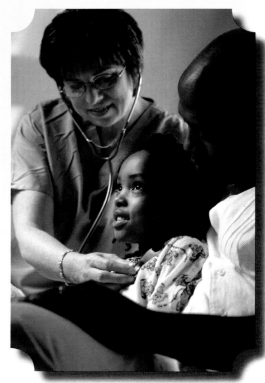

With almost 1,800 beds and over one million patients a year, Florida Hospital treats more patients each year than any other hospital system in the United States. An acute-care health system owned and operated by Adventist Health System, Florida Hospital is one of the largest not-for-profit healthcare systems in the country. Serving Central Florida and the surrounding counties with a comprehensive network of physicians, Florida Hospital has seven campuses in Orange, Osceola, and Seminole counties. Committed to providing superior care in a compassionate environment, Florida Hospital offers an exceptional array of Centers of Excellence, including the Florida Hospital Cardiovascular Institute;

the Florida Hospital Cancer Institute; the Florida Hospital Neuroscience Institute; the Florida Hospital Orthopedic Institute; Rehabilitation and Sports Medicine, Diabetes, Women's Medicine and more.

Almost 100 years ago, Florida Hospital's Seventh Day Adventist leaders were committed to extending the healing ministry of Christ to all patients in need. With an eye toward continual improvement, they began renovating existing Sanitarium structures to be used for medical healing. In the 1950s, patients no longer came to the hospital to "rest," but came for specific medical treatments. The emergence of many new surgical and medical treatment options, along with newly installed air conditioning offered them a better chance for recovery. By 1970, the hospital grew to nearly 500 beds and underwent even more dramatic changes as specialty programs including cardiology, orthopedic surgery, organ transplants, and cancer treatment were added.

State-of-the-Art Facilities

As their centennial year draws closer, Florida Hospital has recognized the enormous increasing growth in the Central Florida community. In order to continue their tradition of superior care, Florida Hospital is excited to initiate an innovative expansion project to support their state-of-the-art treatment centers. With a

dedication to providing patients with a total healing environment, Florida Hospital is extending this massive project to impact all seven of their campuses. Improvements will span every aspect of patient care, from expanding Emergency Rooms, Labor and Delivery, and In-Patient beds to adding a new Sleep Disorders Center and improving diagnostic imaging services at four of the campuses. Driven by their faithful commitment to providing comprehensive medical care to Central Floridians, Florida Hospital strives to anticipate their future healthcare needs.

One example of Florida Hospital's creativity in originating healthcare solutions for its unique population is Florida Hospital Celebration Health. A thoughtfully planned, continuously innovative, comprehensive facility, it serves as a model for future facilities across the country and around the globe. Created in the style of a Mediterranean luxury hotel, Florida Hospital Celebration Health's mission is to soothe the spirit as well as the body.

In addition to having some of the latest technological advances available in Central Florida, from diagnostic imaging and joint replacement to minimally invasive surgery and neurosurgery, Florida Hospital Celebration Health is a full-service hospital providing

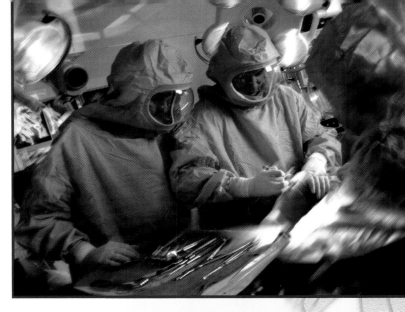

inpatient and outpatient services, and even includes a 60,000 square foot state-of-the-art Fitness Centre on-site. Florida Hospital also continues to meet the needs of Central Floridians where they need it the most by maintaining fourteen convenient Centra Care urgent care centers. Professional walk-in medical care is available for all kinds of urgent medical needs, including colds, flu, sore throats, earaches, stomachaches, broken bones, and stitches.

As a not-for-profit hospital, Florida Hospital gives back to the community by providing accessible and technologically advanced healthcare services, medical screenings, education programs, and more. As a Christian hospital, their mission is to extend the healing ministry of Christ to all patients who come to the hospital, while delivering high quality service and showing concern for patients' emotional and spiritual needs as well as their physical condition.   Responsible to the community both as an organization and as individuals, Florida Hospital has a rich legacy in the community, pioneering the Partners in Education program with area schools; providing mentors and support to health educators; as well as coordinating a mobile medical van program that provides medical care to disadvantaged communities. By embracing a holistic approach to patient care, Florida Hospital joyfully ministers to not only the mind, body, and spirit of their patients but also reaches out to nurture and support the health needs of Central Florida as well.

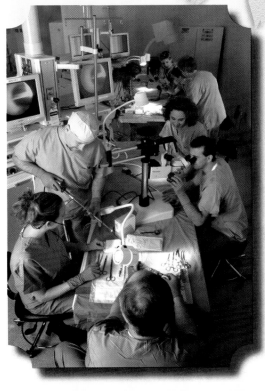

In 1918, a group of Orlando residents and physicians recognized the need to improve community health care services. Under the name of the Orange County Hospital Association, the group invested its time and money, collected donations, purchased land, and hired a team to build the 50-bed Orange General Hospital, one of the first modern health care facilities serving Central Florida.

ANGE GENERAL HOSPITAL, ORLANDO, FLORIDA

The association built more than a hospital. It established the foundation for what would become the city's premier health care network—Orlando Regional Healthcare. Today the 1,572 bed, community-owned, not-for-profit organization serves more than 2 million Central Florida residents and 6,000 visitors annually. As Central Florida's only Level I trauma center and statutory teaching hospital system, Orlando Regional is renowned for excellence in surgery, cardiac care, trauma and emergency medicine, cancer care, and pediatrics.

The downtown building that once housed Orange General Hospital now operates as Orlando Regional Medical Center, one of seven hospitals and numerous health care services united under the Orlando Regional Healthcare umbrella.

Healthcare through Teamwork

Orlando Regional Healthcare has been consistently voted one of the country's top 100 hospital systems by HCIA Mercer, as well as one of the top family-friendly companies in the area by *Central Florida Family* magazine. The more than 12,000 Central Florida employees of Orlando Regional Healthcare make up a team that is committed with a focus on excellence.

Prominent among the organization's facilities is Arnold Palmer Hospital for Children & Women, one of only six such facilities in the nation. More than 10,000 babies are born each year at Arnold Palmer Hospital, and more than 1,000 babies receive neonatal intensive care. In 2006, the new Hospital for Women & Babies will be completed, moving the labor and delivery as well as neonatal intensive care unit to a new facility that can accommodate the ever-growing population of Central Florida. Arnold Palmer Hospital will continue to be a leading pediatric facility with more room to serve children's needs in our community. The addition of the Bert Martin's Champions for Children Emergency Department & Trauma Center, an extension of the Level I Trauma Center at Orlando Regional Medical Center further elevates Arnold Palmer Hospital as a global leader in pediatric care.

Another high-profile facility is M. D. Anderson Cancer Center Orlando, which provides state-of-the-art cancer care in a program jointly sponsored by Orlando Regional Healthcare and The University of Texas M. D. Anderson Cancer Center in Houston. M. D. Anderson-Orlando's specialized multidisciplinary approach means each patient benefits from the expertise of a team of professionals, including medical, radiation, surgical oncologists, pathologists and radiologists, nuclear medicine physicians and research nurses, along with support staff such as social workers, counselors, dieticians and pharma-

cists. M. D. Anderson-Orlando is a patient-centered organization so all services, even down to the physical design of the building are focused around our patients' needs. Before the building was constructed, a design team met with our patients and medical staff to determine their needs and incorporate them into the building's design. As a result, all details were arranged around our patients, from the water-themed chemotherapy area, to a bathroom between the gynecological oncology exam rooms to the sky lit radiation vault waiting room. Also, M. D. Anderson-Orlando welcomes each patient and his or her family with a tour of the facility on their first visit and invites all patients to weekly high teas every Thursday afternoon. Our affiliation with M. D. Anderson in Houston, named again as the top cancer treatment hospital in the U.S. by *U.S. News & World Report*, means our patients have access to cutting-edge clinical trials and research and can have their medical case reviewed by both medical teams in Orlando and Houston during weekly collaborative telemedicine sessions. Additionally, because of our affiliation, all M. D. Anderson-Orlando physicians must meet the high accreditation standards of M. D. Anderson in Houston. This affiliation ensures our patients that they are truly receiving world class cancer care right here in their own backyard

Other major Orlando Regional Healthcare facilities include Orlando Regional Medical Center, specializing in trauma, emergency care, cardiology, orthopedics, neuroscience, diabetes care, and critical care; Orlando Regional Lucerne Hospital; Orlando Regional Sand Lake Hospital; Orlando Regional South Seminole Hospital; Orlando Regional St. Cloud Hospital; and South Lake Hospital. Also part of the network are the Orlando Re-

gional Healthcare Foundation, benefiting community health care programs, and the Hubbard House, which offers affordable and convenient living accommodations for families of patients.

A Mission to Serve

Orlando Regional Healthcare's mission statement promises a commitment to "improve the health and quality of life of the individuals and communities we serve." Orlando Regional Healthcare has earned a reputation as a health care system that looks beyond profits, reinvests its services and funds back into Central Florida, and embraces a mission of long-term services to all members of the community. Orlando Regional Healthcare continues its mission through advanced science research and by expansion of services through new facilities and partnership programs.

"Since 1918, Orlando regional Healthcare has grown hand in hand with Greater Orlando," says President and CEO John Hillenmeyer, "In this age of high-tech hospitals, our goal remains to provide patients, and families with individualized care and treatment. We plan to continue this tradition for generations to come."

Hubbard Construction Company

For over three-quarters of a century, Hubbard Construction Company has been the leader in quality heavy construction work in Florida. Headquartered in Orlando, the company performs in both the private and public sectors. Our work includes complex highway interchanges, drainage systems, roads, bridges, underground utilities, paving, building foundations, airport site work and runways, real estate development, and golf course site work.

Special projects requiring creativity and ingenuity continue to come to Hubbard following a successful history on specialized tasks such as the launch pads at Cape Canaveral, the people mover tracks at the airports in Orlando and Tampa, the foundations for Disney's monorail system and the laser range at Lockheed-Martin.

When your customers are the Florida Department of Transportation, the US Corps of Engineers, Walt Disney World, Florida's top developers, cities and counties throughout Florida including Tampa, Orlando, and Jacksonville, an unusually high standard of excellence is required. It happens during every working day at Hubbard with computerized costs controls, contemporary equipment, ample bonding capacity, precise workmanship, and on-site supervision

and evaluation. This was why Hubbard was the only Florida contractor to be chosen by the U.S. Corps of Engineers to participate in the enormous cleanup after Hurricane Andrew in 1992.

Although the company's headquarters are in Orlando, Hubbard has four construction divisions, three paving divisions, and a materials division located in various parts of the state. The Orlando area, which is among the nation's fastest growing metropolitan regions, is serviced by the Orlando Construction Division, the Orlando Paving Division, and the Mid-Florida Materials Division, which operates a construction debris landfill in Orange County. The paving division, which alone oversees four plants, is the largest producer of hot mix asphalt in the central Florida region, operating at a combined

capacity of 1,000 tons per hour. The Jacksonville Construction Division has made improvements to Interstates 95 and 295 in northeast Florida, while the Atlantic Coast Asphalt Division produces and installs hot mix asphalt in that area. Florida's Gold Coast construction and asphalt needs are met by the East Coast Construction Division and the East Coast Paving Division while the Tampa Construction Divisions helps to meet the needs of southwest Florida.

From world-class attractions like Walt Disney World to new residential communities, international airports to interstate highways, the men and women who specialize in the field of heavy construction at Hubbard have completed every contract awarded with pride, creativity and an unwavering com-

mitment to cost efficiency. It is this proven tradition of excellence that supports our eagerness to meet the challenges that await us.

As always, Hubbard performs its work with a healthy respect for the environment, an attitude of providing lasting improvement in our home state, and with a strong sense of good stewardship for the construction budgets we are privileged to manage for our valued customers.

*T*hanks to reliable, affordable and innovative electric, water and business service, the Orlando Utilities Commission (OUC–The Reliable One) is continuing its more than 80-year history of being a community leader in Orlando and Central Florida and one of the highest-rated municipal utilities in the country.

Since 1923, OUC—The Reliable One has served the citizens of Orlando with dependable utility services at competitive rates.

OUC's slogan, The Reliable One, is nowhere more apparent than in the utility's Electric Distribution Business Unit, where OUC trouble technicians even take bucket trucks home to respond quickly to emergency calls.

OUC was created in 1923 by a special act of the Florida Legislature and has full authority over the management and control of the electric and water systems of the City of Orlando. Over time, the Legislature has given OUC approval to offer services in Orange County and portions of Osceola County.

Florida's second largest municipal utility, OUC has long been an industry leader in using state-of-the-art environmental power production and water treatment technologies. Acting as good stewards of Central Florida's natural resources has been part of OUC's philosophy for decades, which is why its reputation as an environment-friendly utility is so strong.

Electric Reliability

Keeping power on is the primary goal of all electric utilities—the importance of reliability cannot be overstated. Beyond typical day-to-day operations, reliability also means being prepared to keep the lights on in times of unplanned crisis.

OUC has worked hard to build reliability into its system from design and maintenance standpoints. At OUC, being reliable also means making a commitment to providing a superior level of service to its customers. OUC also utilizes the highest level of environmental equipment available when building power plants and has a diverse portfolio of assets for fuel flexibility.

What specifically makes OUC so reliable? It's part planning, part personnel. OUC believes that to be an outstanding utility, you must prepare for the future. That can involve building a new substation in a fast-developing community or replacing an aging transformer before it fails.

Planning ahead is critical for a high-growth region like Central Florida, where new projects break ground almost daily. OUC is there to provide the crucial infrastructure to facilitate this growth.

OUC also provides its employees the tools and flexibility to perform their jobs well. For example, trouble technicians take their bucket trucks home with them so they can respond to service calls at a moment's notice. These "troublemen" don't have to stop at our operations center before heading to work.

Award-Winning Water

The American Water Works Association has named OUC's drinking water the best in Florida. The judging is rigorous, as a panel tests water from utilities across the state and checks for taste, color, clarity, and odor.

The award proves hard works pays off. Through an initiative called Water Project 2000, OUC replaced its older water-treatment plants with new, state-of-the-art facilities. As part of the process, the utility began using an ozone-treatment process that produces water of such high quality and great taste that they proudly dubbed it H2OUC.

As a strong oxidant, ozone removes smelly hydrogen sulfide and leaves the water with a fresh taste and sparkling appearance. Ozone also reduces the amount of chlorine that must be added to the water, improving the taste even more.

And that's not all. OUC operates a state-certified water quality laboratory where OUC staff performs more than 20,000 chemical and bacteriological tests annually to ensure the quality and safety of OUC's drinking water. Customers can enjoy OUC's award-winning water with confidence, knowing the water is regularly tested and surpasses the highest quality standards.

OUC's water supply is obtained from thirty-four deep wells that tap the lower Floridian Aquifer, a naturally high–quality source of water hundreds of feet below the surface. OUC is committed to investing in conservation initiatives and alternative water supply while working with all of its regional partners to develop solutions to safeguard Central Florida's water future.

Innovative Business

As well as its award-winning electric and water operations, OUC offers a wide variety of inventive solutions to local business needs.

From new home communities to apartment complexes to industrial park projects, OUConvenient *Lighting* works with commercial partners to plan, install, and maintain streetlights for various types of developments. To ensure solutions that work for individual customers, customized service packages are available that combine dozens of fixture/pole groupings.

OUCooling, a chilled-water division of OUC, houses all the equipment used to cool water for air-conditioning systems in a central facility. Environmentally

friendly chillers cool water to 37 degrees, sending it to participating buildings before returning to the central chiller plant at 52 degrees to repeat the cycle.

In addition, building owners using *OUCooling* can benefit from smaller mechanical rooms, which results in more rental space, no insurance requirements, federal income tax savings, and improved property resale value.

Community Outreach

There's no doubting how much OUC employees care about their Central Florida community. Every year OUC volunteers assist civic organizations and charities with generous contributions of time, money, and expertise. From working with the Heart of Florida United Way, United Arts, March of Dimes, and many others, OUC takes its roles as a community leader seriously.

OUC also sponsors many of its own events, including the OUC Half Marathon and 5k and the OUC Downtown Orlando Triathlon. Additionally, OUC's own programs, Project Care and Friendly Neighbor, help customers who are having short-term problems paying their utility bill due to job loss, family emergencies or other problems.

For the length of its more than 80-year history, the Orlando Utilities Commission's primary objective has been to deliver safe, reliable, and low-cost electric and water services to its hometown customers. It's clear that mission has been—and continues to be—a resounding success.

Part of the utility's ongoing dedication to energy conservation, OUC's energy auditors work with area residents to maximize energy efficiency in their homes and apartments.

No matter what nature may have in store, OUC's linemen and field personnel are always ready to provide responsive, reliable service to the utility's water and electric customers.

One of OUC's two OUCooling plants in Downtown Orlando circulates chilled water to office towers, hotels and other commercial buildings, reducing air-conditioning costs.

Correct Craft

After eighty years in the marine industry, family-owned Correct Craft is proud to be more than just a boat manufacturing company. Passionate dedication to quality, performance, and value has established Florida-based Correct Craft as an industry pioneer in the design and manufacturing of world-famous water ski, wakeboard, and recreational watercraft. Committed to raising the bar for innovations in marine technology and hull design, Correct Craft was awarded, for the third time in a row, the J.D. Power and Associates award for Highest Customer Satisfaction with Ski and Wakeboard Boats Survey (2002 and 2003), and the 2005 Boat Competitive Information Study. With single-minded dedication, Correct Craft has perfected their line of Nautique boats to ensure that their customers spend their free time on the water—not waiting for repairs.

An Entrepreneurial Spirit

Spurred by the promise of the 1920s real-estate boom, New Hampshire native, W.C. Meloon moved his family to Central Florida in 1924. Though the real-estate market fizzled out, W.C. turned his steadfast determination to forming a boat manufacturing company based on his personal values: commitment to producing the absolute best product on the market, and using superior materials and unparalleled craftsmanship. While the early years were lean, the Meloon sons exemplified the Correct Craft tradition of innovative thinking. They traveled up and down the eastern seaboard with their boat in tow on a hand-built trailer, selling boat rides for a quarter. Besides contributing much needed funding to the family business, the trip spread the Correct Craft name as far north as New England. The Meloon sons' creative use of a homemade trailer led to Correct Craft pioneering a new delivery standard for the marine industry swiftly replacing delivery by train.

Aiding the War Effort

Having supported the U.S. Armed forces during the First World War by providing construction services, the government called upon Correct Craft again during World War II. To fill the demand, Correct Craft opened their second facility in Titusville, Florida, soon adding larger cruisers to the production schedule. When the Allied Forces reached the Rhine River sooner than anticipated, officials scrambled to procure the plywood vessels needed. Concerned that they would be unable to fill their contract for three hundred boats in just twenty days, the government insisted manufacturers toil seven days a week. Refusing to compromise their strong Christian values, the Meloons insisted they could fulfill their contract while still observing Sunday as a day of rest. The famous Meloon innovation prompted them to engineer a new jig and machinery to aid production. They were able to streamline production by closing off Orange Avenue, one of Orlando's main roads, to expand their facilities. Without compromising their faith, Correct Craft amazingly surpassed their contract and produced an amazing four hundred assault boats in just fifteen days. Upon reaching Germany, the boats

built with the heart and soul of the Correct Craft family of employees carried Allied Forces across the Rhine to victory over the Nazis.

From Military Vessels to Luxury Boats

In that proud tradition, Correct Craft continues to reinvent the marine industry with unsurpassed ingenuity. Realizing that their customers are seeking nothing short of perfection, Nautique designers constantly strive to provide them with responsive handling, championship-grade performance and a quiet, smooth ride—even using the same sound and vibration dampening materials as U.S. Naval submarines. Focusing on the needs of today's extreme sports enthusiasts, Correct Craft has honed the unrivaled Nautique line into a superior collection of luxury inboards that also exceed the U.S. Coast Guard standards for safety and flotation. Recognizing that creature comforts are as important as performance to those living the Nautique lifestyle, available options include a depthfinder, satellite-ready sound system, and variable wake control. Correct Craft has truly changed the way people play on water.

Innovation alone is not enough to satisfy Correct Craft, however. True to the values of company founder, W.C. Meloon, Correct Craft is also committed to perfecting every boat that comes out of their factory. By water-testing every Nautique for a minimum of fifty-five minutes prior to delivery Correct Craft ensures a smooth, hassle-free ownership experience. Their eighty-year history of impeccable quality is so consistent that the International Water Ski Federation has committed to a five-year agreement with Correct Craft to be the sole towboat provider for their 3-event world water ski championship events.

Longevity and Family Values

In order to continue to produce these thrilling and versatile crafts, Correct Craft is currently constructing their new International Headquarters, scheduled for completion in winter of 2005. The new 200,000 square foot facility will house corporate offices, research and development as well as 140 acres dedicated to a new factory. Enabling them to increase employment, the new facility will have the potential to increase production by up to 70 percent. The gem of this expansion, however, is the fifty acres dedicated to twin lakes. While the east lake is earmarked for water-testing each Nautique before delivery, the west lake will be used for research and development purposes as well as championship waterskiing, wakeboarding, and wake skating competitions. Though they investigated sites in other states, Correct Craft decided to remain in Central Florida. While moving might save money on paper, nothing could replace the commitment, skill, and experience of dedicated staff and craftspeople. With an average employment term of at least seven years, many employees spend their entire working lives at Correct Craft—often following in the footsteps of their parents or other family members. Reminiscent of the family values of W.C. Meloon, Correct Craft realized that their loyalty belongs to their real asset, their superb workforce. Correct Craft's commitment to providing a comfortable, enjoyable work environment has instilled their employees with pride in their work—and happy craftspeople simply build better boats.

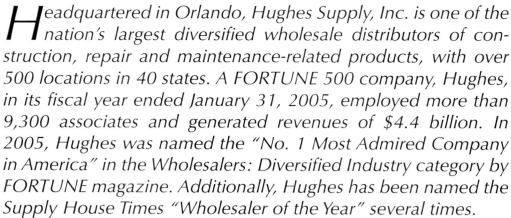

*H*eadquartered in Orlando, Hughes Supply, Inc. is one of the nation's largest diversified wholesale distributors of construction, repair and maintenance-related products, with over 500 locations in 40 states. A FORTUNE 500 company, Hughes, in its fiscal year ended January 31, 2005, employed more than 9,300 associates and generated revenues of $4.4 billion. In 2005, Hughes was named the "No. 1 Most Admired Company in America" in the Wholesalers: Diversified Industry category by FORTUNE magazine. Additionally, Hughes has been named the Supply House Times "Wholesaler of the Year" several times.

A Solid Foundation for Success

Founded in 1928 as a Florida partnership by Clarence Hughes and his son Russell, Hughes Supply started as an electrical distributor of supplies and equipment. Today, Hughes is headquartered in a 150,000 square foot facility in downtown Orlando, part of a larger initiative to revitalize the Parramore community.

Since selling its first electrical part more than 76 years ago, Hughes has concentrated on offering customers superior solutions, an extensive line of high-quality products and exceptional customer service. The company consistently upholds its "12 Commitments to Customer Service": keep your promises; put customers first; have a service attitude; provide solutions; provide prompt credit; provide emergency service; alert short orders; return calls promptly; provide personal service; provide 24-hour service; provide assistance; and treat everyone equally.

Hughes possesses a rich tradition, a solid reputation in the marketplace and a strong leadership team led by President and CEO Tom Morgan, COO Neal Keating, and EVP and CFO David Bearman. Together with a dedicated management team and a highly engaged and motivated workforce, they are achieving dramatic growth by remaining true to Hughes' core values, while also recognizing and embracing new opportunities to increase sales, accelerate earnings growth and develop best in class operations.

Giving Back to the Community

As a respected, long-standing corporate citizen, Hughes has continually answered the call when Orlando citizens and charity organizations need help. In 1999, the company founded the Hughes Supply Foundation, a non-profit entity that supports organizations and individuals in areas where Hughes does business. In 2004, the company started the Hughes Family Fund, which is designed to financially aid employees in urgent need. The company is actively involved in the Boys & Girls Club, as well as numerous community-related and philanthropic organizations. When a flurry of hurricanes blew through Orlando in fall 2004, Hughes Supply was one of the first companies to assist with major contributions to the American Red Cross, Salvation Army and Hughes Supply Foundation. Hughes also matched employee donations to aid victims of the devastating Asian tsunami that struck in December 2004.

Albin Polasek's "Harp" statue, Winter Park, Florida. Photo by Randa Bishop

Daytona Beach International Airport

*A*s Orlando continues to grow, an increasing number of companies are setting up shop just north of the city in the Greater Daytona Beach/Volusia County area. These companies get the best of both worlds—an enviable quality of life and an equally healthy business climate.

Daytona Beach/Volusia County, where Orlando gets down to business

While Volusia County may not be a household name, it has legitimate claims to fame. Daytona Beach is the home of Embry-Riddle Aeronautical University, the world's preeminent aviation and aerospace

Daytona Beach International Airport is among the most passenger friendly in the world, with direct and connecting service to hundreds of domestic and global destinations.

university. The wide, smooth, sandy beaches of the Daytona Beach/ Volusia County area are known the worldwide. Daytona International Speedway is the world center of racing. The LPGA is headquartered in Daytona Beach, as is NASCAR. And the St. Johns River in west Volusia County offers some of the best bass fishing in the world.

Among the businesses here are Boston Whaler, a nationally known boat manufacturer; Hudson Tool & Die Company, a leader in deep drawn metals; Florida Production Engineering, an original equipment

manufacturer for the world's leading automobile companies; Raydon Corporation, which provides simulation software for military and industrial applications; and Crane Technologies, a leader in the high performance automotive aftermarket and many more.

These companies have enjoyed steady growth along with global acceptance of their products. They are supported by the Volusia County Department of Economic Development, which helps local businesses grow and also works with companies from across the nation and around the world that are interested in relocating to or expanding in the area.

"Our community is committed to economic vitality," said Volusia County Council Chair Frank Bruno, "new roads, new industrial parks, new meeting and convention facilities, and new hotels all contribute to a healthy business climate and our emerging reputation as a business location."

Bruno pointed out that the Ocean Center, the area's beachside convention, meeting, and events facility in the heart of Daytona Beach, is undergoing an expansion of approximately $57-million that will add 130,000 square feet of meeting and exhibit space. The project is expected to be finished in 2007.

If traffic at the Web site of the Volusia County Department of Economic Development is an indication, it appears the world is beginning to beat a path to Volusia County.

Ocean Center, a meeting, convention and sports complex, currently undergoing expansion hosts events more than 300 days per year and is considered a preferred venue among meeting planners.

A Great Flying Experience

One of the area's most appreciated assets is Daytona Beach International Airport (DBIA). The complex is extremely user-friendly and gets high marks from business travelers, vacationers and residents.

"Daytona Beach International Airport is critical to our success on many levels," said Volusia County Economic Development Director Richard Michael. "Its importance cannot be overstated and we constantly are improving the facility to add to the ease of travel into and out of the area."

Passengers can fly nonstop to Atlanta, New York (Newark), and Cincinnati, with connecting service to hundreds of other cities here and abroad. Delta Air Lines and Continental Airlines provide the most flights, with Vintage Props & Jets offering additional charter flights including daily runs to the Bahamas and the Florida Keys.

DBIA is a state-of-the-art airport in every way, but its convenience is what places the airport well above larger, more congested airports. Passengers can park, go through security and be at the gate in five minutes. "This is what makes DBIA Central Florida's preferred airport," said Daytona Beach International Airport Director Dennis McGee.

DBIA passengers enjoy an open and airy environment. The airport's gift shop gets high marks from travelers and locals. Several new

eateries are have been added to DBIA's food court including Subway, Nathan's Hot Dogs, Java Coast Coffee Shop, Buckhead Grill, and Ben & Jerry's Ice Cream. Even the security area has been restructured to enhance the flow of passengers and the efficiency of the screening process.

Airport officials have added other conveniences. The complex is a wireless "hot spot" which gives travelers unfettered access to the Internet and email at no charge. They also offer an innovative mail back program where items that do not clear security (items such as scissors and other objects prohibited under security guidelines) are mailed to passengers free of charge.

Flying in and out of DBIA is an experience appreciated by business and leisure travelers and underscores the airport as a convenient gateway to all that Central Florida has to offer.

Parts for the world's leading automobile, aviation, aerospace and medical companies are produced in Volusia County, in the heart of Central Florida's High Tech Corridor.

Ponce DeLeon Inlet and a historic lighthouse add to the allure of Volusia County's magnificent beaches.

Publix Super Markets, Inc.

*S*hop in any of Publix Super Markets' more than 850 stores and you'll instantly notice the courteous service and family atmosphere among the employees. While many of today's top grocery chains have beautiful, high-tech stores, what sets Publix apart is its unyielding commitment to customer service, its family oriented environment, its clean and orderly appearance, and its multiple amenities that make shopping pleasurable and convenient.

Publix's late founder George W. Jenkins envisioned a new kind of grocery store when he opened the first Publix in Winter Haven, FL in 1930.

Publix's late founder George W. Jenkins was affectionately called "Mr. George" by all.

Publix was built on a philosophy that focuses not only on customers, but also on associates—Publix's term for employees. This philosophy is based on the idea that if a company creates the proper environment, attracts the best people, and instills the desire to serve, it will prosper in good times and bad. No doubt, the philosophy has been wildly successful for Publix, which is the largest employee-owned grocery chain in the United States. Company recognitions include ratings as one of the top fifty companies in *FORTUNE's* list of "100 Best Companies to Work For," and one of the top ten companies in Currency/Doubleday's book, The 100 Best Companies to Work for in America.

Simply put, motivated, happy associates at Publix create a positive, service-first atmosphere that shoppers find pleasingly different. One customer, who has shopped at Publix for more than sixty years, is still enamored with the difference from other supermarkets.

"The main thing about Publix is courtesy. I was shopping one day and a lady asked me what made Publix so different. I told her that the priceless ingredient is courtesy. And do you know—two employees were delivering some cases of soft drinks to the store and overheard what I said. One of them said to me, 'They treat us that way, too. At other stores we're like numbers, but here they treat us well.'"

In Fifty Years of Pleasure—a company history published in 1980—a customer in Tallahassee, Florida told of returning from her Publix and having a bag break just as she walked in the door of her home. She called Publix to complain about the poor job the front-service person did with her groceries. Within minutes, a young man arrived at her door with mop in hand and cleaned up the mess.

Publix Now and Then

One of the ten largest-volume supermarket chains in the U.S., Publix has store locations in five states—Alabama, Florida, Georgia, South Carolina, and Tennessee and more than 129,000 employees. In 2004, retail sales totaled $18.6 billion.

Publix founder George Jenkins opened the first Publix Food Store in Winter Haven in 1930 several months after the stock market crash. He later opened a second store in 1935. However, it wasn't until 1940 that Publix began to take off. Jenkins closed his original markets to open his state-of-the-art dream store with air conditioning,

electric-eye doors, wide aisles, terrazzo floors, a modern design, and the latest in equipment. That store, at the corner of Central Avenue and Second Street in Winter Haven, was the first Publix supermarket in the Southeast. Shortly after that, the Publix family was born along with the Publix philosophy "Where Shopping is a Pleasure," which later became the company's slogan.

Since that first grand opening in 1930, Publix has remained on the cutting edge of innovation in U.S. food retailing while staying true to Jenkins' ideas of what a supermarket should be. Today Publix's ingenuity continues with its commitment to growth, recycling, and other innovations like scanning, ATMs, high-quality bakeries and delicatessens, flower shops, in-store banks, and debit card use.

In a constant quest to make the grocery shopping experience pleasurable and convenient, Publix continues to introduce new, innovative ideas. It recently debuted its first in-store Meal Solutions Center, Apron's, designed to show customers how to prepare easy, tasty meals. Publix has opened liquor stores next door to its supermarkets in central and south Florida, selling liquor and some wine and beer. Another new Publix venture, Pix, is Publix's convenience store with gas pumps.

Culture of Giving

George W. Jenkins founded Publix with the spirit of giving in mind. He was once asked, "If you hadn't given away so much, how much do you think you would be worth today?" His response, without hesitation: "Probably nothing."

Jenkins, who passed way in 1996, established a foundation with his own stock as a means of investing in the needs of communities. The foundation benefited from the growth of the company,

which was the result of hard work by Publix associates. Publix Super Markets Charities focuses on youth and education. It helps propel the Take Stock in Children student learning and mentoring program and the George W. Jenkins Scholarship Program for college students. Publix Charities contributes and participates in a broad group of organizations, including the Urban League and the Food Industry Crusade Against Hunger.

In addition to giving to thousands of local projects, Publix annually supports five organizations in company-wide campaigns: Special Olympics, March of Dimes, Children's Miracle Network, United Way, and Food Industry Crusade Against Hunger.

Publix Super Markets is continually recognized as one of the nation's most giving companies. Among its many awards are America's Second Harvest Grocery Distributor of the Year in 2001, the Outstanding Industry Partnership Award for Contributions to the Food Industry Crusade Against Hunger in 1999, the March of Dimes Million Dollar Club Award in 1999, and the United Way of America national Spirit of America Award in 1996.

Publix Super Markets has earned a reputation for being clean and having friendly associates.

Publix erected a birthday cake at the top of its water tower in celebration of its 50th anniversary. It received an award for most unique water tower design in 1980.

Publix's new corporate office in Lakeland, FL opened in 2002 and houses approximately 1,000 associates.

ABC Fine Wine & Spirits

*H*eadquartered in Orlando, ABC Fine Wine & Spirits is the nation's largest privately owned fine wine and spirits merchant with nearly 150 stores and 1,500 employees. Rooted in Florida tradition and family owned and managed, ABC's stores span the Florida peninsula, from Tallahassee and Jacksonville to Naples and South Miami.

Florida-friendly architecture and landscaping help to create the overall shopping experience. Larger stores, averaging nearly 10,000 square feet, are designed as destinations, carrying everything from wine to gourmet cheeses.

Stores Aplenty

ABC's store line-up features a combination of "neighborhood stores" which are typically less than 8,000 square feet in size and focus on a pleasant, convenient shopping environment for every-day needs and the "superstore," a multi-faceted complex averaging almost 10,000 square feet, offering a wide array of wine, spirits, and food products and services.

Approximately 50 percent of ABC's locations are "superstores." A quick stroll through an ABC "su-perstore" and one quickly realizes

customers can store their wine and keep the key. ABC carries more than 4,000 fine wines, a selection of more than four hundred cigars, and both rare and popular spirits. In addition, larger stores carry a variety of gourmet foods, including cheeses and chocolates, as well as custom gift baskets and gift wrapping.

One of the keys to ABC's long-standing success and continual growth is its ability to serve a di-verse customer base. Among the services available at ABC stores are: trained wine consultants who will answer questions and track down hard-to-find wines, special order-ing for items not regularly carried by the store, party and celebration planning, custom gift basket design and assembly services at all larger stores. They also offer a compli-mentary Advantage Buying Card Club and WineISIT membership featuring in-store discounts. Same day delivery is available in several major markets.

Another driving force in ABC's corporate success story is the com-pany's focus on the future. Their flexibility and foresight allows ABC to adapt to continually evolving and changing customer tastes and wants. For instance, in the mid-1980s when wine popularity start-ed to soar in the United States, ABC began putting a strong emphasis on wine education for its employees. Today, ABC has a full time training staff, teaching hundreds of classes a year focusing on wine and spirits. Every new employee takes a "Wine 101" class and larger stores have full-time wine consultants. In addi-tion, ABC has six wine supervisors

ABC stores carry not only popular spirits and beers, but a selection of harder to find items as well. Custom gift baskets are available in the larger stores.

this is not your grandfather's liquor store. "Superstores" often include walk-in cigar humidors brimming with selections from cigar making countries such as the Dominican Republic, Honduras, and Nicara-gua; temperature-controlled wine cellars and massive cold space for imported and micro-brewed beers. Some locations feature a tempera-ture-controlled wine vault where

throughout the state who assist in training and organize wine tastings.

In response to other changing buying habits, ABC created a Direct Sales Center, which provides services such as catalog sales of gift baskets, wine and cigar accessories, and other merchandise. Other specialized services include a custom corporate gift program, Wine of the Month and Cigar of the Month Clubs, pre-sells of special wine and spirit releases, and sales of wine futures.

An increasingly important and successful component of ABC's service-first strategy inside and outside of its stores is its Web site, a well-designed, easy-to-explore site that features new product information, wine picks by ABC experts, upcoming events information, online catalog ordering, new store notices, employment opportunities, and wine travel articles.

A History of Friendly Service

ABC Fine Wine and Spirits was founded in 1936 in Orlando by Jack Holloway, a cigar store manager who saw the end of Prohibition as an opportunity to expand from cigars into spirits. His employer disagreed with his idea, however, and Holloway went into business for himself. The original store, Jack's Friendly Neighborhood Bar, which was situated in downtown Orlando at the corner of North Orange Avenue and Wall Street, attracted customers instantly with Holloway's friendly and service-first attitude. By the mid-1940s, Holloway's company had grown to about a half dozen stores.

Holloway created ABC Liquors in 1950. The simple company name was selected because Holloway wanted something that local residents could easily remember and one than many visitors from other states would immediately associate with spirits. (Many states

have state controlled liquor stores, frequently referred to as ABC stores — Alcoholic Beverage Commission or Alcoholic Beverage Control).

Holloway was a genius at adapting his stores to changing trends and the needs and desires of his customers. During the 1970s, ABC increased the number of retail stores as well as the number of attached "lounges" in styles from basic neighborhood bar to country and western dance clubs to discotheques.

In the late 1980s, ABC embarked on an aggressive growth

Walk-in humidors provide a climate-controlled location for premium cigars, allowing customers to easily find their favorites. ABC's Cigar of the Month Club is a popular means for customers to try new labels or give cigar gifts.

Florida's best selection of wine and spirits greets customers when they step through the doors. Displays feature seasonal items or special promotions.

plan expanding from Central Florida into the northern part of the peninsula with its purchase of Jax Liquors. Reflecting its style of innovative stores and products, the company changed its name in 1993 from ABC Liquors to ABC Fine Wine & Spirits.

One thing that hasn't changed is ABC's staunch commitment to its mission statement which recognizes that growth depends on meeting customers' needs through friendly, competent staff, a broad product selection, and competitive prices. ABC has proved those cornerstones never go out of style even in the fast-paced, constantly evolving wine and spirits market.

Temperature controlled wine cellars allow stores to display more rare wines in a secure, attractive setting. With choices from Australia to New Zealand, customers can find a wine for every occasion and every taste.

*M*ost of the world's important museums are typically located in major international capitals like Rome, Amsterdam, and New York. Consequently, it surprises many people to learn that the Charles Hosmer Morse Museum of American Art, which houses the world's most extensive collection of the works of Louis Comfort Tiffany, is located in the town of Winter Park, just north of Orlando.

World Renown

Quite simply, you can't fully understand Tiffany without visiting the Morse Museum. Alice Cooney Frelinghuysen, curator of decorative arts at the Metropolitan Museum of Art in New York, has called the collection "...the most comprehensive and most interesting collection of Tiffany anywhere." It has been described by Vivienne Couldrey in her book *The Art of Louis Tiffany*, as "... the most important collection of Tiffany material in the world today."

Louis Comfort Tiffany (1848-1933) was an innovator whose enormous glass inventory of more than 5,000 different colors and textures enabled him "to paint

with glass" and imbue his interior designs, windows, and lamps with light and color effects people had not seen before.

A stunning kaleidoscope of colors and shapes, the vast collection of The Morse's holdings includes Tiffany jewelry, pottery, paintings, art glass, leaded-glass windows and lamps, and the chapel interior he designed for the 1893 World's Columbian Exposition in Chicago. The Morse's collection is not only distinguished by its quantity, but also by numerous personal objects from Tiffany, especially those created or exhibited at his Long Island home, Laurelton Hall. The Morse's collection of Laurelton Hall objects, architectural elements, and ornaments is the largest single collection anywhere of surviving materials from this important estate that Tiffany designed himself.

One of the highlights of any visit is to spend time in the famed Tiffany Chapel which was reassembled at the museum in 1999. All of the windows, columns, arches, decorative moldings, altar floor, and furnishings (with the exception of two of the four benches) are original to Tiffany and most date from Chicago, 1893.

While the visually magnificent and historically invaluable Tiffany collection dominates Morse's holdings, the museum also has other important offerings including late 19th and early 20th century American paintings by artists such as Robert Henri, John Singer Sargent, and Maxfield Parish; American decorative art from the mid-19th century to the early-20th century

with especially rich holdings from the Arts and Crafts Movement; and an extensive American art pottery collection featuring Rookwood and other illustrious potteries of the period such as Grueby, Wheatley, and Teco.

Morse has a well-trained, highly professional staff, and it follows strict international guidelines for conservation, storage, and exhibitions.

More about the Morse

Set on North Park Avenue, the Charles Hosmer Morse Museum of American Art is a stately, modified Mediterranean style building. The museum devotes more than 10,000 square feet to exhibitions.

Outwardly, the Morse Museum looks like any other high-level museum; however, it differs in several key ways. The Morse is private in nature and does not receive or accept taxpayer funds directly or indirectly. It does not rent shows like most museums, relying instead on its permanent collection of more than 4,000 objects to create changing exhibitions that deepen the knowledge and appreciation of the collection. Surprising, too, are its low admission prices ($3 for adults, $1 for students and free for children under 12), which afford access to all art lovers, tourist or local. All visitors are admitted free 4-8 p.m. on Fridays, September through May.

Making sure the museum would be accessible without reliance on public funding was the dream of the late Jeannette and Hugh F. McKean, who built the collection over a 50-year period. Jeannette McKean founded the museum in 1942 in memory of her grandfather, Winter Park philanthropist Charles Hosmer Morse. Her husband, Hugh McKean, was the museum's director until his death in 1995. The Charles Hosmer Morse and Elizabeth Morse Genius foundations were set up to operate the private museum in perpetuity.

The scope and quality of the collection reflect the interests, personalities, and ideals of the collectors. The McKeans began their collection with objects already assembled by their families whose collecting activities have been traced back to the 1820s. Undoubtedly, the couple continued shaping the collection to its present size and quality because of their dedication to building a world-class collection of American art designed for the community's aesthetic appreciation and education.

Over the years, objects from the collection have been exhibited at the Metropolitan Museum of Art in New York, the M.H. deYoung Memorial Museum in San Francisco, the Museum of Science and Industry in Chicago, the Renwick Gallery in Washington D.C., and other important institutions.

Community Involvement

Referred to as a "National Treasure and Community Resource," the Morse Museum strives to involve the Orlando community in a variety of ways. Highlighting each year's event schedule are: Christmas in the Park in early December, featuring the lighting of the century-old Tiffany windows in Central Park with a free outdoor concert of holiday favorites; and the three annual open houses in which the museum provides free admission on the family-centered holidays of Christmas Eve, Easter weekend, and July Fourth.

On-going community efforts include a lecture series, film and video series, and a school and art education program, which, among other things, sends a mobile museum out in the Metro Orlando area to visit thousands of school children each year.

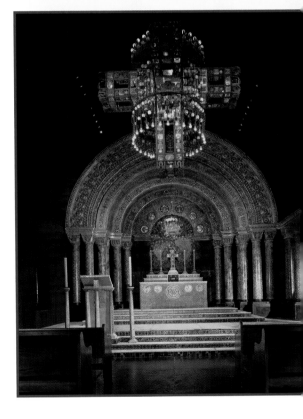

Florida's Blood Centers

Anne K. Chinoda is President and CEO of Florida's Blood Centers. She has been largely responsible for the significant growth and expansion of mission of FBC in the past decade.

*T*he idea for Florida's Blood Centers came about when a group of physicians and local community leaders in Orlando saw the need for a centralized collection and distribution center for blood. Under the name of Central Florida Blood Bank, Inc., it was affiliated with what was then called Orange Memorial Hospital—now Orlando Regional Healthcare—and was chartered in 1942, one of the first in the country and the first in the state of Florida.

From its humble beginnings serving just one hospital, Florida's Blood Centers now is the supplier of blood and blood products to fifty health care facilities in eighteen counties. It provides more than 250,000 pints of blood each year and is one of the largest independent blood banks in the United States.

Blood has been collected and stored since 1938. Before that time, doctors would draw blood from a donor, usually a family member of the patient, and transfuse the blood directly to the patient. In the early 1940s, the process of separating red blood cells and plasma, then freezing the two parts separately, was developed. After that came the process for breaking down the plasma into components, which is now referred to as blood manufacturing. With the onset of World War II and the return of physicians to the U.S. who had seen the benefits of blood transfusions in field hospitals, the demand for blood for the non-combatant patient rose.

The term "bank" is actually misleading, for once collected, blood, which is perishable, does not sit in a vault in plastic bags kept until future use. Although collected blood has a shelf-life of forty-two days, it rarely is stored for that long. After a donor has given blood, that valuable pint is processed into its various components and made available to hospitals within thirty hours. Most of the blood collected on a specific day is used within two to three days.

Florida's Blood Centers was among the first blood banks in the U.S. to establish a network for exchanging blood throughout the country. During the Gulf War, it was the second largest civilian supplier of blood to augment the military's supply. When terrorists attacked on September 11, 2001, it was the first blood bank to respond - within fifteen minutes. Four hundred units of blood were sent to the victims in New York City and the Washington, D.C., area.

Florida's Blood Centers, along with the other blood banks in the country, is regulated by the U.S. Food and Drug Administration (FDA). Because blood components are a special type of pharmaceutical product called biologics, similar to drugs, the FDA licenses blood banks to manufacture and

One of the easiest, fastest ways is to donate on the Big Red Bus bloodmobile when it comes to your business or church. The donation process takes less than an hour, and provides the donor with the knowledge that he or she just saved up to three lives.

ship them across state lines. Blood banks, including Florida's Blood Centers, are inspected by the FDA for compliance with the Good Manufacturing Practices published in the Code for Federal Regulations. These inspections guarantee that the blood being donated and the components used for transfusions are free of contaminants or infections. The American Association of Blood Banks also provides guidelines that must be followed in order for Florida's Blood Centers to operate as a blood bank.

With the discovery of viruses and diseases that were unknown a few short years ago, it is comforting to know that testing and deferrals from donating blood are in place. Those who have traveled to Europe, particularly the United Kingdom, and spent an extended period of time there are not allowed to donate blood because of vCJD, variant Creutzfeldt-Jakob Disease, the human form of Mad Cow Disease. NAT, or nucleic-acid amplification testing, which identifies the genetic material of a virus and then amplifies it millions of times so that it can be detected by sensitive instruments, is used for analysis of a potentially infected blood donation. This test identifies viruses such as HIV, hepatitis C, and West Nile Virus.

Florida's Blood Centers is a registration site for the National Marrow Donor Program. Through this program, potential donors or bone marrow and stem cells are found for those patients who have no genetically matched family member. For thousands of adults and children each year, this procedure may be their only chance for survival.

Patients who rely on this important program may have a number of life-threatening diseases of the bone or blood such as acute or chronic leukemia, inherited metabolic disorders, stem cell disor-

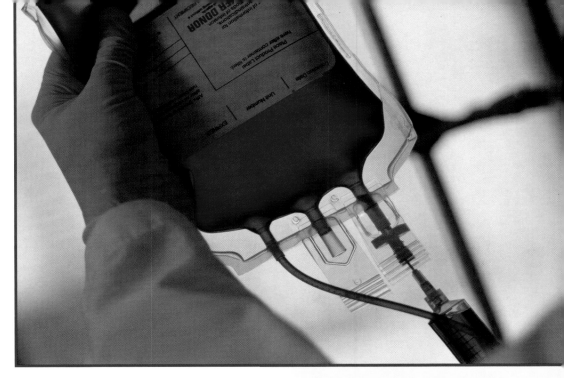

ders, and other malignancies. For children and their parents these diseases can be especially devastating. Robin and Chris Cerquone's son Perry was only 18 months old when he was diagnosed with acute lymphocytic leukemia and they learned he might be helped by an unrelated blood stem cell transplant. Working closely with the NMDP, the Cerquone family endured many trials and tribulations as they went through a donor search, marrow procurement, and the transplant. Perry received his transplant when he was seven years old and today he continues to do well.

The National Marrow Donor Program (NMDP) has an international reach and maintains relationships with medical facilities and other registries in twenty-two countries. Florida's Blood Centers supports NMDP's national and international efforts with the delivery of peripheral blood stem cells all over the world.

A subsidiary of Florida's Blood Centers is the Central Florida Tissue Bank, incorporated in 1985. This organization collects and stores bone and soft tissue for transplants and grafts. Patients who have cancerous bone tumors benefit from

There is no substitute for blood - it can not be manufactured. If each eligible donor committed to donating blood three times a year, there would be no blood shortages.

Only five percent of the population donates blood, however 60 percent of us will need blood in our lifetime. Blood may be donated every eight weeks (56 days) up to six times a year.

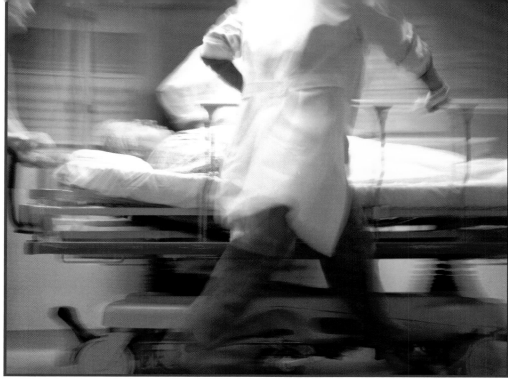

Every three seconds an American needs a pint of blood. One of the most frequent needs is for patients who have suffered trauma, burns, or other life-threatening injuries. Once a blood donation is received, it is usually transfused to a patient within 72 hours.

In 2002, Florida's Blood Centers was fortunate to purchase its new headquarters from another company, which was in decline. This opportunity enabled FBC to centralize its management functions and add a beautiful new donation center near the intersection of John Young Parkway and Sandlake Road in south Orlando.

Donated bone is the second most frequently transplanted tissue after blood. Because it regenerates, it is used to replace bone lost to cancer, for strengthening areas weakened by arthritis or fractures,

bone transplants. Accident victims or vascular disease patients are saved through transplants of bone, soft tissue, or blood vessels. Skin grafts help burn victims. Children with congenital heart defects are able to run and play after a transplant of a heart valve.

for joint replacement, spinal fusion, and oral and facial reconstruction. Bone can be freeze-dried or frozen, and then stored whole, in segments, in small blocks, or crushed, and then re-hydrated when needed. Tissues and bone are donated after death, and a single donor can help as many as fifty people.

Central Florida Tissue Bank also is an eye bank. The cornea is the only part of the eye that is transplanted. With this procedure, thousands are able to see again.

Florida's Blood Centers is on the cutting edge of research and blood collection. In 1986, it was asked by NASA to participate in experiments with blood products in zero gravity. Units of blood were placed aboard the space shuttle Challenger. Unfortunately, they were subsequently lost in the resulting tragedy. However, paper certificates that were to be presented to each blood donor were also on board. One certificate was recovered from the debris at the bottom of the ocean and is on display in Florida's Blood Centers' medical library.

While FBC has grown steadily throughout the years, in 2005 the organization grew significantly with the addition of the former South Florida Blood Bank's opera-

tions to its system. This addition provided the ability for FBC to expand its live-saving mission into South Florida. FBC's intervention circumvented a potential health-care crisis as the previous organization was nearly to the point of being unable to meet the needs of

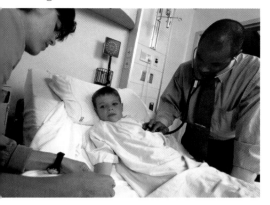

Lifesaving blood is useful in treating a number of conditions that afflict children and adults including cancer, anemia, and hemophilia..

Florida's Blood Centers is on the leading edge of research and technology. In 1986, FBC was asked by NASA to participate with blood products in zero gravity on the ill-fated Challenger mission.

area residents. Today, under FBC's strong leadership, South Florida's residents can rest easy in the knowledge that FBC is providing a safe, ample blood supply to twenty area hospitals.

Across the state, the need for blood is constant. Blood is pulled through the system as fast as it is donated and processed. The increasing populations and constant influx of visitors and winter residents strains the healthcare system and fuels the intense demand for blood. Florida's Blood Centers is committed to meeting these needs through the addition of cutting-edge technology, trained and caring staff, and comfortable facilities. FBC never forgets that the residents of the communities it serves are the reason for its existence.

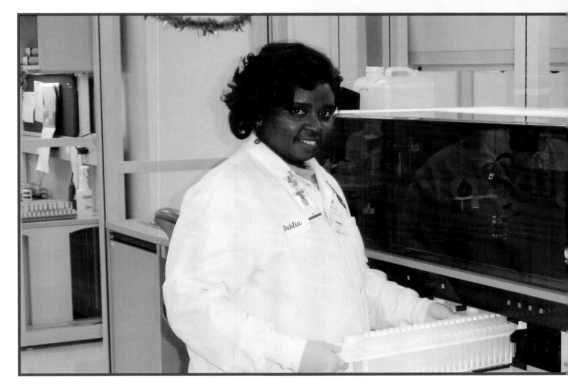

Precious units of blood are sorted by type and stored in industrial size refrigerators prior to being distributed to patients in need. The blood supply must be constantly replenished as red blood cells have a shelf life of only 42 days.

Florida's Blood Centers is on the cutting edge of research and technology. It was among the first to implement testing for West Nile Virus. Every pint of blood donated undergoes 18 hours of processing, testing and labeling and must pass 11 rigid screening tests to assure safety.

Blue Cross and Blue Shield of Florida

*A*t a time when the cost of health care has become a national priority, consumers are demanding more from their health plans. Blue Cross and Blue Shield of Florida, (BCBSF) not only meets its policyholders' needs today, but is also committed to anticipating how the changing world of health care will affect members tomorrow and in the years to come.

Blue Cross and Blue Shield of Florida

Homegrown and Policyholder-Owned

Blue Cross and Blue Shield of Florida is Florida's leading health plan. BCBSF and its subsidiaries serve more than 6.6 million Floridians in all sixty-seven counties in the state. It is the most recognized health plan in the state of Florida, serving its members with a wide array of health care choices and extensive provider networks.

BCBSF is an independent licensee of the Blue Cross and Blue Shield Association, an association of independent Blue Cross and Blue Shield companies. BCBSF is a financially strong, tax-paying, not-for-profit, mutual life and health insurance company. It is an independent organization governed by its own community-based Board of Directors.

Unlike many national health insurers, BCBSF is a Florida company. This unique local presence enables the company to better understand its members' individual needs on a community level. Understanding that customers in Orlando may have different health care needs than their southern neighbors in Miami, BCBSF has fourteen regional offices—each supported with medical directors, health plan administrators and community relations teams. Knowing that their efforts are improving lives in their own communities fosters a sense of pride and satisfaction in employees. As many at BCBSF like to say, they are home-grown, policyholder-owned and here to serve!

When searching for a new career, most potential employees dream of working at an organization that is supportive of their needs and has room for professional and personal growth. Others hope to be a part of a dynamic, trendsetting company that continuously redefines the cutting edge within its market. Still others have a vision of being a part of a major partner in the community, a business that focuses its resources on improving the lives of those around it. In those ways and many others, Blue Cross and Blue Shield of Florida is an employee's dream come true.

With a strong commitment to enriching the lives of its employees, BCBSF strives to create a rewarding work environment that not only encourages its employees to grow within their professional roles, but also enables them to contribute to the well-being of their communities. Through the distinctive Blue Community Champions program of community involvement, BCBSF places volunteers in many local programs that share a focus on health, education, cultural, or quality of life issues affecting all Floridians. By donating their time to local programs such as Shepherd's Hope Health Centers for the uninsured, Speaking of Women's Health symposiums, Habitat for Humanity, local mentoring programs, and Meals on Wheels, BCBSF employees bring hope, health, and happiness to members of their respective communities.

Recognizing the unique blend of cultures throughout Florida, BCBSF endeavors to not only offer culturally and linguistically sensitive customer support but also provides

a supportive environment for its diverse workforce of 9,500 employees and contributes time and funding to programs improving the health and well-being of Florida's minorities. By supporting programs such as Hispanic Health Initiatives, Inc., the LBS Foundation, and the Lisa Merlin House, as well as assisting the elderly, young, homeless, and abused within its communities, BCBSF strives to improve the quality of life for its neighbors.

BCBSF also devotes time and resources to educational programs from preschool to college level students. Concerned with the dramatic nursing shortage threatening health care nationwide, BCBSF has chosen to designate a significant portion of its philanthropic investments in support of nursing and allied health educational programs. BCBSF has provided substantial financial support for nursing education at the University of Central Florida in Orlando. And by helping to create a permanent endowment to Foundation for Florida's Community Colleges, tuition and laboratory fees for two hundred nursing and allied health students will be covered annually in perpetuity.

Helping the Uninsured

Unfortunately, as health care costs continue to rise, the number of uninsured and underserved Floridians is rising as well. Recent statistics show that approximately 2.8 million or 17.5 percent of Florida's workforce are unable to afford medical coverage. Some are temporary or part-time employees ineligible for the coverage offered by their employers, while others are struggling to pay for dependents whose coverage has been reduced or eliminated by strapped employers. In addition, many senior citizens face choosing between their medications and paying their bills. Trying to get by, some seniors

simply do not purchase their medications, or cut their pills in half to make expensive prescriptions last longer.

True to its commitment to improving the health and well being of all Floridians, BCBSF proudly established The Blue Foundation for a Healthy Florida. With the help of BCBSF, this philanthropic organization has brought quality health care and health education to many needy individuals and families. Focused on the unique needs of Floridians, The Blue Foundation works on a community level to identify local at-risk populations and implement programs to address their specific needs. Dangers of being uninsured include premature death from breast cancer, colon cancer, and under-treated hypertension, in addition to complications resulting from unmonitored diabetes.

In order to better serve these populations, The Blue Foundation has made ninety-five grants—nine of which are in the Orlando metro area—totaling nearly $5 million

"The Blue Foundation for a Healthy Florida provides funds for Shepherd's Hope expansion."

"Jeppesen VisionQuest and The Blue Foundation giving children a clear look at the future."

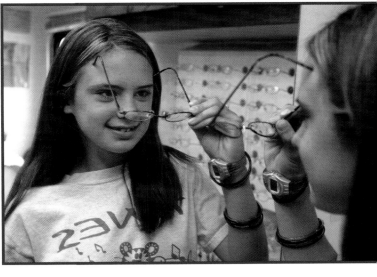

"Blue Cross and Blue Shield of Florida volunteers make a difference in Orlando."

"The UCF School of Nursing continues to explore new paths to good health as a result of support from BCBSF."

since its inception in 2001. One recipient of these grants is the Shepherd's Hope organization, a faith-based group of health centers providing quality non-emergent care to persons in need. Thanks to The Blue Foundation's grant and the coordinated efforts of volunteer physicians, health-care professionals, schools, hospitals, and churches, Shepherd's Hope has provided more than 22,000 patient visits in the past six years. Each of the eight Shepherd's Hope Health Centers grows out of a union between faith communities or schools, providing volunteer staff and clinic space, and hospitals, which accept referrals without compensation for routine laboratory and radiology services. The Blue Foundation shares its vision of compassionate, first-rate care for those who would otherwise go without.

Another recipient of the Blue Foundation's philanthropy is Jeppesen VisionQuest, a not-for-profit charity focusing on meeting the vision needs of Florida's most vulnerable children. In 1994 Nancy

and Richard Jeppesen purchased vision examination equipment with the intention of bringing it overseas to help the populations of third world countries. To test drive the equipment, the Jeppesens offered free eye exams to the children of Florida's migrant farm workers. Appalled by the vast need for visual care on their own doorstep, the Jeppesens changed their plans. After buying a Winnebago and installing the equipment on board, Jeppesen VisionQuest was born. With the help of The Blue Foundation's annual grants and by providing on-site vision examinations and free quality glasses,

"A diversified work force offers opportunities to grow personally and professionally in a supportive environment."

Jeppesen VisionQuest will care for more than 14,000 pairs of young eyes this year.

The Blue Foundation is proud to support organizations such as the SeniorsFisrt, the Hispanic Health Initiatives, and the United Cerebral

Palsy, which innovatively meet the needs of Florida's medically poor. Through these and other community based programs, underserved and uninsured Floridians are able to obtain screening, treatment, and preventative care for conditions such as diabetes, heart disease, hypertension, cervical cancer, mental health, hepatitis C, pediatric asthma, as well as vital OB-GYN, nutrition, vision, and prescription drug services.

"BCBSF's local presence means a better understanding of members' needs on a community basis."

With the generous financial contributions and dedicated employee volunteers of BCBSF, The Blue Foundation will be able to continue to improve the lives of Florida's underserved and uninsured for years to come.

In addition to its work within the community, BCBSF is passionately committed to providing customers with access to a wide array of affordable health plans and broad networks of physicians, hospitals and health care facilities. Focusing on education and communication, BCBSF works closely with local physicians and health care providers to improve access to quality care. BCBSF assists physicians in providing their patients with the tools they need to manage their care by offering on-site training for medical office staff, as well as online reference tools for health care providers and patients alike. In order to better support health care providers, BCBSF has also created a doctor-staffed Physician Advisory

board to review potential programs prior to rollout.

Providing Information

Thanks to the availability of the Internet, consumers today choose to educate themselves before making choices. BCBSF appreciates this need for valid, reliable health information and has designed programs to help members take charge of their care. In addition to 27,000 pages of online reference information about 1,900 clinical topics, BCBSF also provides its members with free audio, video, and printed information on specific health conditions to help them weigh the risks and advantages of treatment options. Health Coaches and Chronic Disease Management programs are also available to help patients and their families meet the challenge of managing their health and wellness choices.

"Adding value, one member at a time."

Health insurance is a purchase that needs careful thought and attention. Some of the most frightening and wonderful events in our lives, like treating a chronic or debilitating disease or giving birth to a baby, are shaped by the choices we make regarding insurance. By choosing Blue Cross and Blue Shield of Florida as your health plan, you are buying security in the knowledge that the person overseeing your coverage issues or taking your service calls isn't halfway across the country. They are Floridians, serving Floridians ... because they believe you deserve only the best.

Blue Cross and Blue Shield of Florida

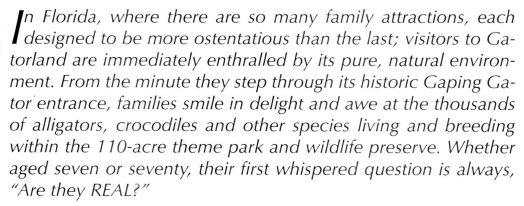

Gatorland

In Florida, where there are so many family attractions, each designed to be more ostentatious than the last; visitors to Gatorland are immediately enthralled by its pure, natural environment. From the minute they step through its historic Gaping Gator entrance, families smile in delight and awe at the thousands of alligators, crocodiles and other species living and breeding within the 110-acre theme park and wildlife preserve. Whether aged seven or seventy, their first whispered question is always, "Are they REAL?"

Known internationally as the Alligator Capital of the World, and voted Best Florida Non-Major Attraction in 2003 by Florida Monthly magazine, family-owned Gatorland is an exotic oasis nestled between Orlando and Kissimmee, just fifteen minutes from the Orlando Airport. In its pristine all-natural setting, Gatorland's helpful staff specializes in welcoming guests for days of fun, smiles, and special memories. Completely free of animatronics, Gatorland provides visitors with a chance to see the park's exotic residents in their true habitat.

For the Love of Gators

In the 1930s, the late Owen Godwin built a gatorpit in his backyard as a way to share the beauty of an alligator family as tourists began to explore Florida.

It was a small step towards his dream of an attraction that would showcase Florida's wildlife in a family-friendly, natural setting. After World War II, Owen purchased a sixteen-acre "borrow pit" created from the paving of a new highway. A family labor of love, the Godwins worked together for two years to excavate and construct Central Florida's first major attraction, finally opening to the public in 1949. In addition to observing regional alligators and snakes, visitors could also watch breathtaking displays of Seminole alligator wrestling.

By 1954, the park had gone through a number of incarnations, finally settling on the name Gatorland. With its popularity boosted by taking the giant alligator, Cannibal Jake, on the road, tourists began flooding through the concrete Gaping Gatorjaw entrance. After adding the Swamp Walk in 1978, guests were able to walk along a two-thousand foot boardwalk through enclosure-free Florida wetlands, observing the headwaters of the Everglades much as they existed thousands of years before.

As the park grew, the Godwin family worked together to maintain a lush haven for all-natural family fun and in 1979 expanded their interests to support crocodilian research and education by teaming with the University of Florida and the Florida Wildlife Commission. Through ground-breaking onsite research and an annual $20,000

grant to the University of Florida, Gatorland has helped usher the science of breeding alligators and nurturing their hatchlings into the new millennia, thus ensuring propagation of a number of endangered species.

With their most recent expansions in the 1990s, 110 acre Gatorland has grown to include over one hundred breeding alligators, four species of crocodiles, regional snakes, birds, turtles, and a petting zoo. New depth was brought to Owen Godwin's vision of a showcase of Florida wildlife when the Alligator Breeding Marsh opened. In a stress-free natural environment, the park's alligators found the safety needed to mate and raise families. As an added bonus, thousands of aquatic birds were drawn to the abundant vegetation of the Breeding Marsh and have established a permanent breeding rookery, protected by the alligators from natural predators. One of the largest and most accessible rookeries in Florida, it was chosen in November 2000 by the Florida Fish and Wildlife Conservation Commission as part of its "Great Florida Birding Trail." Awestruck visitors are able to observe this one-of-a-kind, balanced habitat from the near-by walkway and observatory. To better share their one-of-a-kind habitat with the world, Gatorland has also opened their doors to film crews for hundreds of movies, natural documentaries, and television series.

Combining Education with Entertainment

Families are enthralled by Gatorland shows, combining thrills with a healthy dose of education. In addition to learning more about man-eating jungle crocs and enjoying daring displays of Gator Wrestlin', guests are delighted by the exciting Gator Jumparoo, where

alligators leap four to five feet out of the water to snatch food from their trainers' hands. For those in search of even more adventure, the Rookie Wrestlin' and Trainer for a Day programs give guests a glimpse into the dangerous daily life of Gatorland staff. Finally, families can stop by the Aviary to hand feed exotic lorikeets or experience an Up Close Encounter Show to meet both local wildlife and fascinating creatures from around the globe.

Striving to be a community leader in educating the public about Floridian wildlife, Gatorland's recently expanded educational program includes snake and crocodilian safety and awareness classes for children and adults, including firefighters, police, emergency medical service professionals, and environmentalists. To reach more people across Florida, Gatorland has produced a twenty-minute alligator and snake safety video, offering do's and don'ts to help adults and children avoid dangerous encounters with Florida wildlife.

The welcoming, warm staff of family-run Gatorland continues to hold fast to Owen Godwin's vision of providing visitors with a precious journey into the heart of Florida natural habitats. More importantly, however, thanks to Gatorland's contributions to education and research these amazing creatures will be here for future generations to enjoy as well.

WFTV-9

*T*he television station with the answers to these questions is WFTV and Channel 9 Eyewitness News: Coverage You Can Count On.

What's happening in Central Florida? What's the new information on the big story? Will it rain tomorrow?

The long-time experience of WFTV makes it the station to turn to in order to stay informed on a daily basis. Since it sent out its first broadcast on February 1, 1959, WFTV (Wonderful Florida Television) has been an influential force in the Orlando area. As an ABC affiliate, it carries all the network news and entertainment programming, but its heart is in Central Florida. With twenty reporters covering all the important events in the area,

the station has been rated the #1 news TV station in the market for the past twenty-five years. Five anchors, who also do field reporting, find and tell interesting local stories with depth and detail. Bob Opsahl, the most senior male anchor in the market, has been with the station for twenty-five years; his partner, Martie Salt, is also well known, having been a reporter and anchor for seventeen years. This team, the most recognized and respected news anchors in central Florida, delivers the five o'clock, six o'clock, and eleven o'clock news. At 5:30, Bob Opsahl and Barbara West do a recounting of the day's events. Early birds can catch Vanessa Echols and Greg Warmoth at 5:00 AM. Those who like to get the news with their lunch can see Vanessa Echols once again and Barbara West at noon.

Besides the important local news of Central Florida, the weather is on everyone's mind, and Tom Terry, chief meteorologist, delivers the sunshine along with the clouds. The station's Severe Weather Center 9 keeps track of any storms that might put a damper on the day's events. During the six weeks in 2004 when Florida was ravaged by Hurricanes Charley, Frances, and Jeanne, and threatened with Ivan, the weather center was utilized in dramatic form. The station was the number one choice of viewers during this scary and dangerous time. With weather technology, such as Early Warning Doppler 9000, Storm Tracker, Tornado Tracker, and Future Track, the station's meteorologists were able to plot both short and long range forecasts, and thus helped the community by saving lives and property.

Helping the community is part

of the station's mission of involvement. After the devastation of each of the hurricanes, WFTV Channel 9 held relief efforts—at the T.D. Waterhouse Center, at the M.L. King Center for the Performing Arts, and at Daytona USA. No other TV station in the area attempted such wide-scale relief efforts. As a result, the recovery drives benefited the American Red Cross, Central Florida's Blood Centers, the SPCA, and Second Harvest Food Bank. Over $111,000 in cash and 116 tons of non-perishable food and pet food were collected, and more than 4,200 people registered and donated blood.

Besides stepping in to help out during disasters, the station has an on-going community-centered outreach called the WFTV 9 Family Connection. The station supports forty to fifty community events each year, and raises millions of dollars annually to help Floridians improve their lives. The station also received recognition in the 2004 Philanthropy Day Awards for its relief work done during the period of the hurricanes.

As a part of their community outreach, the station also runs a series of family specials on a regular basis. These programs, headlined as "9 Family Connection Specials," concentrate on family-oriented issues and identify real problems that real families face and real solutions to those problems. The criteria for these special programs deal with issues in four areas: safety, education, health, and quality of life. For the past several years, the station has won first place awards for their efforts from such recognized organizations as the Mid-Florida Society of Professional Journalists, the South Florida Society of Professional Journalists, and the Florida Associated Press.

In addition to 9 Family Connection, the WFTV Anchor Bob Opsahl is the driving force behind

"Wednesday's Child," a weekly feature that showcases young people who are looking to be adopted by generous, caring families. These children have usually been in the system of the Department of Family Services for a while and have lived in various foster homes. Through the efforts of Opsahl, 50 percent of the children who have been featured have been adopted.

Of course, a television station would not be complete without reporting on the area sports teams, and WFTV is no exception. Every Sunday night from 11:30 to midnight, Dan Hellie and Zach Klein discuss the week's wins and losses on "Sports Night on 9," a locally programmed show. These "sports guys" also anchor and report on team doings during the week.

From disasters to sunshine to sports, WFTV Channel 9 has a legacy of news reporting excellence and leadership. Owned by one of the oldest, privately-held media companies in the country, Cox Enterprises, Inc., the station is proud of its veteran anchors and its legacy of news reporting. It is the only station in the area that gives back to the community in the form of continual public service. With its commitment to advanced weather technology in a severe weather state, it is the most reliable and trustworthy destination for weather information. It is truly "coverage you can count on."

Arnold Palmer's Bay Hill Club & Lodge

Nestled in a quiet, meticulously landscaped residential community in southwest Orlando, Arnold Palmer's Bay Hill Club & Lodge is reminiscent of a simpler time when private clubs offered accommodations for guests. It is one of the nation's few remaining private clubs with an on-site resort hotel, and the unique situation allows non-members who stay at the 65-room lodge (or nine cottages and guest houses) to receive the best of both worlds—a combined private golf club and an amenity-rich resort experience. Lodge guests are greeted by name and treated as club members during their stay.

At Bay Hill, members and guests will experience classic Palmer hospitality.

Far Right: A perennial landmark at Bay Hill, the Rolex clock stands a vigilant watch over the putting green.

Your Host: Arnold Palmer

Bay Hill undeniably is an extension of the personality of golf icon Arnold Palmer, who owns the property and lives at the community during the winter months. Comfortable and friendly, Bay Hill's design and ambience is everything you would expect from golf's most beloved ambassador. Better still, there's a distinct possibility for a chance meeting with Palmer. Friendly and approachable, "Arnie", as he is affectionately known by golf fans everywhere, can be spotted just about anywhere on the property from the golf course and clubhouse to the dining room and front lobby. Those that aren't lucky enough to meet Palmer can stroll the hallways of the lodge where the walls are brimming with memorabilia and photographs celebrating his miraculous six-decade golf career.

Decorated with rich wood appointments, antiques, and classic colors, the lodge is elegant, but unpretentious. Guestrooms feature

View of the 18th green from the fairway.

Middle Right: Bronze plaque at the entrance near the Clubhouse.

oversized, private patios with views of the golf course as well as the finest quality linens. For corporate meeting groups, Bay Hill offers 7,000 square feet of tastefully appointed and well-designed meeting space.

Repeat Visitors Abound

First-time guests are drawn to the property by their admiration for Palmer and the desire to play Bay Hill's renowned, highly rated course, site of the Bay Hill Invitational, a PGA Tour event held every March. The 27-hole Palmer-designed golf course, just a few steps from the lodge, is truly one of the world's great golf experiences. Bay Hill has an extremely high percentage of repeat guests and what keeps them coming back is the amiable and attentive service staff, amenities such as a full-service salon and spa, fitness center, junior Olympic swimming pool, six lighted tennis courts, and, of course, Arnold Palmer's undeniable presence and appeal.

The Peabody Hotel's doube ducker bus.
Photo by Randa Bishop

Port Canaveral

Although Florida's geography naturally lends itself to containing a number of prime ports of call for both cargo shippers and pleasure seekers alike, the daily effort required to keep such a port running safely and efficiently is staggering. Fortunately for tourists and shippers the world over, the team at Port Canaveral goes above and beyond the call of duty.

There are few places more exciting than a port, and as Port Canaveral is one of the busiest ports in the world, day-to-day life is quite bustling. Whether you are a vacationer boarding a cruise ship to the Bahamas, a merchant shipping cargo to another time zone, or simply an avid fisherman looking to spend a day at the marina, Port Canaveral is the place to be.

Business Matters

Although it would seem that business clientele would increase simply because ships need to dock somewhere, Port Canaveral does aggressively seek new clientele. By maintaining low operating costs, as well as having its desirable proximity to the open sea, the port greets many new and returning customers each year. With more than a dozen deepwater ports on the Florida peninsula, it would certainly be quite easy to get lost in the shuffle, but with many effective methods for sending and receiving cargo (as well as vacationers!), it is no wonder that Port Canaveral is such a successful, bustling commercial port. Port Canaveral's major business dealings come from three separate categories: cargo, cruises, and local businesses.

Port Canaveral is known for having the shortest direct entry in

eastern Florida, with the trip from first sea buoy to berth taking only forty-five minutes. In addition to its easy access, shippers choose the Port because of its cost-effective services and facilities. An attractive feature is that the cargo facilities on the Port are located separately from the cruise docks, resulting in better security and quality assurance of the goods coming in and out of Port. The Port also is well-equipped to monitor bulk and breakbulk cargo, not only with its nearly 4,000 feet of dock space, but also with its tram trains that bring the cargo from shipping vessels to the warehouses, as well as an intermodal gate with modern, fiber optic weighing and tracking technology, allowing trucks quicker access to the loading docks.

Port Canaveral is also home to Foreign Trade Zone 136, which in itself contains three hubs and subzones for cargo shipping. FTZ 136 is the world's first quadramodal zone, handling cargo from sea, land, air, and space. Strategically located adjacent to the Kennedy Space Center and Cape Canaveral, the port fosters an ongoing relationship with these two hubs of the nation's space program.

If you are flying or driving to Florida to board a vacation cruise ship, there is a very good chance that you will be meeting that ship at Port Canaveral. As one of the world's busiest cruise ports, second only to that of Miami, Port Canaveral is home to such illustrious cruise lines as Carnival, Royal Caribbean, and Disney Cruises, as well as other gaming vessels including the Sterling Casino and

SunCruz Casino ships, which offer gaming "cruises to nowhere" twice a day. The Port's proximity to the Orlando International Airport also is advantageous—it's only about a forty minute drive east on the Beeline highway/SR S28.

The major focus of the Canaveral Port Authority, the governing body of Port Canaveral, is to foster a healthy economy for residents and businesses in the region. It accomplishes its task through the dozens of businesses that make their home near the docks. The commercial park, which offers an appropriately maritime flavor, has business tenants that include seafood processors, restaurants, and boat manufacturers. These businesses stimulate the local Florida economy by employing at least 30,000 people throughout Central Florida, resulting in an economic boost of more than $808 million.

Security Measures in Today's World

Centuries ago, a man stationed aloft in a lighthouse with a beacon was considered the height of security. These days, it takes a lot more manpower and highly sophisticated security measures to keep the open sea and its ports safe.

Prior to the September 11th attacks, only four to five percent of Canaveral Port Authority's budget was earmarked for security. Since then, the Port has allocated approximately 20 percent of the budget to upgrading and maintaining security. J. Stanley Payne, CEO, states that security infrastructure continually is being added to the Port, citing such measures as automated access points and biometric identification cards for the employees of the Port Authority, its tenants, and customers, as well as experimental radar and closed-circuit televisions to monitor strategic parts of the entire area.

Charting a Course

When Stan Payne came on board, first as chief operating officer, then as CEO, his mission was not only to continue the success the Port has been enjoying since 1953, but to broaden its image as a "growing, vibrant commercial port."

"This is a port that grew up quickly," Payne says, suggesting that the port never truly "caught its breath" due to its success during the past decade. In addition to restructuring the organization to make it "lighter on its feet," Payne is planning to reform the brand of the Port so that it is established clearly in the minds of Floridians and everyone what already is there: an independent, fully functioning Port that provides not only world-class cargo shipping services, but also has a colorful community of businesses, restaurants, parks, marinas, and recreational facilities, among others.

It seems that the team at Port Canaveral has found the right recipe for success. As it continues to grow and adapt to the evolving needs of its customers, the Port will continue to shine as one of Central Florida's true gems.

Ron Jon Surf Shop

A stroll through the world's largest surf shop, the two-story, 52,000 square foot Ron Jon Surf Shop in Cocoa Beach is as much of an entertainment as shopping experience. The ocean-front landmark, which attracts nearly two million visitors annually, is synonymous with the surfing lifestyle and is the ultimate destination for any beach lover.

Open 24 hours a day, the sprawling, two-acre store is filled floor to ceiling with everything one could possibly need for the sun and fun lifestyle. From surfboards and wetsuits to swimsuits and sandals, the choices are endless.

"Obviously not everyone who visits our stores is a surfer and some may never get on a surfboard, but lots of people are enamored with the beach and surfer lifestyle," says Ed Moriarty, president of Ron Jon Surf Shop, describing the appeal of Ron Jon. "Our customers come from all parts of the world and they love the American surfing lifestyle."

The finest quality merchandise and recognized popular labels including Ron Jon, Quiksilver, O'Neill, Rip Curl, Billabong, Oakley, Volcom, and Hurley are at the core of Ron Jon

Surf Shop's product appeal. "From the beginning, Ron Jon's has always been about offering the best quality possible, whether it's a surfboard, shirt or suntan lotion," says Moriarty. "Our t-shirts are made to wear and last a long time, they're not just souvenirs."

The Cocoa Beach shop is the flagship store of Ron Jon Surf Shop, which includes the original store in Long Beach Island, New Jersey, an 8,100 square foot shop famous for its "world's largest surfboard," which weighs more than 200 pounds and is twenty-four feet in length; a 25,000 square foot shop in Orange, California located five minutes from Disneyland; a 22,500 square foot shop in the Oasis at Sawgrass Mills Mall in Fort Lauderdale, Florida; and a store in Orlando. In addition, the Ron Jon Surf Shop Web site

features a live surf web-cam and an e-commerce store that allows web surfers to shop for hundreds of brand-name items from the Ron Jon online marketplace.

Surf's Up in Orlando

Ron Jon Surf Shop has a strong presence in Orlando with its store in the Festival Bay shopping complex on International Drive, which opened in 2003. Featured is a stunningly realistic beach scene with a 1934-replica Ford woody wagon favored by surfers, piles of white sand and a 1960s-style Ron Jon billboard. Thatched bamboo structures, sand textured walkways, a 60-foot-long, surf wave mural, and island-themed surf shacks give the surf emporium an authentic island look and feel.

Expansion through Licensing

Ron Jon Surf Shop's popularity has continued to grow and is expanding through licensing opportunities both in the U.S. and around the world. In April of 2004 Tampa, Florida based Stellar Partners opened a Ron Jon Surf Shop in the Orlando International Airport. With the success of the Orlando location, Stellar Partners is planning additional airport shops in Tampa, Newark and Miami. In September of 2004 Tiendas Tropicales of Mexico opened a new Ron Jon Surf Shop at an outdoor shopping area, Puerta Maya, adjacent to the Carnival and Princess Cruise Lines terminal in Cozumel, a perfect tropical location for the world's most famous surf shop.

Going Back in Time

It was 1959 and on the New Jersey shore, a bright young man named Ron DiMenna was just discovering the sport of surfing with fiberglass surfboards. His pastime soon became a passion, and homemade surfboards would no longer do. When DiMenna's father heard that his son wanted his own custom surfboard from California, he suggested, "Buy three, sell two at a profit, then yours will be free." His dad was right, and Ron Jon Surf Shop was born.

The original Ron Jon Surf Shop opened in Long Beach Island, New Jersey in 1961. DiMenna sold surfboards out of that tiny Jersey shore shop, supplying former customers with surfboards to open their own surf shops on the East Coast. When he headed to Florida two years later and opened the "One-of-a-Kind" Ron Jon Surf Shop in Cocoa Beach, he sold even more.

The Ron Jon Surf Shop logo and name has been recognized around the globe for more than forty years with only minor revisions. It has been spotted on the space station Mir 200 miles above the earth, and has purportedly embraced one of the long slender legs of the Eiffel Tower. And every day, it is seen on vehicles ranging from '65 Ramblers to '04 Lincoln Navigators.

The University of Central Florida has come a long way in a short time. Barely forty years into its history, UCF is one of the fastest-growing universities in the country, both in the size of its student body and the quality of its academics and research.

The Student Union building, at the center of the campus, offers a wide selection of eateries for students, as well as stores and office facilities for student government and various student organizations.

Founded in 1963, UCF has quickly become a leader in lasers and optics, modeling and simulation, computer science, biomolecular and life sciences, nanoscience, education, and hospitality management, all of which are essential to the regional and state economy.

The university has one of the world's top research programs in lasers and optics, a focus of which is developing the next generation of ultra-small computer chips, and one of the top hospitality management programs, located in the heart of one of the world's top tourist destinations. In 2004, the university created the Florida Interactive Entertainment Academy, a partnership with Electronic Arts that will train future video-game developers. While becoming a leader in research and a partner with industry, UCF has continued to maintain its goal to provide the best undergraduate education possible to its students.

Under the leadership of President John C. Hitt since 1992, the

The fountain in the Reflecting Pond is something of an icon on campus. The grass provides a comfortable place for students to sit and study on sunny days. The fountain is in front of the Library, which houses more than a million volumes.

university has become a major factor in the economy and technology-based areas of Florida. Annual sponsored research funding at the university is approaching $100 mil-

lion, and UCF's estimated impact on the Central Florida economy is more than $1.3 billion a year.

President Hitt asked leaders at the University of South Florida in 1996 to join him in forming the Florida High Tech Corridor Council to help attract, retain, and grow high-tech industry and the workforce needed to support it. The corridor, which has since expanded to include other universities, has partnered with more than 200 companies and generated more than $128 million in applied research in key industries.

Located on 1,415 acres in East Orlando, UCF is one of the ten largest employers in Central Florida, with almost 2,000 faculty and several thousand additional staff. Another 10,000 employees work in the adjacent Central Florida Research Park. UCF has partnered with Orange County and Orlando to develop the park into a showplace business hub for the region.

With 43,000 students in fall 2004, UCF has the second-largest enrollment among Florida universities and one of the brightest student bodies. SAT scores and grade-point averages for incoming freshmen and the number of National Merit Scholars rank among the highest in the state. More than half of UCF's students come from outside the university's eleven-county service area in Central Florida, including all fifty states and more than 140 countries around the world.

With nine colleges, including the Burnett Honors College for top-ranking honors students, UCF offers more than 180 bachelor's, master's, doctoral and specialist degrees. The university has awarded more than 140,000 degrees since classes began in 1968.

Other colleges include Arts and Sciences, Business Administration, Education, Engineering and Computer Science, and Health and Public Affairs. Three colleges have been added in recent years: the Burnett College of Biomedical Sciences, the College of Optics and Photonics, and the Rosen College of Hospitality Management.

The College of Optics and Photonics has been hailed as one of the top three optics programs in the nation, and its faculty and students are conducting research in laser system development, optoelectronics, X-ray science technology, and other areas. The Rosen College of Hospitality Management, located on its own campus off Universal Boulevard, is home to 1,000 students who are forging the future of hospitality management.

Meanwhile, the recently named Burnett College of Biomedical Sciences is expanding UCF's research in biomedicine, including treatments for cancer, diabetes and neurodegenerative conditions such as Alzheimer's. The college establishes a solid foundation for a proposed medical school that could be in place before the end of the decade.

UCF also serves Central Florida through a dozen regional campuses, including educational sites at community colleges in Brevard, Lake, Marion, Orange, Osceola, Seminole, and Volusia counties.

Ultimately, UCF is most proud of its students, past and present. Prominent alumni include Michelle Akers, captain of the 1996 Olympic gold medal soccer team; Daunte Culpepper, starting quarterback of the Minnesota Vikings; George Kalogridis, president of Disneyland; Bill Parsons, manager of NASA's Space Shuttle Program; and Al Weiss, president of Walt Disney World.

UCF film students created "The Blair Witch Project," the low-budget thriller that proved creative, independent films could be highly successful. Daniel Myrick and Eduardo Sanchez, the "Blair Witch" directors, and Gregg Hale, Robin Cowie and Michael Monello, the film's co-producers, met as UCF film majors in 1990.

In spring 2003, Tyler Fisher, a double major in English and Spanish, became UCF's first Rhodes Scholar. Later that year, advertising and public relations major Ericka Dunlap was crowned Miss America.

UCF's campus is one of the most attractive in the nation, with large expanses of green lawns, flowering trees and shrubs, and untouched conservation areas. UCF continues to expand its Orlando campus to better serve students, faculty, alumni, and friends in the community. In the coming years, new academic buildings, an alumni hall, and a convocation center will become fixtures on campus. Student housing and a retail area will be added next to the convocation center, which will also host basketball games and serve as the centerpiece of a state-of-the-art athletics complex being developed and expanded for the nine women's and seven men's sports at UCF.

Great universities cannot succeed without the help of the community in which they are based. UCF's close relationships with Orlando, Orange County, and the region have ensured its rapid rise as a world-class university that proudly serves its community, state, and nation.

UCF conducts more than $80 million a year in research, much of it in high-tech areas such as lasers and optics in the College of Optics and Photonics.

One of the newest buildings on campus is the Welcome Center, which houses undergraduate admissions and is the first stop for new and potential students and their families.

The Rosen College of Hospitality Management is located near International Drive in the heart of one of the world's top tourist destinations.

Ryland Homes

A cursory drive through any Ryland Homes community reveals a concerted commitment to quality, from impressive entranceways to a variety of architectural styles to impeccable landscaping. At the core of Ryland Homes' successful formula is an unwavering dedication to prime locations, an extensive product line, quality craftsmanship, intelligent and practical designs, in-house design services, step-by-step financing and a 10-year homeowners' warranty.

Ryland has a home for everyone, whether you're a first time homebuyer, moving up to your second or third home, or an active adult starting the second half of your life. Our homes range from the mid $100s to over $400,000. Ryland Homes is your builder for life.

After a hard day at work, take refuge in your living room, cozy up with a good book, a hot cup of tea and let the worries of your day drift away. Ryland Homes knows your satisfaction is the best measure of our success.

More than thirty-seven years ago, Ryland Homes debuted with 220 homes in the acclaimed master-planned city of Columbia, Maryland. Since then, Ryland, with headquarters in Calabasas, California, has built more than 225,000 homes in approximately 350 communities in twenty-seven cities throughout the U.S and financed more than 195,000 mortgages. Today, in addition to Orlando, Ryland is building new homes in cities all across the country in areas like Austin, Texas; San Francisco, California; Charleston, South Carolina; Charlotte, North Carolina; Chicago, Illinois; and Cincinnati, Ohio, just to name a few.

Orlando Presence

Ryland has been building homes in the greater Orlando area for more than twenty years. Mirroring Orlando's meteoric growth pattern, Ryland built 1,150 homes in 2003 and more than 1,300 homes in 2004 with annual increases of 25 to 30 percent since 2001. Ryland Homes can be found in several well known Central Florida communities including Avalon Park, Vista Lakes, Summerport, Rybolt's Reserve, Markham Forest, Vizcaya, Westfield, Oak Hill Reserve, and Northshore at Lake Hart.

Elsewhere in Florida, Ryland is building homes in Jacksonville, Tampa Bay, and the Fort Myers/ Naples area. New Ryland markets include Brevard, Lake and Volusia Counties.

America's Home Builder

Ryland Homes' motto is "America's Home Builder," which describes the company's goal to fulfill home ownership needs for buyers throughout their lives—from a first home purchase to an active adult residence. With a diverse product line, ranging from townhouses and single-family homes to estate homes at various price points, Ryland can accommodate a wide range of buyers.

Enhancing Ryland's appeal to all types of potential homebuyers in various stages of life is the homebuilder's extensive list of floorplans, exceptional amenities packages, in-house architects adept at designing for changing needs and lifestyles, and Ryland's own mortgage and title companies that make the purchase process less stressful and less time-consuming.

Ryland's value is perhaps what appeals most to its many repeat buyers. Ryland's size and strength as one of the nation's largest homebuilders allows it to partner with national companies to secure top-quality materials in bulk and hire the best subcontractors to make a Ryland home one of the best values on the market. Simply put, with Ryland's national purchas-

The kitchen is often described as the heart of the house. It should be warm, inviting and yet functional. Ryland Homes offers over 85 different floor plans, each with a kitchen as unique as the individual that calls it home.

ing power, it builds a higher-quality home for less than many of its competitors. By offering a superior product complemented by superb customer service, Ryland attracts an impressive number of buyers who, indeed, consider Ryland their homebuilder for life.

The Ryland Difference

What sets Ryland Homes apart from a typical production homebuilder? Lots of things. First, Ryland handles each aspect of the homebuying process, from design, construction and sales to competitive mortgages, financing programs and title search, settlement and escrow services. The Ryland home buying process is truly one-stop shopping. Sales counselors and design consultants are present to assist in the selection and personalization of each home. With home decorators on staff, Ryland offers buyers a world of options and upgrades and the ability to customize through its design center. Ryland Mortgage helps customers find the mortgage that is right for them, and Ryland Title, Ryland Escrow, and Ryland Insurance Services handle all the final details.

To make the homebuying process easier, Ryland's Web site offers buyers a wealth of information on the company as well as details on new home possibilities in Ryland communities throughout the country.

Ryland Homes places a strong emphasis on acquiring land in the most desirable areas, where homebuyers want to live, shop, and work. In all of its communities, Ryland creates common areas with attractive entry features, ample green space and appealing landscaping.

Just as important as the bricks and mortar aspect of the homebuilding experience, Ryland Homes is dedicated to providing the highest quality of customer service in the industry. All Ryland homes are backed by a 10-year warranty program.

While it is a large, national company, Ryland's local operating divisions are an integral part of the cities in which it builds. Its regional and divisional management teams offer an average of 20 years' experience in the homebuilding business and they fully understand local homebuyers' needs. That expertise enables Ryland to build communities in the areas where buyers want to live and create homes and neighborhoods with outstanding features to fit every lifestyle.

Can't you just envision Cole Porter entertaining guests in this intimate music room? At Ryland Homes, we offer those little extra features that make a house YOUR home.

Many people are surprised to learn that Valencia Community College (VCC) was named the 1998 National Community College of the Year by the National Alliance of Business, or that is has more Bright Futures Scholars than any other community college in Florida, or that it transfers more students to the University of Central Florida than the other three Central Florida community colleges combined.

"Although we teach more than 55,000 students a year, we're still an unknown entity to some of our Central Florida citizens," says Sanford Shugart, president of Valencia Community College. "Beyond our excellent facilities and faculty and wide-ranging degree programs, our success is based on a deep commitment to teaching undergrads versus research or graduate work. Learning is our first priority and I think that is why students gravitate toward Valencia."

Shugart is obviously VCC's number one supporter; however, other highly respected educators around the nation are strong believers in the school's mission. "Valencia Community College is a place where exceptionally talented and committed people are striving in a thoughtful way to place students and learning at the center of everything they do," says Kay McClenney, director of the College Survey of Student Engagement and the Community College Leadership Program at the University of Texas at Austin. "This is harder work than most people realize, as it involves exercising the courage to examine college performance, question prior assumptions, challenge traditional practices and look constantly for ways to improve."

Valencia was chosen by *Time Magazine* in 2001 as one of the nation's best schools at helping first-year students thrive.

Making a Difference

What began as a few portable buildings in 1967 on West Oak Ridge Road in Orlando has grown to encompass five campuses and centers and 2,539 faculty and staff in the Orlando area. Valencia is now the third largest of Florida's twenty-eight community colleges. The main 180-acre campus (West Campus) is located on South Kirkman Road. As Orlando has grown, so has Valencia Community College, which opened the East Campus in 1975, the Osceola Campus in 1997, and the Winter Park Campus in 1998. Plans for the future include two new campuses in rapidly growing regions southwest of metro Orlando and southeast of the airport.

Since its inception, Valencia has allowed the marketplace to guide their educational programs toward the broader needs of the Central Florida economy. It offers eighty career programs and forty pre-university majors in a wide variety of disciplines ranging from accounting and architecture to computer engineering, and from film production to radiography, and restaurant management.

To enhance its strong connection with Central Florida's business community, Valencia builds relationships with high schools and universities to strengthen academic scholarship and economic de-

velopment. Valencia has close to 500 corporate education/training partnerships, including those with AT&T, Florida Hospital, Lockheed Martin, NationsBank, Sea World, SmithKline/Beecham, Universal Studios, and British Airways.

Under the Associate in Arts degree, Valencia offers preparation for nearly 200 majors in the state university system. The Pre-Majors Program combines general education requirements with course prerequisites for specific majors offered at the university level. Valencia produces the second highest number of associate degrees in the nation and 72.4 percent of its A.A. graduates transfer to a state university

Program Highlights

Universities like Duke, Georgetown, Vanderbilt, and John Hopkins are just a few of the many high-profile institutions that have accepted graduates from Valencia's highly regarded Honors Program. Inaugurated in 1990, the program serves over 1,000 students on four campuses. The program annually attracts dozens of students with SAT scores in excess of 1400 (including perfect 1600 SAT scores) and ACT scores in excess of 32. Among the unique features of the program is its "holistic" approach, which seeks to develop social and leadership skills in addition to intellectual and academic abilities. The University of Florida has designated the Valencia Honors Program as the "premier two-year honors program in the state."

One of Valencia's more celebrated departments is Entertainment Technology which includes disciplines in film production, digital media, graphics, music production and theater and entertainment. Valencia's Film Production program has been called "one of the best film schools in the country" by re-

nowned director Steven Spielberg. Notable graduates from the Entertainment Technology department include two of the creators of the award-winning Blair Witch Project, Gregg Hale and Ben Rock; Howard Muzika, a digital artist who worked on special effects for the movie *Titanic*; and pop group members Howie Dorough of the Backsteet Boys, Chris Kirkpatrick of 'NSync and David Perez, Brody Martinez and Raul Molina of C Note.

The Right Choice

President Shugart says there are numerous and varied reasons why students choose Valencia Community College to pursue higher education goals. "Our student body is extremely diverse and runs the gamut from high-school students enrolled in our dual enrollment program to academic stars attracted by our honors program to middle-age students transitioning to other careers," says Shugart.

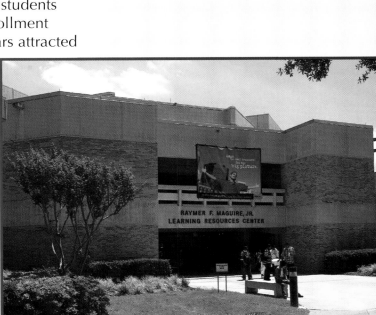

Lower tuition costs than a 4-year school is certainly at the top of many student's list of reasons for selecting Valencia, says Shugart, "however, many people falsely assume that means lower standards."

"Nothing could be further from the truth," he says adamantly. "Valencia has professors with PhDs or masters degrees teaching our freshman classes. Many universities often relegate graduate assistants to the job. When you combine our superb faculty and program offerings, with smaller classes of twenty-one students on average and tuition savings of up to 50 percent versus the first two years at a 4-year school, Valencia is a phenomenal choice."

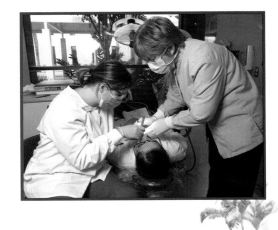

Newland Communities

*T*he most desirable new homes today are being built within master-planned communities offering lifestyle amenities that are carefully integrated into a well-designed community plan. In the Orlando area, several communities already exist. Vista Lakes is one of the newest of these communities. It offers the lifestyle, wide range of housing types, and rich amenities that homebuyers desire.

Creating a special Sense of Community at Vista Lakes in Orlando

Vista Lakes entry fountain greets residents and visitors alike.

Vista Lakes is one of numerous communities across the nation created by Newland Communities. They have been creating desirable, livable communities across the nation for nearly four decades and have the expertise to create that special "sense of community" by bringing to life the unique history, culture and traditions of the land they develop. Vista Lakes is an example of this.

Nestled within a pristine setting of lakes, parks, nature preserves and recreational facilities, Vista Lakes combines amenities with the environment creating a community that is beautiful, functional and truly enjoyed by its residents. Fountains and lush plantings abound. Visitors can easily find their way to the Residents' Club located in the heart of the community. This multi-functional facility includes the Welcome Home Center, where visitors and prospective homebuyers first visit the Vista Lakes community.

The Residents' Club is staffed with an activities director who, along with dedicated staff members, ensures all visitors receive a community overview. Homebuyers also get details about the community, its amenities, and numerous activities. Parties, picnics, holiday events, fitness walks, and exercise classes are just a sample of the types of activities and events the activities staff can coordinate for residents.

Adjacent to the Residents' Club is the Fun Pool. A two-story, spiral waterslide, a kiddie pool with an elephant spray fountain, and a new junior Olympic pool with six lap lanes offer residents water sports fun all year round. Tennis courts and a pavilion and sundeck for lounging provide more options for recreation and relaxation for community residents. These types of amenities and gathering places are what make Newland Communities so special and are what inspire residents to say they feel at home the moment they move in.

Boaters pedalling next to the Pirate Ship at Vista Lakes.

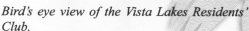

Bird's eye view of the Vista Lakes Residents' Club.

80-acre Vista Lake

Prospective homebuyers at Vista Lakes will find homes to suit most lifestyles and budgets. Single-family homes, townhouses, and apartment homes located amid a setting of lakes are perfect spots for fishing, canoeing or kayaking. Another signature Newland amenity are the open space and parks that have been set aside, providing miles of walking and jogging trails, pathways for rollerblading and bicycling as well as tot-lot parks and sports fields. Vista Lakes also offers a middle school and a proposed elementary school conveniently located within the community.

The Vista Lakes Town Center, Vista Lakes Village, features an array of shopping choices for its residents. It includes a Publix supermarket, as well as a video store, cellular phone store, dry cleaners, eye care center, dentist, and choice of banks. Dine-in and take-out options are available, with an Italian and Chinese restaurant and a sandwich shop for residents on the go. And for animal lovers, a veterinarian clinic is provided.

Through ongoing customer research, Newland Communities has discovered that homebuyers are seeking a greater sense of place and connection with neighbors and community. Some of this is achieved through the community amenities and design, and some of this is achieved using technology. With the dissemination of broadband technologies, Newland Communities has found a new method of addressing these needs.

Using one of the most technologically advanced communications tools, residents at Vista Lakes are entitled to utilize the community private network, "Intranet." This network, called Life At Vista Lakes, allows them to connect with their neighbors and have access to the latest community news and events. Locating a babysitter, meeting announcements, or a garage sale are communicated through the community Intranet. Most importantly, the Intranet allows residents to feel like part of a family. Through this technology, neighbors can come together to connect and share ideas with others.

Headquartered in San Diego, California, Newland Communities is currently developing communities across the country in states including Florida, Georgia, North Carolina, South Carolina, Texas, California, Colorado, Oregon, Washington, Minnesota, and Maryland.

An afternoon fishing on 80-acre Vista Lake.

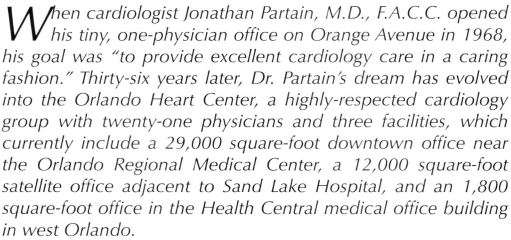

*W*hen cardiologist Jonathan Partain, M.D., F.A.C.C. opened his tiny, one-physician office on Orange Avenue in 1968, his goal was "to provide excellent cardiology care in a caring fashion." Thirty-six years later, Dr. Partain's dream has evolved into the Orlando Heart Center, a highly-respected cardiology group with twenty-one physicians and three facilities, which currently include a 29,000 square-foot downtown office near the Orlando Regional Medical Center, a 12,000 square-foot satellite office adjacent to Sand Lake Hospital, and an 1,800 square-foot office in the Health Central medical office building in west Orlando.

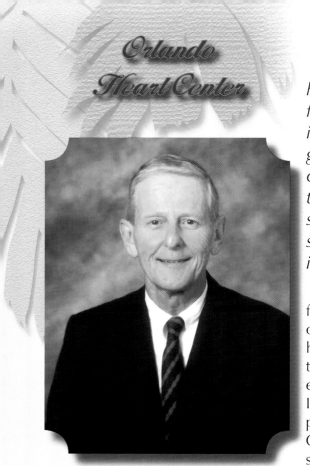

The Orlando Heart Center is a full-service cardiology center that offers cost-effective care and the highest quality in the diagnosis and treatment of cardiovascular diseases as well as prevention programs. Included in the many services provided by the Orlando Heart Center are nuclear and exercise stress testing, echocardiograms, vascular care, cardiac catheterization (coronary angiogram), percutaneous transluminal coronary angioplasty (PTCA), stenting, electrophysiology and arrhythmia care, external counterpulsation therapy, coumadin management and consultative services.

The Orlando Heart Center has the distinction of being one of the few cardiology practices in the nation that has its nuclear laboratory, echocardiography laboratory, and vascular laboratory accredited by the respective national accrediting organizations.

Putting Patients First

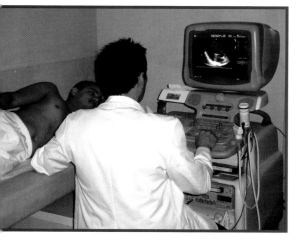

Since its inception, the underlying philosophy at the Orlando Heart Center has been to treat each patient in a private, individualized, and personal manner, using the latest technological advances available. "We have state-of-art cardiac care technology, but equally important, we have impeccably trained physicians who combine first-rate care with excellent interpersonal communications skills," says Partain.

In recruiting new physicians, the Orlando Heart Center insists on those with excellent interpersonal skills that enhance the physician/patient relationship. In addition, it seeks those with specialized training in the emerging methods of cardiac care and technologies that expand the Center's abilities to treat and prevent heart disease. "Changes are very dramatic in the cardiac care field," says Dr. Partain, "and we are constantly reinventing ourselves by bringing in specialty-trained physicians who impart new skills and technologies to patients who need it."

All physicians at Orlando Heart Center are certified by the American Board of Internal Medicine and by the Specialty Board in Cardiovascular Diseases.

Focus On Research

The Orlando Heart Center physicians are enthusiastically involved in cardiac care research through the Orlando Cardiovascular Research Institute, a subsidiary of Orlando Heart Center, which focuses on specific areas of interest such as coronary artery disease, electrophysiology, interventional cardiology, nuclear medicine, congestive heart failure, and myocardial infarctions.

Crealde School of Art sculpture and art garden. Photo by Randa Bishop

Park Maitland School

*V*oted the "Best Private School" in the elementary school category by the readers of Orlando Magazine, Park Maitland School offers an exceptional education program with a commitment to teaching values, manners, and strength of character.

Located at the corner of Hwy. 17-92 and Magnolia Road in Maitland, Park Maitland's new Early Childhood Center offers passers-by a glimpse of the creativity that permeates the school.

The new Arts and Athletics Center houses the school's art, music, and drama classrooms as well as a gymnasium and stage for school shows and special events. Its unique design incorporates notes from Park Maitland's alma mater depicted as windows on the upper level.

Founded thirty-seven years ago by Patricia M. (Nell) Cohen, a highly respected Maitland elementary school educator, and her husband William H (Bill) Cohen, Park Maitland provides a well-rounded, enriching educational experience with emphasis on academic, social, emotional, and physical development. Beyond its strong focus on academics, arts, culture, and athletics, Park Maitland retains an engaging, family-centered environment of warmth and caring that welcomes children and parents.

In 2003, four graduating seniors who were former Park Maitland honor students were the Valedictorians at their respective high schools. Park Maitland has also produced two Presidential Scholars, the highly prestigious national academic award. Among notable alumni are actress and recording star Mandy Moore, Orlando Opera singer Jeanette Zilioli and comedic actress Beth Littleford.

Academic Excellence

Situated on a flower-laden campus shaded by large oak trees, Park Maitland School is located between the communities of Winter Park and Maitland.

Park Maitland School has evolved from a small house with thirty-two students nearly four decades ago to a multi-functional, multiple structure campus serving 630 students from four years old to sixth-grade. There are currently sixty teachers on staff and class sizes are typically sixteen students.

The curriculum is broad to give children opportunities to enhance skills in a wide variety of subjects and interests. In addition to taking primary classes, students start learning Spanish in kindergarten and take drama, music, and art. Because the school is departmentalized, each teacher works in the subject area where he/she has credentials and experience. Classes run the gamut from the academic-reading, English, math, math lab, science, social studies, writing lab, language arts lab, and grammar lab, to personal enrichment-computer, library, art, drama, music, swimming, physical education, and Spanish.

"Our classes are small and our teachers are very involved with each student," says Head of School Carolyn Cappleman, "We have a team approach that enables us to quickly address student needs and concerns. Every student receives personal attention in a caring, family-oriented environment."

Outside the classroom, Park Maitland offers a wide variety of educational experiences through hands-on science experiments, arts and drama performances, and field trips, to name a few. Among the field trip destinations are Williamsburg, Virginia; Washington D.C.; St. Augustine, Florida; and the Kennedy Space Center.

Exceptional fine and performing arts programs, with art, drama, and music classes beginning in Kindergarten are highlighted by an annual full-scale, Broadway style production at the Bob Carr Performing Arts Center in Orlando.

Third grade social studies students enjoy a fabulous "Native American Festival" as one of their special activities each year.

Albin Polasek Museum and Sculpture Gardens, statue of "Elizabeth."
Photo by Randa Bishop

Trinity Preparatory School

*W*ith a beautiful campus on 100 acres between Lake Martha and Lake Burnett, Trinity Preparatory School boasts a rigorous curriculum, highly qualified and caring faculty, low student/teacher ratio and exceptional college guidance program and has long been recognized as the premier college preparatory institution in Central Florida.

Trinity Prep was founded in 1966 as an independent Episcopal school by the late Reverend Canon A. Rees Hay and a group of Orlando community leaders who wanted to provide a top-quality secondary education for students in Central Florida.

During the last five years, the National Merit Scholarship Competition has recognized 21 percent of Trinity Prep's graduates. The average SAT score for the Class of 2005 was 1301 and 100 percent are attending colleges and universities across the United States. In 2002-03 and 2003-04, Trinity Prep was named the 2003-04 Dodge Sunshine Cup FHSAA Class 2A Floyd E. Lay All-Sports award winner, a prestigious honor that signifies the strength of a school's overall athletic program.

On the playing fields, Trinity athletes, benefit from the school's well-designed, collegiate style sports facilities are annually among the highest rated in the state in numerous sports. Trinity offers 49 teams in fifteen different sports, with 71 percent of the student body participating in competitive athletics. In 2003, nine varsity teams finished top ten in the state of Florida.

Beyond the numerous impressive academic statistics and accolades, Trinity Prep, with students in grades 6-12, owes its success to an unwavering commitment to four core values: educational excellence, both academic and extracurricular with challenging programs and exemplary instruction in outstanding facilities; character development through high standards for ethical behavior, personal responsibility and honor; Trinity family, a school community that values traditions, respects each individual regardless of race, ethnicity, gender or faith in a safe, caring and supportive environment; and spiritual growth, a school community where all are allowed to explore and deepen their own faith. Character development is further enhanced through Trinity's outstanding community service program, which teaches students the value of being an integral part of their community. In 2002-2003 Trinity completed its fourth Habitat for Humanity House—becoming the first school in the nation to record this achievement.

With an enrollment each year of approximately 800 students, Trinity Prep's class sizes average sixteen to eighteen students and teacher to student ratio is 11 to 1. All classes are honors level and taught by highly credentialed and dedicated instructors who teach only in their field of expertise.

Trinity Prep's exceptional fine arts program is designed to encourage success in a wide variety of fields with fourty-five courses available and activities such as instrumental music, strings, chorus, photography, art, theatre, and publications. A state-of-the-art, 800-seat on-campus auditorium serves both student activities and many community functions.

In the classroom, on the athletic fields and in the community, Trinity Prep serves as an undeniably strong foundation for success in college and beyond.

Scenic boat tour, Winter Park, Florida.
Photo by Randa Bishop

Central Florida Investments

Westgate Resorts

With its rather generic sounding name, Central Florida Investments (CFI) belies the fact it is one of the fastest growing, most dynamic companies in Central Florida. CFI has a compounded average growth rate in excess of 20 percent over the last decade. As the largest privately held corporation in the area with over $500 million in annual revenues and over 8,500 employees and independent contractors, CFI is an integral part of the Orlando and Central Florida business community.

CFI's President and CEO, David Siegel, started the company in 1970 as a small real estate firm with limited funds and its headquarters situated in the corner of his garage. Today, Siegel's far reaching empire encompasses timeshare, real estate, construction, hotel and apartment management, dude ranch, retirement golf village, travel services, telecommunications, insurance, retail, and much more.

Timeshare Innovators

The cornerstone of CFI's portfolio is Westgate Resorts, a timeshare vacation concept Siegel has helped bring to people of all economic and social status. Before corporate giants like Disney, Marriott, Hyatt, and Hilton entered the timeshare business; it was Siegel who used the sunny weather, palm trees, and attraction-laden landscape of Central Florida as a lure to vacation ownership buyers around the world.

"Our philosophy has always been simple," says Siegel. "We fulfill our guests' dreams by providing a quality vacation experience that exceeds all expectations. What makes us different from any other timeshare product is we know middle America's idea of a dream vacation and we do everything possible to provide them with more than they could ever expect. We always go the extra mile, whether in the quality of products used in our villas, the amenities we provide, the treatment of our customers, or our involvement in the community."

He continues, "Our resorts are not pretentious but they are decidedly upscale and designed to overwhelm visitors with amenities galore like large-screen televisions, leather furnishings, granite countertops, fully equipped kitchens, jetted Roman tubs, and screened-in patios or porches."

The process of finding out exactly what the timeshare consumer wants has been a long one that Siegel has perfected after more than twenty-five years in the business. With its meteoric growth pattern, Westgate Resorts has evolved as experts in many key aspects of the timeshare industry.

In timeshare development, Westgate Resorts has expertise in strategic marketing, land planning, unit design, detailed project management, and forming solid financial partnerships. The company builds over 300 units annually with associated amenities and resort facilities.

Westgate Resorts' marketing team has over a hundred guest service locations across the country. Included is a 210,000 square foot, state-of-the-art call center in Orlando. They have a proven track record of targeting potential buyers

and converting them into timeshare owners with closing percentages that significantly exceed the industry average. Recognized as a world leader in sales training, with one of the largest and most comprehensive training programs in the industry, Westgate Resorts has the ability to service different nationalities and market sources. The major hub for all customer and marketing activities, the Orlando Call Center processes, on average, 100,000 inbound and 500,000 outbound calls per month. This is only one of several Westgate call centers around the country.

With the ability to service and support more than $1 billion in timeshare mortgages and over 200,000 active accounts, Westgate Resorts has expertise in mortgage servicing and corporate collections that is considered the gold standard in the industry. It is the only timeshare company that Standard & Poor's has rated.

The Information Technology Department (IT) at Westgate Resorts is comprised of technology and business unit experts with more than a hundred combined years of timeshare and technology expertise. The company has formed strategic relationships with technology leaders such as Oracle, Microsoft, Computer Associates, Davox, Sun Microsystems, CMC, Lucent, Cisco Systems, Ciber, Kronos, and Dell Computers.

Westgate Resorts' operations are on par with luxury resorts with a focus on every detail of the upscale resort experience resulting in high levels of guest satisfaction. Their motto is "Good Enough is Never Good Enough."

The Early Years

Siegel got started in the timeshare business in 1980. He had acquired quite a bit of real estate in Central Florida, including an 80-acre orange grove alongside U.S. Highway 192, just west of Disney World. Siegel saw timeshare as an opportunity that no one had fully realized, and he decided to develop the property as a timeshare resort, starting with sixteen villas. He named it Westgate Vacation Villas.

Those sixteen villas have since grown to more than 2,500— making the resort the largest single-site timeshare resort in the world. In the twenty-five years since, Westgate Resorts, a subsidiary of CFI, has expanded to include over 8,000 villas at twenty-four timeshare vacation resorts.

Westgate's family of resorts includes: Westgate Vacation Villas; Westgate Town Center; Westgate Lakes Resort & Spa; Westgate Towers; Westgate Blue Tree Resort;

Westgate Palace; the Ramada Plaza Hotel; all in Orlando, FL; Grenelefe Golf & Tennis Resort in Haines City, FL; River Ranch, near Lake Wales, FL; Harbor Beach Resort in Daytona Beach, FL; Westgate Miami Beach and Westgate South Beach, both in Miami Beach, FL; Westgate Park City Resort & Spa in Park City, UT; Westgate Smoky Mountain Resort in Gatlinburg, TN; Westgate Historic Williamsburg in Williamsburg, VA; Westgate Flamingo Bay in Las Vegas, NV; Westgate Painted Mountain in Mesa, AZ; Westgate Branson Woods Yacht Club and Westgate Emerald Point in Branson, MO; Westgate Tunica Resort in Tunica, MS; Westgate Myrtle Beach in Myrtle Beach, SC.

The Siegel Way

The driving force behind Westgate Resorts is David Siegel, a self-made entrepreneur who started out as a television repairman. Innovative and focused with a strong vision and penchant for risk taking, the personification of an entrepreneur, Siegel has propelled Westgate Resorts to become the largest pri-

vately-owned timeshare company in the world. Through a combination of hard work, persistence, and a hands-on management approach, Siegel, who has been dubbed "The King of Timeshare" by local media, has literally changed the face of the timeshare industry in the past two decades.

Many of Westgate Resorts' employees are a reflection of Siegel's entrepreneurial personality. "Our company is only as successful as the people who work for us," says Siegel. "More than 200 of our employees make six-figure incomes and that says a lot about the dedication, heart and resourcefulness of the people that work for us."

Siegel loves to talk about the numerous rags to riches stories of Westgate Resorts employees, former teachers, carpenters, housewives, etc., who started at the company almost penniless and have risen to become big earners.

Other Entities

Since its inception, Westgate Resorts has continually diversified under Siegel's entrepreneurial leadership. The company has interests in a wide variety of pursuits, including: Westgate Hospitality Organization, a marketing organization with over 125,000 members and 600 local sponsors designed to stretch the Central Florida hospitality worker's paycheck. I Love Orlando and I Love the Smokes Magazines, publications that produce over 1.5 million readers annually; Florida Vacation Store, a full-service travel agency that highlights Florida as the travel destination choice and establishes lead generation; Florida Visitor's Bureau, with several locations in Central Florida providing tourist information and discount attraction tickets; CFI Travel, a full-service travel agency offering discount travel packages; Las Vegas Visitors

Bureau; WWFL 1340, a 1,000 watt AM radio station; Papillion the Spa at Westgate Lakes and Westgate Park City; Westgate Grill, a full-service restaurant in Park City, Utah; and Westgate Smokehouse Grill, an old-fashioned barbecue house at Westgate Lakes Resort & Spa in Orlando.

Community First

Like everything else in his company, David Siegel is intimately involved in the vast number of Westgate Resorts charitable endeavors. Siegel, who holds an honorary doctorate from Florida A&M University for his work in community service, is also holder of the National Community Service Award presented by ARDA, the timeshare industry association.

Siegel and his employees donate thousands of service hours and financial contributions to numerous local charities, including Give Kids the World, Boggy Creek Gang, Children's Wish Foundation, Edgewood Children's Ranch, and Tangelo Park Foundation.

In 2001, Siegel started the Westgate Resorts Foundation to raise monies given primarily to charitable organization in communities where Westgate Resorts employees live and work. In the three years since the Foundation was created, nearly $4 million has been raised and distributed to more than a hundred different groups that are improving the quality of life for the people who need it most. It's important to note that 100 percent of the funds donated to the Westgate Resorts Foundation are distributed to the charities. This is possible because David Siegel pays all of the organization's expenses.

"It's important to our company to be a responsible and conscientious corporate partner in the communities which are home to our resorts as well as our employees and their families," says Siegel. "Westgate Resorts Foundation reflects the diversity of our company's people. Employees on every level have been involved in each step of the process in setting up the foundation, as well as reviewing grant applications and making recommendations."

Siegel's personal acts of charity are wide reaching. He helped start the Inner-City Games in Orlando. He donates about one-third of the money used for Christmas presents in the Shop-With-A-Cop program. He's helped load up trucks with household items, canned food, blankets, and furniture for the Lisa Merlin House. He supports the Special Olympics. Sharing his wealth, Siegel has helped all sorts of people along the way.

One group on the top of his list is Westgate Resorts employees, who benefit from an innovative program called the David's Dollars Foundation, which provides grants and support to Westgate Resorts employees in need. This

provides a safety net for all of his employees so that no matter what catastrophe occurs, they will receive help. One example was after the devastation of the 2004 hurricanes over 1,500 employees received free housing at the Westgate resorts for as long as four months until their homes were repaired. Last year, Paul, an employee in the food and beverage department at Westgate Lakes Resort & Spa, lost everything to an apartment fire. Within days, the David's Dollars Foundation was able to place Paul and his family into a new apartment and furnish it. Paul also received a $1,000 gift card to Wal-Mart so he could replace other household items and clothing, as well as purchase food.

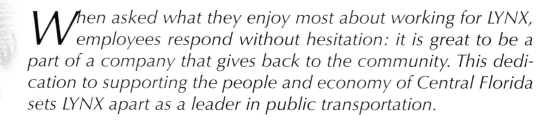

LYNX

When asked what they enjoy most about working for LYNX, employees respond without hesitation: it is great to be a part of a company that gives back to the community. This dedication to supporting the people and economy of Central Florida sets LYNX apart as a leader in public transportation.

The American Public Transportation Association (APTA) recognized this tradition of excellence by naming LYNX as the Public Transportation Company of the year for service improvements that resulted in record rider-ship increases in both 1996 and 1998.

Founded in 1972 as the Orange-Seminole-Osceola Transportation Authority, LYNX now supports over 2,500 square miles and 1.8 million people. By providing transportation to businesses, hospitals and educational institutions as well as a considerable number of hotels and tourist destinations, LYNX is the nervous system that keeps Central Florida's commerce moving and breathing. To guests from around the world and commuters alike, LYNX is a vital part of their day.

In addition to decreasing roadway traffic and exhaust emissions, LYNX is responsible for transporting the thousands of employees that run Central Florida's many businesses, hotels, and theme parks. Recent studies have determined

that halting LYNX's services for one day would result in half a million dollars in lost wages. Research by the University of Central Florida also identified that for every dollar invested in LYNX, $2.40 is returned to the local economy.

Decisions at LYNX are not based solely on economics however. LYNX team members work together to create an overall riding experience that is comfortable and pleasant for daily commuters and visitors alike.

Paying tribute to the vibrant spirit of Central Florida, LYNX proudly boasts a fleet of 238 brightly painted motorized coaches. Instantly recognizable, the buses' artwork is created with the flamboyant color and flair people have come to associate with Central Florida. This conscious effort to incorporate innovative style into LYNX's image is evident in the newly opened LYNX Central Station, whose graceful lines are reminiscent of a ship sailing through ocean waves.

Described by the Orlando Sentinel as "downtown Orlando's first architectural icon", the 20,000 square foot LYNX Central Station now provides patrons with air-conditioned waiting areas, a highly visible arrival/departure screen and enhanced lighting to ensure pedestrian safety. This new structure was carefully designed to decrease foot-traffic congestion while providing commuters with a more spacious and attractive environment.

LYNX's impressive Central Station is merely the most recent in a long line of innovations implemented to improve the Central Florida commuting experience.

Embracing modern technology, LYNX's free Lymmo line is both environmentally and economically beneficial. Running on low-emission compressed natural gas, the Lymmo line is a frequent shuttle system servicing the downtown Orlando area. Traveling in their own designated lane, Lymmo buses help support local employers by delivering both employees and customers in a safe, timely manner.

The Carpool and Vanpool programs also benefit local employers by providing employees with an inexpensive, reliable mode of transportation. Aside from the environmental impact of fewer cars congesting Orlando's roadways, patrons are able to save money by taking advantage of the free Carpool matching program or joining with other commuters to rent a low-priced LYNX Van through the Vanpool program. The Guaranteed Ride Home offers emergency transportation to both Carpool and Vanpool participants via taxi services up to four times per year.

Faced with the daunting task of providing transportation to patrons across four large counties, LYNX adopted two programs in an attempt to support additional commuters. Through Rack 'N Roll, travelers are able to safely lock their bicycle on specially designed racks fixed to the front of each bus. Upon arriving at the new Central Station, patrons are able to lock their bicycles in weatherproofed bins before they continue on to their destination. In addition, at Park N' Ride lots in all four counties LYNX offers free parking for commuters and visitors.

Recognizing the value of time spent in transit, LYNX has installed flat-screen monitors in their motor coaches to provide both information and entertainment. The Transit Television Network (TTN) delivers daily news, weather, and trivia along with route information and stop announcements. This effective use of technology enables LYNX to contact their patrons easily regarding changes in service and other commuter information.

Through these and other programs, LYNX is working hard to fill the travel needs of Central Florida. As one proud employee stated, "Although you may not use the LYNX transit system, you can be sure someone you depend on does."

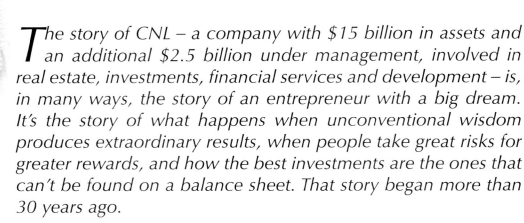

CNL

The story of CNL – a company with $15 billion in assets and an additional $2.5 billion under management, involved in real estate, investments, financial services and development – is, in many ways, the story of an entrepreneur with a big dream. It's the story of what happens when unconventional wisdom produces extraordinary results, when people take great risks for greater rewards, and how the best investments are the ones that can't be found on a balance sheet. That story began more than 30 years ago.

Left to right: James M. Seneff, Jr., Chairman/ CEO and Robert A. Bourne, President.

Developing a Vision

The vision began in the heart and mind of a college graduate and Vietnam veteran who, sitting across from his father at a kitchen table, asked for a $5,000 loan to start his own business. His name was Jim Seneff, the year was 1973 and his destination, with his young wife Dayle, was Orlando, Florida. To fuel the new business, Jim resolved to live frugally, believing, according to Dayle, "that every dollar not spent today would be worth more

than five dollars in a few years." Jim then set out to buy real estate, reasoning that if he liked a piece of property, he could convince others to join him in the investment. Several did and together, Jim and his partners invested in an 11-acre site in downtown Orlando – at a time when downtown property was in decline and out of favor. Around the same time, Jim partnered with a young Coopers & Lybrand accountant named Bob Bourne to manage properties for a variety of clients.

Executing a Strategy

When he began CNL, Jim's strategy was contrarian, i.e., buying out-of-favor properties in undervalued markets. He then decided to add the strategy of long-term, triple-net leases - a leasing agreement in which tenants pay the taxes, insurance and maintenance costs, in addition to rent. By focusing on this conservative, long-term approach, CNL was able to create consistent income for shareholders.

Offering triple-net leases, CNL developed relationships with operating partners in the restaurant, hospitality, retirement, retail and leisure industries that wanted to expand their business. CNL's tenants include nationally-recognized brands such as Pizza Hut, Wendy's Hamburgers, and Golden Corral restaurants, as well as Marriott, Hilton, CVS, Office Depot, and Barnes and Noble and other top retailers.

By the end of its third decade, CNL's contrarian, conservative strategy took hold and CNL's assets grew to more than $15 billion. The foundation of that strategy was compounding, a phenomenon that Albert Einstein had called *"the eighth wonder of the world."*

"Seeing everything through the filter of compounding was the secret to success," said Jim. "I didn't visualize business as much as I visualized the impact of compounding."

Compounding the Results

From its humble beginnings at a kitchen table, to two office towers in downtown Orlando, the companies CNL has formed or acquired have built enduring value. Today, CNL is noted for its ability to incubate young companies and grow them into significant businesses that generate consistent, long-term results for investors. Two of the companies that CNL has launched are now publicly traded on the New York Stock Exchange. And the company continues its innovating approach and adjusts to the business environment as it positions itself for future growth.

The success of CNL has been a dynamic factor in the success of Orlando. Growing from a two person office to employing nearly 1,000 associates, CNL and its related and heritage companies are a major force in the city's job market, as well as an important contributor to the community's non-profit organizations. CNL has been placed in the top twenty of the *Orlando Sentinel's* annual listing of the "Top 100 Companies for Working Families," and is involved in community outreach through its community giving as well as its hundreds of associates. CNL's Community Giving Program focuses on three key giving areas: investing in

education, investing in *leadership & entrepreneurship* and investing in *arts and culture.*

CNL associates participate in community outreach through CNL's Workplace Giving Campaign that enables them, through payroll deductions, to support charities of their choice. The company is also very involved with Junior Achievement of Central Florida, and in 2004, Jim Seneff received JA's Spirit of Achievement Award.

As CNL looks to the future, it will continue to explore new investment opportunities, yet it will remain a company that continues to invest in people. "In looking back over the years," said Jim, "it's humbling to see how far CNL has come. We've moved from a one-man company to a team of very talented, highly dedicated professionals. We've moved beyond being a company involved in transactions to being a company focused on people and how they work together to better serve our stakeholders. We've also become a company that cares very much about the community of Orlando and its people. When I picture the company, the first thing I see isn't the numbers. What I see are the faces of all the wonderful people who make CNL what it is today. I'll always be grateful."

CNL corporate headquarters, located in downtown Orlando, Florida.

SeaWorld Orlando

SeaWorld Orlando is the world's premier marine adventure park with 200 acres of world-class shows, thrilling rides, and unforgettable animal encounters. Millions of visitors have explored the mysteries of the sea with up-close animal interactions and exhilarating experiences. State-of-the-art rides give guests unprecedented thrills, while amazing animal encounters include killer whales, dolphins, sea lions, sharks, and more.

SeaWorld Orlando is the world's premier marine adventure park with 200 acres of world-class shows, thrilling rides and unforgettable animal encounters.

Shamu the killer whale spins SeaWorld animal trainer Caroline Gibbs during the Shamu Adventure show. SeaWorld trainers have worked for years to build a special relationship with these majestic animals.

"At SeaWorld Orlando and Discovery Cove, our commitment to quality shines above all else," says Jim Atchison, Executive Vice President and General Manager for SeaWorld Orlando and Discovery Cove. "Guests continue to tell us what they want, and we will continue to provide them more than they expect. From our world-class shows and attractions, to our special events like Bud & BBQ and Viva la Musica, there is something for everyone at SeaWorld Orlando."

SeaWorld Today

Constant growth has been a key concept at SeaWorld Orlando. Since 1973, millions of people have experienced the park. In its expansion efforts, SeaWorld Orlando has continued to add exciting and informative attractions and animal habitats, as well as entertaining shows. In 1989, Anheuser-Busch Companies acquired the park and set in motion a new era of transformation.

The park made waves in 1998 with a fresh new look, sensational shows and the latest in thrill technology. Guests were introduced to the new Journey to Atlantis, a water-coaster thrill ride plunging riders into the middle of the lost city of Atlantis.

SeaWorld's commitment to innovation continued in 2000, when SeaWorld Orlando opened its newest thrill, Kraken, a monster of a coaster that is the fastest, tallest, longest, and only "floorless" roller coaster in Orlando.

Great food has always been a staple of the SeaWorld experience. In 2002 the park raised the bar on theme park dining with the upscale Sharks Underwater Grill and Dine with Shamu. These unique eateries afford guests the opportunity to enjoy a delicious meal alongside sharks and killer whales.

The year 2003 brought another addition to the park with the opening of The Waterfront at SeaWorld Orlando. Inspired by the sights, sounds, and character of vibrant seaports around the world, this nautical neighborhood bustles with activity and immerses guests into a rich tapestry of festive entertainment, dining, and shopping.

The summer of 2004 completed what is one of the most comprehensive shopping and dining areas inside any theme park. The expanded Waterfront now covers seven acres and includes three new restaurants—SeaFire Inn, Voyagers Pizza and The Spice Mill, and an array of new shopping experiences. Also new in 2004 was the summertime extravaganza, Mistify—the largest and most spectacular finale in SeaWorld Orlando history. Mistify soared through the nighttime sky with larger-than-life marine creatures, towering fountains, fire on water and dazzling fireworks. Mistify will return for summer and special appearance shows throughout the year.

In 2005, SeaWorld opened an all-new dolphin spectacular, Blue Horizons. This awe-inspiring new show seamlessly blends the sea and the sky with amazing special effects and awesome animal experiences.

The park's killer whale and other marine mammal shows have also undergone transformations. Marine mammal shows such as "The Shamu Adventure" and the multi-species "Clyde and Seamore Take Pirate Island" have eclipsed expectations of early marine mammal training and feature these amazing creatures performing natural maneuvers and showcasing their individual talents.

Discovery Cove–Nowhere Else on Earth

In 2000, Anheuser-Busch opened Discovery Cove in Orlando, Florida. Discovery Cove is an all-inclusive tropical island where guests may snorkel through a colorful reef with exotic fish, hand feed hundreds of tropical birds, float down a river through waterfalls and lush landscaping, relax on white-sand beaches, and swim in refreshing pools. The Discovery Cove experience peaks with an extraordinary opportunity to swim and play with bottlenose dolphins.

Edutainment

Mixing entertainment and education has always been a staple at SeaWorld and Discovery Cove. In 2002, SeaWorld began offering two of the most exciting and unusual animal interaction programs in the world, Sharks Deep Dive and Marine Mammal Keeper Experience.

Located at the Shark Encounter attraction, Sharks Deep Dive im-

merses guests into the realm of these perfect predators. Participants don SeaWorld wetsuits and either snorkel or scuba dive in an authentic shark cage during their close encounter. The cage traverses through a 125-foot-long underwater habitat teeming with an array of more than fifty sharks and thousands of schooling fish.

During the eight-hour Marine Mammal Keeper Experience, guests feel the thrill of working alongside marine mammal experts. From bottle-feeding orphaned manatees to interacting with seals and walrus, participants learn first-hand how SeaWorld animal care specialists work with SeaWorld animals.

At Discovery Cove, participants in the popular Trainer for a Day program work side-by-side with Discovery Cove animal experts as they interact with dolphins, birds, sloths, anteaters, sharks, stingrays, and tropical fish. From training sessions to food preparation, participants learn how the Discovery Cove zoological team maintains the health and well being of these incredible animals.

Discovery Cove, Orlando's newest vacation destination, offers families the ultimate up-close and hands-on dolphin experience. Guests wade into shallow water and become acquainted with their dolphin through hugs, kisses and rubdowns. Guests then swim and play with their dolphin in deeper water, and may receive an exciting dorsal tow or belly ride.

Thrill seekers enjoy a spin on Kraken, SeaWorld Orlando's "floorless" roller coaster. Named after a legendary sea monster, this wickedly fast serpent coaster breaks all Orlando records, including tallest, fastest, longest and wildest.

SeaWorld plunges guests into the realm of the shark during the park's newest most daring animal interaction program, Sharks Deep Dive. Participants don SeaWorld wetsuits and snorkel or scuba dive in a shark cage during their close encounter with more than 50 sharks and an array of fish.

Moore Stephens Lovelace, P.A.

*M*oore Stephens Lovelace, P.A. (MSL), a leading provider of accounting, business advisory, assurance, consulting, and financial services, has been a highly-respected part of Orlando's financial community since 1974.

MSL President William (Bill) Miller, Jr. CPA.

As one of Florida's largest non-national CPA firms, MSL prides itself on the exceptional level of personal service it delivers to its clients. The Firm's professionals combine extensive technical competence and industry experience with proactive and innovative thought to assist clients in improving their businesses. Known for its expertise, professionalism and reliability, MSL is a rarity in the world of mid-sized accounting firms, where it is an unusual achievement to endure and prosper for thirty years.

The Firm has grown to over eighty employees with offices in Clearwater, Miami, and Tallahassee, as well as its headquarters in Orlando. To meet national and international client needs, the Firm is affiliated with Moore Stephens North America and Moore Stephens International Limited, a network of independently owned and operated accounting firms and correspondents with a combined strength of more than 12,000 partners/owners and staff, 273 member firms and 440 offices in 91 countries. In size, fee income, reputation, and longevity, Moore Stephens is the 18th largest accounting and consulting organization in the world. Annually, MSL is ranked as one of the largest accounting firms in Florida by *Florida Trend*, as well as one of the largest firms in Central Florida in 2004 by the *Orlando Business Journal*.

Diverse and Dynamic

Headed by William (Bill) Miller, Jr., CPA, who assumed the role of President of MSL in 2004, the Firm is embarking on an exciting expansion era with plans to double in size by the year 2010. Miller, a graduate of Florida A & M University, joined MSL in 1985 as a senior manager after working at a national firm. In 1986, he was elected head of the Firm's accounting and auditing department and was admitted as a shareholder two years later. He has served on the Firm's Board of Directors since 1998 and was elected as the first chairman of the board in 2001.

Named that same year as one of Central Florida's 100 Most Influential People by the *Orlando Business Journal*, Miller is a proven leader, who serves on the City of Orlando's Finance Committee and the Board of Directors of the Metro Orlando Economic Development Commission and the Florida Chamber of Commerce and is the former chairman of the Greater Orlando Aviation Authority.

Specialists in Performance

Fueling MSL's growth is its ability to assist clients in a wide variety of industries. The Firm has dedicated practice groups in the areas of governmental, healthcare and clinical consulting, SEC/corporate finance, not-for-profit, hospitality/timeshare, employee benefit plans, and fraud examination.

Topping the list of MSL's areas of focus is the Florida healthcare market. The most respected, expe-

rienced, and knowledgeable Florida-based accounting firm when it comes to Florida healthcare accounting and financial issues, MSL has counseled and assisted a wide range of healthcare entities, including skilled nursing facilities, hospitals, hospice and home health agencies, long-term rehab facilities, independent/assisted living facilities, intermediate care facilities for the developmentally disabled, healthcare management companies, psychiatric hospitals, mental care facilities, large physician practice groups, regional health planning councils, not-for-profit agencies, and healthcare provider associations.

Complementing its healthcare specialty, is the Moore Stephens Lovelace Broussard Clinical Consulting, LLC team that provides solutions to the long-term industry with emphasis on developing the highest level of quality healthcare services and optimum levels of financial reward.

To serve our clients' needs for outsourced accounting services, MSL developed the OASIS (Outsourced Accounting Solutions & Information Services) group that works with companies of all sizes, from small and emerging businesses to medium and larger organizations. Among its long-term and turnkey solutions are financial reporting, internal audits, budgeting, strategic financial and business planning, advice on tax issues, payroll services, cash management, accounts receivable, and accounts payable.

Helping Others

An annual event that personifies the caring nature of MSL's employees is the Ray Bolt Classic Golf Tournament. Staged every April 16th, the event is held in tribute to a former Firm shareholder, Ray Preston Bolt, who died of colon cancer in 2001. April 16th is the selected date because Ray had a ritual of celebrating the close of tax season with a round of golf. Proceeds from the tournament are donated to charity.

Employees of MSL are dedicated to improving life in the Orlando area by actively assisting more than twenty-five civic and charitable organizations, including the Alzheimer's Association, Coalition for the Homeless, Seniors First, Winter Park Library and the University of Central Florida.

Besides caring for others, MSL is concerned about its own employees. For several years, the Firm has been selected as one of the "Top 100 Companies for Working Families" in Central Florida.

Trans Continental Companies

He's got a Bachelor of Arts degree in accounting from Queen's College, New York. He's got a Master of Business Administration degree and a Doctor of Philosophy in Business. He can fly small planes. He can fly helicopters. He can play the guitar. He can leap tall buildings in a single bound. . .well, not quite. But he is The Man, and the brains behind Trans Continental Companies, Inc. His name is Lou Pearlman.

Louis J.Pearlman

Howie Dorough of the Backstreet Boys and Lou.

Chartering Flights for the Stars

It all started in 1975 in New York City with a helicopter charter service. From that simple beginning, Trans Continental Companies has morphed into a corporation that blankets the entertainment and high-end travel industry. It includes an aircraft charter and leasing service, a travel agency for personal and corporate travel and entertainment, a talent search organization, a recording studio, entertainment management, and has branched out into high-end jewelry retail and casual dining outlets, among other ventures.

The helicopter charter service expanded into an air charter service using jetliners to shuttle entertainers like Art Garfunkel, Paul McCartney and Wings, Michael Jackson, Madonna, and Phil Collins to their destinations. This became Trans Continental Airlines, and Trans Continental Travel, a full-service travel agency, developed out of that. When Pearlman received a charter request from the musical group, New Kids on the Block, and learned about the fortune these young men had amassed in record sales, tour proceeds, and merchandise sales, he decided to create Trans Continental Records and discover his own pop music stars. He was already armed with a musical background, for he had played guitar for his own rock band that

had done the club circuit in New York, and had been inspired by his first cousin, Art Garfunkel. In 1991, he moved to Orlando, where the climate was better, and by 1992, he had put together five young men who could sing and whose voices meshed well. The group known as the Backstreet Boys was born. His next attempt, 'N SYNC,

*Bob Fischetti (VP of Trans Continental Records),Joey Fatone (of *NSYNC),JC Chasez (of *NSYNC), Lou and Joey Sculthorpe.*

was another success. Between the two groups, Trans Continental Records has sold over 120 million units worldwide and gone gold and platinum. Other singing sensations under the Trans Continental umbrella include O-Town, a group Pearlman put together for the ABC/MTV award-winning series <u>Making the Band</u>, Aaron Carter, Jordan Knight from New Kids on the Block, LFO, whose hit "Summer Girls" (the Abercrombie and Fitch song) sold several million copies, and a girl group, Innosense, whose youngest, would-be member, Britney Spears, decided to go solo. He has also helped the careers of the Latino quartet, C-Note; the rock band, Natural; Smilez & Southstar, a southern hip-hop duo; Sean Van der Wilt, a solo artist; and up-and-comers, Jasper Sawyer and Kelli Feaster.

Carving a New Niche

After discovering all this talent, the logical thing for Pearlman to do was to provide these singers with a place to record, so he built Trans Continental Studios, a state-of-the-art recording facility. It includes three fully-equipped studios, as well as extra amenities for the artist to use to relax or conduct business. Such well known entertainers as Art Garfunkel, Queen Latifah, Eminem, Ray Charles, Limp Bizkit, R. Kelly, K.C. and the Sunshine Band, Mandy Moore and many others have used the facilities.

Not one to wait for talent to come to him, Pearlman goes out and finds new talent by using his Fashion Rock search events. These events, held over a weekend, draw over 3,000 aspiring models, actors, singers, dancers, and comedians from all over the country, who are exposed to industry professionals. Besides exposure, the attendees are also offered workshops to help hone their art. Many "wannabees" have been discovered through this venue and are pursuing their dream. To give these performers even more exposure, Pearlman also produces the event for television.

His first introduction to the small screen was with <u>Making the Band</u>, the first reality show on network television. The documentary was produced by MTV, debuted on ABC in 1999, and won a Motion Picture Association Award. From there, the next step was to make a movie for the big screen. He came up with the idea of <u>Longshot</u>, starring Hunter Tylo and Paul Sorvino, and featuring cameos by Kenny Rogers, K.C. from K.C. and the Sunshine Band, Britney Spears,

Lance Bass and Justine Timberlake from 'N SYNC, and Kool from Kool and the Gang, just to name a few. The movie ran over five hundred times on Cinemax, HBO, Showtime, and the ABC Family Channel. His Trans Continental Productions is now looking at getting involved in other similar projects.

Maintaining a Love of Flying, and Other Ventures

The entertainment industry has not eclipsed his love of flying, for Pearlman branched out into the blimp or airship business. Other than Goodyear, this is the only other major blimp business in the U.S. The airships are used mainly for advertising by such corporations as McDonald's, Tommy Hilfiger, Budweiser, MetLife, Fuji Film, and Sea World. McDonald's has flown one over Disney World every week, and the others can be seen flying around the rest of the country during good weather from time to time. With a top speed of sixty mph, they are not for transportation, but are perfect for aerial shots at sporting events, for TV promotion and marketing. They have also been used by federal agencies for security at the Olympics and World Series.

Planet Airways, a wholly owned

Lou's "RECORDING STUDIO" in Orlando.

subsidiary of PHC Holdings, the charter airline service, operates a fleet of 727 jets, and they fly all across the U.S., to Canada, to Mexico, and to the Caribbean. Besides flying charter flights for travel companies that arrange tours, the service has also been used by the U.S. Marshal Service and the Department of Defense.

Planet Airways (Lou's Charter Airline-727/200).

NYPD (New York Pizzeria and Delicatessen) Lou's restaurant in Metro West Orlando.

Lou's jewelry store "ROCKS FINE JEWELRY."

Keeping his artists happy is part of making Pearlman's business work. When Nick Carter of the Backstreet Boys complained he couldn't get any good pizza in Orlando, Pearlman decided to start a pizza franchise. N.Y.P.D. (New York Pizzeria Delicatessen) was begun. Themed to look like a New York City police station, the restaurants offer high quality pizza and other types of Italian food on the menu. The restaurants have an agreement with the New York City Police Department to use a police shield as its logo and the N.Y.P.D. acronym. Delivery cars resemble police cars and a Summons Violation shows up as your bill. Several franchises have opened in Florida and other parts of the country with more planned in the future. Merchandise with the logo is very popular. Another venture begun for his artists is Rocks Fine Jewelry, a jewelry boutique at the upscale Mall at Millenia in

Orlando. The store offers the latest styles in gold, platinum, and diamond jewelry, and also includes a selection of rare gemstones. An in-house jeweler and designer are available. Many members of the

Magic professional basketball team frequent the store. More Rocks are planned to open soon.

Reaching Out

With his national and international connections, Pearlman does not ignore the local community. All of his artists do charity work, and he frequently reaches out in conjunction with WFTV-9 on community activities. The Trans Continental Companies is an avid supporter of the Make-A-Wish Foundation. On a more personal note, he supports the Southwest Orlando Jewish Congregation, and recently had the Temple Ohalei Rivka named in honor of his mother, Reenie. Also, the corporation built a large water park for the community.

From finding and managing talent, to travel, to pizza and gems, each of the companies is interrelated through the entertainment industry. They are all doing well and growing as evidenced by the number of awards the companies and the talent they handle have received, such as MTV Awards, American Music Awards, and various international awards. Pearlman himself has been honored by receiving the World Award, a yearly award given to men with ideals and vision, and whose success allows them to help others who have not been as fortunate. The president of the association is Mikhail Gorbachev, and honorees include such people as Paul McCartney, Dr. Craig Venter, discoverer of the DNA genetic code, Steven Spielberg, Christopher Reeve, and even the Pope. Pearlman has also been a keynote speaker at Harvard Business School as part of their Distinguished Speakers Series. His book, <u>Bands, Brands and Billions</u>, published by McGraw-Hill, explains "how to make any business go platinum."

From the corporate offices at historic Church Street Station, Pearlman oversees his musical empire of Trans Continental Companies. In the three decades since he began his helicopter charter service, he's been having a great time. He prides himself on being able to bring a lot of great music to a lot of people around the world. From music to pizza, Trans Continental Companies, Inc. touches the lives of many people.

Hulk Hogan, Lou and David Siegel (President and Chairman of Westgate Resorts) and Brooke Hogan

Aaron Carter and Lou

Datamax Corporation

Datamax's diverse product line can be found in everyday applications such as product labeling, patient file tracking, and event ticketing. These products include top of the line bar code and Radio Frequency Identification (RFID) label printers; software products and services; and label, ticket, and tag materials; all of which are used by an international roster of customers ranging from small manufacturing shops and single-outlet retailers to large government agencies and corporations.

Today, Datamax has an installed base of more than 600,000 printers worldwide. They are used in a variety of environments, including consumer goods, manufacturing, automotive, healthcare, electronics, telecommunications, chemicals, textiles, shipping, warehousing, distribution, government, food packaging, and retail.

Orlando Headquarters

Founded in 1977, Datamax's corporate office and main production facility is located in Orlando with representative offices throughout the United States, Singapore, China, and the United Kingdom, as well as label converting and preprinting facilities in Robinson, Illinois. Datamax is the world's leading international bar code and RFID solutions company and markets its products exclusively through a network of resellers and distributors in more than 100 countries worldwide.

Datamax made its debut in the printing industry twenty-six years ago with the introduction of its "Super 6" and "8" inch dot matrix printers, a product set tailored for high-speed online applications such as event and theme park ticketing. By 1984, the company was designing and manufacturing motor assemblies and printed circuit boards for ticket printers used in state lotteries and gaming applications. In 1985, Datamax began development of direct thermal and thermal transfer printers

for the travel industry's automated ticket and boarding pass applications. The company later won exclusive contracts with major US airline carriers to supply the fastest ticket and boarding pass printers in the industry. By the late 1980s, Datamax was the forerunner in the airline ticketing industry, supplying check-in, baggage tag, and ticket and boarding pass equipment to airlines in Europe and worldwide, as well as major travel agencies in the United States. Many of these high-speed printers are still in service today.

In the mid-1990s, Datamax expanded its product offering by acquiring the bar code printer product line from Fargo Electronics, located in Eden Prairie, Minnesota. Shortly thereafter, Datamax also acquired Pioneer labels, a specialty label-converting business in Robinson, Illinois. These complimentary acquisitions enabled Datamax to offer a wider range of printing products and consumables that address many applications.

Datamax has pioneered numerous advances in bar code labeling technology, resulting in some of the industry's most innovative and reliable product developments. Many of these breakthroughs in printer technology are now patented. At the core of Datamax's tremendous success and widespread market acceptance are the company's technologically advanced product designs, high product value, and ease of integration.

Innovative Products

Datamax offers one of the most diverse lines of thermal printers in the bar code industry, with products ranging from entry-level and mid-range units to high-performance systems and specialty printer platforms. These printers are recognized for their reliability and durability in the industry, while offering more standard features, upgradeable options, and connectivity beyond other comparable products in the marketplace. All products can be deployed off-the-shelf, or customized with a variety of configurations to meet special user requirements.

In the continuous quest to address new technologies that help customers operate their business more effectively, Datamax consistently introduces new features for its printers. Recently, Datamax introduced the first "Intelligent" printer enabled by the unique and exclusive Datamax/MCL Collection. MCL is a Macro Command Language consisting of a client runtime module that is embedded inside the printer. An intelligent printer puts the power of connectivity and communications inside the printer. The Datamax printer then drives the application instead of the printer relying on instructions from a host device, such as a computer. Datamax is also at the

forefront of RFID, a technology designed to streamline tracking applications. RFID is currently featured in Datamax I-Class and A-Class printers.

For printing applications, Datamax features an extensive line of thermal transfer ribbons, along with a large selection of label stock. These consumables offer a wide range of formulations and performance characteristics, making them ideal for general-purpose use, as well as for harsh environments where durable wax/resin and resin inks are required. Datamax also operates a full service label converting facility that transforms labels, tickets, and tags from various papers and synthetic materials to exact customer specifications. Other services available to customers with special labeling requirements include in-house art, plate-making, and preprinting services.

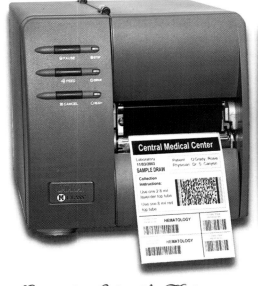

ZOM, Inc

In Robert Frost's timeless poem "The Road Not Taken" one poignant line states, "I took the road less traveled by, and that has made all the difference."

Orlando-based ZOM, Inc. has followed a similar less traveled road as one of the nation's most innovative and visionary real estate companies. By creating, acquiring, enhancing and managing residential and commercial properties with a progressive, think outside-the-box attitude, the approach has indeed made all the difference. Since 1992, ZOM has received sixteen Pillar awards from the National Association of Homebuilders. The Pillars, which are awarded for excellence in development, management, and marketing, are the most coveted and competitive national awards in the housing industry.

Representing the antithesis of the all too prevalent cookie-cutter development mentality, ZOM, Inc. owes its success to a philosophy aimed at forging a trail of innovation and quality rather than following where the well-worn paths may lead.

"ZOM specializes in creating special, one-of-a-kind projects because we strongly believe that is the key to maximizing long-term value," says Steve Patterson, president and CEO. "We are not a brand. Our properties are all different and designed individually to address different lifestyle needs. We find unique, niche opportunities in every marketplace."

Visually striking, ZOM's innovative, stylish building designs, attractive amenities, and cutting edge appointments have strong appeal to renters and buyers. Investors are impressed by a corporate philosophy that emphasizes a disciplined approach to real estate investment. Strict underwriting guidelines and prudent capital structures enable ZOM to minimize the risks associated with developing and operating real estate. Since its inception,

ZOM has built a solid reputation with both lenders and equity partners alike. In 2004, ZOM property sales returned over 20 percent per annum to investors in some instances.

Real estate is, of course, cyclical but we consistently deliver what we promise to investors, says Patterson. "We have a long track record of delivering returns in line with our projections."

Big Picture

A U.S. based company founded by Dutch real estate executives in 1977 and acquired by Patterson in 1997, ZOM has main offices in Orlando and The Hague, Netherlands and regional offices in Atlanta, Fort Lauderdale, Dallas, Tampa and Washington D.C.

ZOM is currently developing projects in Orlando, Tampa, South Florida (Broward, Dade and Palm Beach Counties) and Dallas, Houston and Austin in Texas. Among ZOM's high-profile Florida projects are the recently opened, ultra-luxurious, 91-unit Hotel Victor on South Beach in Miami, a bold, exciting property designed by internationally renowned Parisian designer Jacques Garcia; the Waverly at Surfside, a 111-unit, beachfront project adjacent to the exclusive Bal Harbour community; and The Waverly at Las Olas, a 14-story mid-rise in downtown Fort Lauderdale featuring 304 luxury apartment homes and 25,000 square feet of street level retail shops.

In recent years which have been dominated by low mortgage rates, ZOM has been hugely successful at converting its popular apartment homes into condominiums. Every property in ZOM's portfolio

is underwritten for conversion potential and where suitable, a conversion sale strategy is implemented. "ZOM has an impressive percentage of renters who purchase their units as condos," says Patterson. "The focus on quality, upscale amenities and distinctive design elements is very appealing to condominium buyers who want to increase the value of their investment."

Renters and owners seem to be equally impressed with ZOM's property management services, ZOM Residential Services, Inc., which was awarded the "Property Management Firm of the Year" in 2003 by the National Association of Home Builders. For more than ten years, ZOM Residential Services has served its client base of owners and developers with a dedicated service ethic, innovative management practices and meticulously maintained properties. ZOM manages thirty-seven properties totaling 12,000 units.

Orlando Presence

ZOM's successful projects throughout Orlando are a testament to Patterson's philosophy of constructing buildings that elicit "strong and positive emotions." ZOM has developed 2,597 units and manages 3,155 units in the Orlando area, according to 2003 company compiled statistics.

As part of ZOM's growth strategy to identify urban housing trends, its 230-unit The Waverly at Lake Eola, a sleek, eye-catching high-rise overlooking Lake Eola in downtown Orlando, has been an integral force in the transformation of the area into a 24-hour city where residents can live, work, and play. Honored by the National Association of Home Builders in 2002 as the Best Luxury Multifamily Development, The Waverly at Lake Eola, the first successful, luxury high-rise

residential product in downtown has served as a catalyst for nearby dining and shopping entities. The project was 90 percent sold out in less than six months.

"With the Waverly at Lake Eola ZOM wanted to overwhelm, not underwhelm and make a strong statement that we believed in downtown Orlando," says Patterson. "We set a high standard with the project and are very excited about the future possibilities in downtown Orlando."

That future, according to Patterson, includes another downtown luxury high-rise project with an urban grocery format set to break ground summer 2005 and an urban village concept with a mix of office, retail, and multifamily housing to be built near Loch Haven Park.

Planting Hope

ZOM is a respected corporate citizen committed to enhancing the environment and quality of life in the communities where it builds. For nearly a decade, ZOM has celebrated Arbor Day by planting trees in schoolyards. ZOM always strives to plant more trees than it removes through its development activities, and schoolyards are ideal places to plant those trees and set positive civic and environmental examples.

Rumberger, Kirk & Caldwell, P.A.

*W*hen the founding partners of Rumberger, Kirk & Caldwell encountered an unforeseeable roadblock at a Tampa courthouse in early 1983, they turned what could have been a major disappointment into what is now a memorable victory.

Founding partners J. Richard Caldwell, Jr., E. Thom Rumberger and William L. Kirk, Jr. at the firm's 25th anniversary party.

"After we arrived, we quickly realized we could not get our demonstrative evidence through the doors of the building's elevator," recalls Thom Rumberger. The trial attorneys were representing General Motors, and their exhibit included an entire car (minus the engine and wheels). But that did not stop this team of determined lawyers. Lead counsel Rumberger convinced the U.S. Marshals Office to let them remove the entire window frame of the

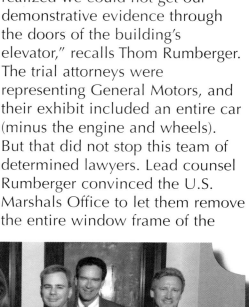

Francis H. Sheppard, William L. Kirk, Jr., Darryl L. Gavin, Lori J. Caldwell, Daniel J. Gerber, J. Scott Kirk and Ernest H. "Skip" Eubanks, Jr.

fourth-floor courtroom, and he hired a crane to hoist the car and push it through.

"Never underestimate the use of imagination and creativity to get the job done," says his longtime partner, William "Bud" Kirk.

William L. Kirk, Jr. and Ernest H. "Skip" Eubanks, Jr. inspect a damaged car in preparation for trial.

Humble Beginnings

On Oct. 2, 1978, Rumberger, Kirk and third founding partner Dick Caldwell began practicing law in a sublet space with a $40,000 loan and a collective commitment that the day they no longer enjoyed getting up and going to work, they'd stop.

Little did they know they were creating an Orlando-based institution. Nearly three decades later, Rumberger, Kirk & Caldwell has grown to twenty times its original size and is staffed with dynamic attorneys committed to doing everything it takes to best represent their clients. And these efforts have not gone unnoticed. Over the years, the nationally recognized lawyers of Rumberger, Kirk & Caldwell have earned numerous awards. The *National Law Journal* named Bud Kirk one of the nation's "Top 10 Litigators" in 1996. The prestigious publication also named Rumberger partner Dan Gerber one of the "Top 40 under 40" attorneys in 2002. In 2001, J. Scott Kirk was one of only seven trial attorneys featured in *Orlando Magazine* as one of Orlando's 55 best attorneys. And in 2004, the Audubon Society recognized Thom Rumberger for his invaluable, ongoing dedication to the restoration of the Florida Everglades.

With offices in Orlando, Miami, Tampa, Birmingham and Tallahassee, the firm's attorneys litigate on behalf of local interests, Fortune 500 companies, and everything in between.

Building a Florida Legacy

One of the leading product liability law firms in the country, Rumberger, Kirk & Caldwell began making a name for itself in automotive product liability. From that base, the firm has grown and diversified its practice to include a broad variety of complex civil litigation matters, including employment, professional liability and commercial clients—ranging from General Motors, Busch Entertainment Corporation, the accounting firm of KPMG, DEI (Dale Earnhardt, Inc.) and The Everglades Foundation, Inc.

"We may be based in Orlando, but our work stretches from coast to coast," says Dick Caldwell. Adds Kirk: "I've tried cases from Maine to California and many places in between. Wherever our clients ask us to go, we go."

While the lawyers of Rumberger, Kirk & Caldwell take great satisfaction in representing corporate America, they also pride themselves on representing environmental interests that are truly Florida based.

Often referred to as the "Defender of the Everglades," Thom Rumberger has been the lead counsel for The Everglades Foundation, Inc. since 1989. A committed environmentalist, Rumberger also has been a leading figure in the effort to save the endangered Florida manatee. In the late 1980s, the prominent legal figure worked to implement some of the first manatee protection laws.

Method of Success

For more than 25 years, Rumberger, Kirk & Caldwell has set the standard for trying small to multimillion-dollar lawsuits—but they've also proven that respect, dignity and fun all play key roles in their success.

"Everyone here has a great sense of humor, and we all care about each other," says partner Lori Caldwell.

Managing partner Frank Sheppard agrees. "We are a family here," he adds. "And because of that, we look forward to coming to work and rolling up our sleeves."

Director of human resources and recruitment Kaye Daugherty has been with the firm since day one, and she still keeps a memo Thom Rumberger distributed to his small staff during those first, challenging days. The memo welcomes everyone to Rumberger, Kirk & Caldwell and stresses the importance of all employees treating one another with respect.

"Still today our partners, associates and staff members have the highest degree of respect for one another," she says. "Thom, Bud and Dick are tough advocates with kind hearts."

Bright Future, Continued Growth

Looking to the future, Rumberger, Kirk & Caldwell intends to maintain steady growth as both national and local counsel, to be progressive with the changing face of the law and to remain invaluable to its clients.

"Our goal is to continue to maintain high-quality lawyers and high-quality clients," says Kirk.

Despite his long tenure as a highly respected, first-rate Florida attorney, Rumberger has no plans of slowing down. "I hope to continue practicing law as long as my intellect permits," he says.

Daniel J. Gerber, J. Scott Kirk, Suzanne Barto Hill, Michael D. Begey and Charles P. Mitchell.

Francis H. Sheppard, Charles P. Mitchell, Lori J. Caldwell and David B. Shelton.

Bogin, Munns and Munns

*B*ogin, Munns and Munns began modestly but with great aspirations. One of its goals was to create a law firm that could meet the legal needs of central Floridians with the utmost competence and integrity. Now celebrating its 25th year of service, Bogin, Munns and Munns (BM&M) has successfully created a full service practice that combines all aspects of corporate and real estate law, along with a comprehensive litigation, commercial and personal injury practice.

Bruce Bogin, Ranier Munns, and Rulon Munns, the founders of Bogin, Munns & Munns, all had a clear vision of Orlando's future when the firm was formed. Ranier and Rulon, who grew up in central Florida, had a feeling that Orlando had a great future. When the three men came together in 1979, they committed the law partnership to provide outstanding service to its clients free from the bureaucracy experienced at so called "big firms." Twenty-five years later, it is apparent that they had the right idea.

The early objectives of the three attorneys have since skyrocketed into a practice with seven offices, thirty-five attorneys, and a total of over 120 employees. Bogin, Munns & Munns provides comprehensive legal services to the central Florida community, with its main office in Orlando, as well as satellite of-

fices in Clermont, Daytona Beach, Deltona, Kissimmee, Leesburg, and Ocala, and with future locations planned in Melbourne, Palm Coast, and Poinciana.

With thirty-five lawyers and a long list of practice areas, BM&M has the classic markings of a large, sophisticated law firm, but has maintained a small firm atmosphere. Clearly, the firm deserves its recognition, having successfully handled numerous matters related to real estate, wills, trusts, probate, intellectual property law, commercial and corporate law, bankruptcy, litigation, family law and adoption, personal injury law, entertainment, labor and employment law, and trademarks and copyrights. The firm's clients are as diverse as these areas of law practice, with clients ranging from individuals to large corporations, from small businesses to Fortune 500 companies. It would

seem nearly impossible for a large firm to handle such a wide range of cases with such a personal touch, but for the lawyers at BM&M, they are merely keeping up with the mission as originally stated by the three founders.

The central Florida region is desirable for those looking to start a business as well as those who wish to raise a family. It is no wonder, then, that much of BM&M's caseload involves real estate, corporate law, and adoption law. Rulon Munns, with over twenty-eight years of experience as an attorney, primarily represents clients with cases involving commercial real estate and general corporate matters, in addition to his work as consultant to the commercial litigation and employment law practice. Ranier Munns, who has nearly thirty years of experience in law practice, bases his practice on plaintiff representation. He also acts as consultant to the firm's adoption law practice, which affects him on both a professional and personal level, as three of his thirteen children are adopted.

Although founder Bruce Bogin has since retired to France, the legacy he created with Rulon

Munns and Ranier Munns is clearly evident in the firm's elite staff of lawyers. These attorneys, a number of whom are multilingual and well-traveled, are fiercely devoted to the clients they represent. In addition to his or her law experience, each lawyer brings to the firm a strong sense of responsibility to the community, with many serving the central Florida region as board members, committee volunteers, and adjunct professors.

What started as a lofty goal shared by three men twenty-five years ago has blossomed into a reality that benefits the entire central Florida community. The people at the law firm of Bogin, Munns and Munns are proud to make the Orlando area their home and even more proud to provide such complete and personal legal assistance to their neighbors.

The hiring of an attorney is an important decision that should not be based solely upon advertisements. Before you decide, ask us to send you free written information about our qualifications and experience.

In 1980 nine attorneys from a large statewide law firm split off to establish a business law firm in Orlando named Dean, Mead, Egerton, Bloodworth, Capouano & Bozarth, P.A. The founding partners were Stephen T. Dean, Robert W. Mead, Jr., Charles H. Egerton, Darryl M. Bloodworth, Albert D. Capouano and Stephen J. Bozarth. With the exception of Mr. Dean, who passed away in August 2000, these founders remain leaders at the firm. Today, the firm has over forty lawyers in three Florida offices serving the legal and business needs of businesses large and small, as well as individuals. The firm is well-known under its abbreviated name, "Dean Mead."

Although becoming a large firm has never been a primary goal of Dean Mead, the firm is committed to the strategic growth that will meet the evolving needs of its clients. In 1987 the firm opened an office in Fort Pierce, part of Florida's Treasure Coast, concentrating in agribusiness, real estate development, estate planning, tax and commercial litigation. The firm opened two more offices during 1992 in Brevard County (Florida's Space Coast) whose primary focus at the time was real estate development. Those offices have now been consolidated into one office in Melbourne. This office continues to concentrate on real estate development, but also practices in commercial litigation, estate planning, elder law, and family law.

By recruiting the most talented attorneys and staffing every project with at least one very experienced lawyer, the firm's focus is on producing the best results possible for its clients at a reasonable cost. The firm places emphasis on the efficiency of its services to clients, ensuring that the time and resources devoted to a project are exactly what it requires-no more, no less. This combination of quality and efficiency in legal services is a hallmark of Dean Mead.

Dean Mead is one of the top-rated business law firms in Central Florida. The firm's lawyers have received national recognition in six core practice areas: corporate/tax, real estate, litigation, estate planning, employee benefits, and health law. The firm has been consistently ranked as one of the top five law firms in Orlando by *Corporate Board Member* magazine. A number of their attorneys are rated AV (the highest rating available from Martindale-Hubbell) and are named in *The Best Lawyers in America* and *Chambers U.S.A.'s America's Leading Lawyers for Business*. Several of the firm's members lecture regularly to both those in the legal profession and to various segments of the business community. Many Dean Mead lawyers hold leadership positions in the bar associations in which they are members, and have served as community leaders in many business and civic organizations.

Dean Mead's clients include some of the area's largest banks, real estate developers, construction companies, and agricultural interests. The firm also represents health care providers and other professional organizations, individuals, trusts, and estates. The industries of the firm's clients include health care, financial institutions, agribusiness, commercial real estate, and professional service firms.

Dean Mead lawyers recognize that to provide high quality legal representation they must take the time to learn the client's business. This helps them identify future legal issues that may arise due to new legislation, court decisions, and changes in the client's business or personal situation.

To better serve its clients who have business in other areas of the United States, or internationally, Dean Mead has recently joined ALFA International, an international network of law firms. The individual law firm members of ALFA have been rigorously scrutinized to ensure the highest quality of legal representation. While Dean Mead is proud to have been selected to serve the Central Florida area, they are also pleased when the need arises to be able to quickly refer their clients to quality legal representation in various parts of the nation and world.

For over 25 years, Dean Mead has prided itself on the quality of its lawyers and staff. It is a mid-sized firm, but clients receive the breadth and experience of a much larger firm and do not get "lost in the shuffle." Each client receives individual attention while receiving the benefits of a diverse team. The services, background, and experience of the attorneys at Dean Mead make it uniquely qualified to serve the Central Florida community.

Greenspoon, Marder, Hirschfeld, Rafkin, Ross & Berger

*F*rom his office in the Capital Plaza One building overlooking Lake Eola in downtown Orlando, Michael Marder, co-managing partner of Greenspoon, Marder, Hirschfield, Rafkin, Ross & Berger, says his statewide law firm has a distinct personality all its own. "We are a medium-size firm but with the same quality of talent as larger firms," says Marder. "Our environment is much less bureaucratic, which allows us to give a higher degree of personal service."

"We are a very creative and hard working firm that doesn't just blindly accept what everyone else is doing," continues Marder. "Our philosophy is to combine years of legal expertise with common sense to solve our client's problems."

Marder says the firm's mission statement is followed closely by all of its attorneys and staff. It states: "To proactively serve and satisfy clients' needs by consistently providing superior services delivered by a team of professionals committed to achieving the highest standards of the legal profession."

Strict adherence to its mission statement has been immensely successful for the 23-year old firm. Regarded as one of Florida's most respected law firms, Greenspoon Marder has offices in Orlando, Fort Lauderdale, West Palm Beach and Boca Raton with more than 150 lawyers and support staff. Following the recent merger with Abrams Anton, a well-established 35-year old South Florida firm, Greenspoon Marder plans to add eleven more lawyers and twenty support staff members in 2005. The combined firm will be known as Greenspoon, Marder, Hirschfeld, Rafkin, Ross, Berger, Abrams & Anton.

Areas of Expertise

Greenspoon Marder's clients engage in numerous and diverse business endeavors. The firm's attorneys and support staff serve clients throughout Florida, the nation and the world. As a broad-based practice, the firm concentrates its efforts in the areas of real estate, commercial litigation, bankruptcy, estate and trust planning, personal injury, taxation law, labor and employment law, immigration law, international law and family law.

Real estate activities are emphasized at Greenspoon Marder, which is involved in sophisticated transactions with buyers and sellers of real property, lenders and borrowers in mortgage financing, loan restructuring, title examinations, zoning and land use issues and leasing. Greenspoon Marder is regarded as one of the leading firms to specialize in vacation ownership issues with a national practice in the areas of condominium development, condominium conversions, timeshare development and land sales.

Because of its expertise in a wide range of corporate and commercial services, Greenspoon Marder assists clients in the negotiation, structuring and implementation of business acquisitions, mergers, dispositions and financing. The firm handles a broad spectrum of corporate work ranging from day-to-day corporate activities from initial incorporations and the monitoring of corporate minute books to assisting with major issues such as company mergers and acquisitions. In the commercial field, the firm drafts and negotiates contracts, licensing and franchise agreements, and prepares venture documentation, including the formation of general and limited partnerships

and limited liability companies. The firm's corporate department provides consultation and advice on federal and state taxation issues, including tax planning and structuring.

Greenspoon and Marder's philosophy on litigation, according to Marder, "is to provide aggressive, effective, practical and cost-conscious litigation for every client." The firm's litigation practice covers a wide area that includes debt restructuring and foreclosures as well as disputes involving financial institutions, commercial and real estate litigation, construction defect and condominium, governmental, labor, estate, civil rights and employment discrimination.

Historical Perspective

Gerald Greenspoon and Michael Marder were young, hard working lawyers when they met in Miami more than two decades ago, and quickly discovered they shared the same ideology on practicing law and building a practice. In 1981, they opened their own firm in Miami focusing on real estate, corporate and hospitality law. Five years later, they relocated the office to Fort Lauderdale to better serve their growing client base. In April 1992, they opened a small office in Orlando with a staff of three people. The highly-successful Orlando office now has 40 attorneys and support staff, and the firm recently added a title insurance branch in Maitland to address housing growth in the area. As a result of the recent merger with Abrams Anton, the firm will have a total of 52 lawyers statewide with support and administrative staff of approximately 200.

Marder attributes the firm's steady growth to its relationship with long-term clients, a loyal and stable staff and the high-level of legal talent the firm recruits. "Our longevity is a direct result of how we treat our clients and staff members," says Marder. "We always keep our clients' best interests in mind and our staff has been extremely loyal since we started." Marder says two administrative assistants that started in 1981 are still with the firm and several staff members have 10, 15 or 20 years of service with Greenspoon Marder.

The future looks bright for the firm. Plans call for expansion by serving additional markets and extending its title insurance services as Florida housing demand continues. Greenspoon and Marder are considering Vero Beach, Port St. Lucie, west Florida and South Florida for expansion. Additionally, they are seeking to extend their Equity Land Title operation to Lake County, Daytona Beach, Sarasota, Clearwater and Jacksonville.

Greenspoon and Marder's legacy of helping the less fortunate will continue in the future. The firm has provided pro bono services to disadvantaged persons and has contributed in numerous ways to various charitable organizations, including the Westgate Resorts Foundation, which distributes funds to more than 100 different groups.

Gerald Greenspoon

Orange County Convention Center

With its premier attractions and world-class hotels, it's no wonder that the Orlando area is a top US tourist destination. You may be surprised to learn, however, that there are just as many business-suit clad people as there are swimsuit-clad vacationers arriving each day. While the vacationers are heading off to any one of the numerous theme parks and recreation areas, there's a good chance that the majority of those coming to Orlando for business purposes are making their way towards the Orange County Convention Center, (OCCC) known for its expansive function spaces and overall Florida charm.

Booking an event at the Convention Center at first seems merely the logical thing to do. There are over 100,000 hotel rooms nestled in the Orlando area, and the OCCC happens to be within a short walking distance of about 8,000 of them.

Since the opening of its West Building in 1983, over 15 million visitors have passed through the palm tree-flanked entrances of the Center. The OCCC has since expanded the West Building, as well as doubled its overall size with the addition of the North/South building. These buildings offer clients over two million square feet of exhibition space. The West Building houses forty-nine meeting rooms, 141 breakout rooms, a 160-seat lecture hall, two business centers, four food courts, and a full-service restaurant. The impressive North/South building boasts two 92,000 square foot general assembly areas, twenty-five meeting rooms, ninety-four breakout rooms, four food courts, two business centers and two full-service restaurants.

In January 2005, the OCCC will be hosting not only its largest convention to date, but also the largest that the city of Orlando has ever hosted. Over 100,000 people will be convening in what clearly will be the most logistically-challenging assignment the Orange County Convention Center's staff has ever faced. But for Kathie Canning, Deputy General Manager, it's all in a day's work.

"Working at a convention center means something different is happening each day," she says of the constant flow of clients. "People from all over the world meet here to learn, buy, and sell. It is always exciting."

Windows at Winter Park, Florida.
Photos by Randa Bishop

KPMG LLP

*O*ne of the world's most recognizable and trusted names in audit, tax, and advisory services, KPMG LLP is the international professional services firm with the strongest growth record over the past decade, and is the largest of the Big Four firms in Orlando. Capitalizing on an unparalleled knowledge base, KPMG is the global network of professional services firms whose aim is to turn knowledge into value for the benefit of its clients, its people, and its communities. KPMG professionals team together to provide clients access to global support, industry insights, and a multidisciplinary range of services. KPMG International has nearly 100,000 professionals in 148 Countries.

Standing (left to right) Dave Dennis, Risk Advisory Services Partner; Steve Elker, Office Managing Partner; Seated (left to right) Paul Stepusin, RAS Managing Director; Matt Donnelly, Tax Managing Director

Left to right: Rick Cloyd, Audit Partner, Kaki Rawls, Tax Managing Director; Katherine Pace, Tax Partner; Steve Appel, Audit Partner

A cornerstone of many KPMG client relationships is the company's Audit and Risk Advisory Services practice, which is committed to managing risk in all of its forms as well as uncovering hidden opportunities for helping businesses become more efficient and profitable.

KPMG's Tax Services practice focuses on finding opportunities for tax savings that can make a significant difference on client balance sheets. Throughout its history, KPMG—with its customized, high-quality tax services—eliminates unnecessary expense by helping companies achieve an optimum tax structure.

KPMG *Orlando*

KPMG's Orlando office has seven partners, who average twenty years experience in the Orlando market, and more than fifty managers and professional staff serving both public and private businesses and organizations throughout the Central Florida region. Adept in delivering quality audit, risk advisory, and tax services, the KPMG Orlando office also offers one of the largest and most comprehensive private client advisory practices of any Big Four firm in Central Florida.

In addition to providing quality services to a client base which includes public and private companies, family businesses, government organizations, and not for profits, the Orlando office also places importance on being an employer of choice.

Giving Back

KPMG has a legacy of volunteerism and community involvement through its innovative Involve program. Partnering with a host of leading non-profit organizations, Involve gives the firm's employees and alumni easy access to carry out their vision of volunteerism. By placing a strong emphasis on community service, KPMG's Orlando office strives to help others in need in Central Florida through volunteerism and fund-raising activities. Among the many local organizations KPMG Orlando supports are Junior Achievement, United Arts of Central Florida, Community Foundation of Central Florida, Coalition for the Homeless, American Cancer Society, Center for Independent Living, Junior League and the Orlando Science Center.

In addition to annual workplace giving, the Orlando office has established a donor advised fund at the Community Foundation with an advisory committee comprised of local office personnel that allocates money to not-for-profit organizations where its partners and employees volunteer.

International Road area, Orlando.
Photo by Randa Bishop

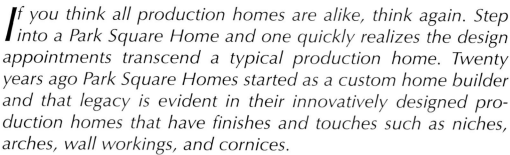

If you think all production homes are alike, think again. Step into a Park Square Home and one quickly realizes the design appointments transcend a typical production home. Twenty years ago Park Square Homes started as a custom home builder and that legacy is evident in their innovatively designed production homes that have finishes and touches such as niches, arches, wall workings, and cornices.

Building Success

Formed in 1984 by a small group of partners with a vision to meet the needs of Central Florida's increasing demand for custom homes, move-up home, second homes, and vacation housing, Park Square Homes is the largest privately owned builder in Orlando. The company operates solely in the Central Florida market.

Enamored by Park Square Homes' stylish designs, unwavering emphasis on quality, and exceptional community locations, home buyers have made the company one of the fastest growing in Central Florida. Park Square Homes was noted in 2000 as one of the five fastest growing companies in Central Florida by Orlando Business Journal. Indeed, the past five years has been a meteoric growth time for the homebuilder. In that time, the company has seen sales volume increase from 250 homes per year to over 1,100 homes per year. Annual sales volume now tops $300 million. Park Square Homes plans to continue this growth through the next three years, with anticipated sales topping well over 1,500 in the next few years.

Park Square Home's success formula is based upon an adherence to the company's core purpose: To build homes and communities that enrich people's lives. Employees of the company adhere to a set of core values that has enabled the company to achieve a high rate of customer satisfaction. The core values are as follows: Have an entrepreneurial spirit, show respect for stakeholders, display honor and integrity in all dealings, always strive for improvement, and work hard and keep it fun.

Abundance of Homes

Since its inception, Park Square Homes has built homes ranging in price from the low $100,000s to over $1 million. In 2004, almost all of the homes built by Park Square ranged from $200,000 to over $500,000. They have built in master planned communities, individual developments, and on self-developed communities. Among the master planned communities where you will find Park Square Homes are Eagle Creek, Tuscawilla, MetroWest, Southern Dunes, Hunters Creek, Vista Lakes, and Summerport at Horizon's West. The company has built homes in a variety of individual developments as well as in their own communities that include Emerald Island Resort, Belmere, Hidden Cove, the Reserve at Bridgewater, Westridge, Terra Verde Resort, Phillips Landing, and the Lake Berkley Resort.

Park Square Homes is also considered a pioneer and innovator in Florida's resort home market with the inclusion of amenities like themed clubhouses, pools, spas, saunas, exercise rooms, cafes, game rooms, and concierge services in many of its resort communities.

Kelly Kibler, American Jewish Ballet, dancing at the Holocaust Memorial, "Remembrance". Photo by Randa Bishop

The Florida Mall

Sprawling impressively on the corner of Orange Blossom Trail and Sand Lake Road in south Orlando, The Florida Mall transcends the stereotypical American mall. A 21st century marketplace where shoppers can buy everything from a lawn mower to a Caribbean cruise to a designer handbag, The Florida Mall offers one of the most diverse retail and dining rosters in the United States. Anchored by a Who's Who list of luxury and moderately-priced large retailers, such as Macy's, Dillards, JCPenney, Nordstrom, Saks Fifth Avenue and Sears, The Florida Mall provides a diverse group of shopping experiences.

The Florida Mall is the largest enclosed shopping mall in Central Florida.

Opened in 1986, the 1.8 million square foot enclosed shopping center encompasses 260 stores, boutique shops and restaurants in a well-designed, bright, airy environment. Located near Orlando's dynamic tourism corridor, The Florida Mall has an international flavor and has become a "must stop" for visiting tourists from around the world who relish the wide selection of stores and restaurants as well as amenities such as multi-lingual staff members at guest services locations, valet parking, motorcoach drop-off locations, and complimentary wheelchairs.

For visitors seeking the ultimate shopper's holiday, the 510-room Florida Mall Hotel, an amenity-rich property with a fine-dining restaurant and 20,000 square feet of meeting space for business groups, is connected to The Florida Mall affording direct access.

Shop Till You Drop

Nearly 50 percent of The Florida Mall's customers are tourists from around the world and the Mall does its best to offer a broad selection of stores and products that are appealing to them as well as to the local market. Few malls anywhere can boast the immense variety of products offered at The Florida Mall. Whether you're in need of a hammer and nails for a home improvement project, a school outfit for a child, or an elegant evening gown, The Florida Mall has the wide selection of department stores and specialty shops to accommodate those and other needs. In addition, special shopping programs are available for business meeting groups seeking spouse or day-trip activities.

Beyond the world class shopping experience, The Florida Mall functions as an important community entertainment venue. A plethora of events are staged throughout the year featuring shows such as the Simon Super Chefs Live demonstration, Soap Opera Digest Revue, and new talent performances by local school and community groups.

Desirable Dining

The dining menu at The Florida Mall can accommodate everybody from the intrepid shopper seeking a delicious quick snack at the food

court in between store-hopping to the shopper that wants to relax at a full-service restaurant with attentive table service.

The Florida Mall's Food Court features eighteen stations offering a fast food menu ranging from hamburgers, tacos, and sub sandwiches to Greek, Italian, and Japanese food in a pleasant, open, dining area.

Few malls in the U.S. can match The Florida Mall's impressive list of full service restaurants. The offerings include: Buca di Beppo, a trattoria-style restaurant offering hearty Italian specialties served family style; California Pizza Kitchen, known for its innovative pizzas, pastas and salads; Le Jardin, a fine-dining experience at the Florida Mall Hotel; Nordstrom Cafe Bistro, a charming, upscale eatery located in Nordstrom; Paradise Bakery and Cafe, where fabulous pastries and frothy cappuccinos can be found; Ruby Tuesday, the national chain restaurant serving American classic fare; and Salsa Taqueria & Tequita Bar, a lively establishment known for its Mexican specialties and Margaritas.

Community Involvement

The Florida Mall takes immense pride in giving back to the Central Florida community through financial contributions, venue donations and employee volunteer hours. Among the charities benefited by Florida Mall are the American Red Cross, March of Dimes, Florida Hospital Foundation, Lisa Merlin House, Ronald McDonald House, Habitat for Humanity, Give Kids the World, Special Olympics, and Center for Hope and Help.

Simon Says

The Florida Mall is owned and managed by Indianapolis-based

Simon Property Group, one of the nation's most influential and innovative ownership, development, and management companies. Specializing in regional malls, Premium Outlet® centers and community shopping centers, the Simon Property Group is the largest publicly traded retail Real Estate Investment Trust in North America and the country's largest owner, developer, and manager of high quality retail real estate. Through its subsidiary partnerships, it currently owns or has an interest in 299 properties in North America containing an aggregate of 204 million square feet of gross leasable area in thirty-nine states plus Canada and Puerto Rico. The Company also holds interests in fourty-nine assets in Europe (in France, Italy, Poland, and Portugal) and four Premium Outlet centers in Japan. Simon manages a retail network that drives approximately $42 billion in annual sales and maintains a portfolio that consistently outperforms the industry.

Simon Property Group owns fifty-two of the top regional malls in the U.S. (malls generating over $2 million in total annual sales) and seventy-eight regional malls located in the twenty-five largest U.S. metropolitan areas. Besides The Florida Mall, other high-profile shopping complexes in the Simon portfolio include, Copley Place in Boston, MA, The Galleria in Houston, Texas, Lenox Square in Atlanta, Georgia, The Forum Shops at Caesars in Las Vegas, Nevada and The Fashion Centre at Pentagon City in Arlington, Virginia.

The only Saks Fifth Avenue in Central Florida is located at The Florida Mall.

Nordstrom opened it's only Central Florida location at The Florida Mall in 2002, joining over 260 other retail and restaurant establishments.

Dynetech Corporation

*D*ynetech Corporation, in the eyes of many observers throughout Central Florida's business scene, is one of Orlando's "best kept secrets." But this moniker requires a closer look. "Secret" is not ordinarily a term one might associate with a company that has more than $200 million in annual sales and more than 500 employees working in four locations throughout the United States.

Not that Dynetech ever sought a low profile. The company has been seen in such prestigious places as the Inc. 500 list of the fastest growing privately-owned companies in the United States and *Florida Trend* magazine's Golden 200 list of the state's largest privately owned companies. Dynetech also steps up each year as a sponsor of the Orlando Regional Chamber of Commerce's HobNob and underwrites the annual *Dynetech Entrepreneur of the Year* awarded by the Roy E. Crummer Graduate School of Business at Rollins College.

Still, even while acknowledging a series of documented achievements and a growing record of community involvement, Dynetech founder and CEO Laurence J. "Larry" Pino admits that his "elevator speech" about the company "is not quite the 15 seconds it should be."

Perhaps that explains the "best-kept secret" sobriquet.

For the record Dynetech is an enterprise development and management company that develops and sells an array of software products and training programs. "Simply put," says Pino, "we create and manage direct-to-market distribution channels for our own proprietary brands and, as an outsource partner, for other companies."

Indeed, Dynetech is a leader in the direct marketing of high-value, consumer-focused products and training. Among Dynetech's proprietary brands are Wizetrade™ software for self-directed investors in the stock market, Options Made Easy® software for self-directed investors in the options markets, 4X Made Easy®, Commodities Made Easy™ and a host of other software products.

Dynetech also provides marketing, logistics, and operational support on an outsource basis to organizations it calls Partner-Clients. Among these Partner-Clients are the Robert Allen Institute for real estate education, the American Cash Flow Institute, author Mark Victor Hansen of *Chicken Soup for the Soul* and *One-Minute Millionaire* fame, Optionetics®, a seminar series created by market guru George Fontenills for individuals interested in understanding the options markets and a score of others.

Dynetech provides technology support to companies such as eBay—contributing to the development of custom-designed auction interfaces—and RCI, providing development and mainframe services for its custom-designed, online timeshare re-sale services.

Dynetech is a strong supporter of work force diversity with about 65 percent of its Orlando associates either members of minority groups or female. Over half of Dynetech's executive staff are women.

Dynetech's direct-to-consumer marketing and fulfillment model for many of its proprietary brands and Partner-Clients includes live sales events held on a weekly basis in dozens of markets throughout the country and outside the United States. Dynetech in-house associates market, manage, and stage

each event, and then fulfill the product or service purchased by customers.

Dynetech conducts more than 150 live sales events per week, drawing an average cumulative monthly audience of 30,000 qualified prospective customers from throughout the United States, Canada, Australia, New Zealand, South Africa, Singapore, and Hong Kong. The company expends, on average, $1.5 million per week in advertising and marketing expenses to create those audiences.

This enterprise management organization conducts business through a number of wholly-owned subsidiaries. For example:

* **MyMediaWorks** is Dynetech's sales and marketing arm. It provides media production, media buying, as well as event management and logistics support for Dynetech's proprietary products and for Partner-Clients.

* **TechWerks** develops and manages e-commerce business solutions applications. It provides software engineering, IT and Internet marketing support to Partner-Clients and other customers. In addition, TechWerks has developed the AGORA Management Series, a unified business platform for organizations that manage memberships, events, and training activities. With one of the largest Web development staffs in Central Florida, TechWerks also has developed more than twenty-five different e-commerce Web sites for proprietary products and Partner-Clients.

* **Emerald Capital Group** provides venture capital financing, commercial business financing and venture management services to companies that require incubation.

* **GlobalTec Solutions** develops user-friendly, state-of-the-art software and training programs primarily for self-directed investors in the equities, options, com-

modities, and spot foreign currency exchange markets. GlobalTec's flagship software products are Wizetrade™ software for stock market traders; Options Made Easy® for options traders; 4X Made Easy® for foreign currency exchange traders, and Commodities Made Easy™ for traders in the commodities markets.

Larry Pino founded Dynetech in 2000 by consolidating the operations of several companies that he had been running since the early 1990s. A commercial litigation lawyer by training, Pino was educated at the University of Notre Dame, New York University Law School, L'Alliance Francaise, University of Madrid and Centro Linguistico Italiano Dante Alighieri. He got his start in the direct-marketing of training services with the cash-flow industry, which he literally created.

As a private attorney, Pino bought dozens of real estate parcels by taking back privately held notes. Unimpressed with the time-consuming nature of managing real estate, Pino began selling off parcels for long-term wealth creation. Upon realizing the potential size and the scope of the privately held mortgage market, he began developing a series of practices and procedures to empower other entrepreneurs around the country to take advantage of investment opportunities with privately held mortgages. Soon after, he launched and then perfected the *Certified Mortgage Investor Training Program*.

The impact of the resulting network of trained consultants and their contact with funding sources was almost immediate. Then, having identified similar economic dynamics in factoring and other privately held debt instruments, Pino created the *Diversified Cash Flow Specialist Training Program* to train consultants in all debt instruments. In the establishment of this

program, Pino brought the multitude of debt instruments under one umbrella and gave a name to the burgeoning industry—*the cash flow industry.*

The business was successful. But the best was yet to come. Pino's development of the cash-flow industry led him to the realization that the same direct-to-market process used to market the cash-flow industry could also be used

to market other high-value, consumer-oriented products and training programs.

Thus, Dynetech was born, and the breakthrough occurred.

In addition to being named to the 2004 Inc. 500 list, Dynetech also was recently named to *Inc.* magazine's Inner City 100, a list of the fastest-growing privately owned companies headquartered in urban core areas. The company also was recently named to *Orlando Business Journal's* Golden 100 list of the largest privately owned companies in Central Florida. And, for two years in a row, Dynetech was singled out as an eBay Star Developer in recognition of its efforts to contribute to eBay's custom-designed auction interfaces.

While growing his business, Pino has been engaged in other passions, too, chiefly the study and promotion of entrepreneurship and enterprise development. As an inveterate entrepreneur himself—having started and run more than forty-five companies throughout his career—Pino acknowledges a fascination with how small start-up companies morph themselves into large sustainable and scaleable enterprises.

That's one reason why Pino personally donated $100,000 to the Roy E. Crummer Graduate School of Business at Rollins College in 2002 for its Entrepreneur Center and why he underwrites the annual *Dynetech Entrepreneur of the Year* award, presented by the Crummer School each year to a successful Central Florida business.

Pino serves as co-chair of the myregion Economic Leadership Workgroup, a collection of local business leaders seeking to implement strategies to grow and diversify the economy of the seven-county Central Florida region.

Pino's other passion is his family. He is married to the former Janet Horvath, Dynetech's executive vice president, and the couple are parents to three children, two boys and a girl. The Pinos are heavily involved in a variety of activities on behalf of their sons' school and spend much time together with the children. It is not uncommon to see the couple on weekends bicycling with their children around Winter Park or boating on one of its lakes.

As Dynetech looks to continue its growth, Pino and his 500 associates constantly scan the horizon for new Partner Clients that "fit" the Dynetech sales model. On tap for expansion are new ventures in business-to-business consulting, a probate-business training program and a family-oriented consumer product that strives to improve communication between parents and children.

"We've proven that the Dynetech model works," Pino says. "We need only to continue finding new ways and new ventures to put it to use."

And in the process, perhaps sooner than later, Dynetech will cease to be Orlando's "best kept secret."

Crealde School of Art sculpture and art garden. Photo by Randa Bishop

In the late 1980s, a couple of young mortgage loan originators, Douglas F. Long and Jeffery J. Vratanina, met regularly at a small doughnut shop and talked about how emerging technology and the Internet would eventually change the face of the mortgage loan business. With an unabashed, take-on-the-world entrepreneurial spirit and a commitment to stay ahead of competitors with new technologies, they founded Pinnacle Financial Corporation in 1988.

Today, the Orlando-based company is one of the East Coast's largest independently-owned mortgage lenders. Amazingly, Pinnacle Financial, a full-service lender licensed in forty-eight states, has increased year-over-year closings by 6,000 percent since opening its doors.

In 2004, the Pinnacle family of companies closed over $3.5 billion in residential mortgage loans. "From the day we opened, our company has always been customer driven, not transaction driven," says Pinnacle Financial CEO & Director Doug Long, who grew up in Orlando and graduated from the University of Central Florida. "The principles we started with, a strong entrepreneurial spirit and heavy reliance on new technology, are still the cornerstones of our success philosophy."

Pinnacle Positives

It's no secret that homebuyers these days have a multitude of mortgage financing choices. How has Pinnacle Financial been able to distinguish itself from your average mortgage company?

"By utilizing technology and our proprietary underwriting software to expedite the entire process and by offering broad product choices, the customer always comes out the winner at Pinnacle Financial," responds Long. "We created nearly 50 percent of our product mix and our company maintains a street-savvy culture that keeps a flat-line management structure. Everyone on our team is close to the street and never loses touch with current trends in the market."

Pinnacle Financial also works directly with Wall Street investors to design residential and commercial mortgage products that are unique to the industry. The company has created its own proprietary underwriting system for Alt-A and subprime loans. In addition, Pinnacle Financial is a direct lender that processes, underwrites, and funds their loans locally. This gives each of its branch offices the ability to provide customers with unmatched, personalized service.

Calling itself "The Home of the Stress Less Mortgage," Pinnacle Financial's primary menu includes FHA/VA, conventional, Alt-A, and subprime. They looked closely at their customers' unique needs and developed expanded loan features that include condo programs that overcome the obstacles of traditional underwriting guidelines, 100 percent LTV investor properties, LIBOR-indexed adjustable-rate mortgages, interest-only option,

no mortgage insurance option, genuine no documentation loans, condotel properties, and foreign national borrowers.

Pinnacle Financial recently introduced their No Income/No Asset (NINA) commercial mortgages. The small-balance loans are offered to borrowers with quality credit and collateral without the burden of income and asset documentation. The innovative product opens up a traditionally underserved and untapped market for community banks, mortgage bankers and brokers, and commercial real estate agents. "It's a phenomenal new product because it can help banks salvage the 30 to 35 percent of commercial mortgages that they traditionally decline due to insufficient documentation from the borrowers," says Long. "Banks can fill a huge market void for a wide range of commercial properties."

To service mortgage brokers, Pinnacle Financial offers its products through its wholesale division, Tri-Star Lending Group. The company also has several joint venture companies and recently debuted Pinnacle Financial Group, a financial services firm with offices in Winter Park, Florida and Bermuda offering annuities, mutual funds, managed money, and other services.

Core Values

"We offer more than 1,200 products," says Long, "but at the end of the day, our business is really about relationships more than anything. Our mission at Pinnacle Financial is to go beyond customer satisfaction to create customer delight."

Long cites three fundamental values that guide his company toward the goal of providing a stress less mortgage experience. The SPA formula includes Speed—Making quick decisions, responding to

questions and delivery via technology; Personal Service—Putting the customer first, helping not selling and doing more than is expected; Accessibility—24/7 online status and multiple contact methods.

Helping Others

Pinnacle Financial is a generous corporate citizen that reaches out to help others in need. In fall 2004, when Florida and Alabama were ravaged by four violent, destructive hurricanes, Pinnacle Financial responded with an innovative $1 billion, one-year program called FIX-FLA/FIX-BAMA, to assist people in rebuilding, remodeling, or relocating their home. Homeowners in affected counties who had their homes destroyed or made uninhabitable could qualify for up to 100 percent financing and a 0.125 interest-rate reduction for the life of the loan. Renters who had been forced from their dwellings could qualify for a mortgage to purchase their own home. Due to the immediacy of the financial need, all of these loans were given top priority.

"We had a lot of our employees who were affected by the hurricanes and we got together and decided we wanted to do something to help others," says Long. "The dedication of our employees to this project is symbolic of the hard work and commitment they put in every day to make Pinnacle Financial successful."

Avalon Park

Set on 1,860 acres in east Orlando along the banks of the Econlockhatchee River, Avalon Park is a traditional neighborhood community where residents can live, learn, work, and play. The antithesis of suburban sprawl, Avalon Park is master-planned to evoke an inviting small-town charm with classic home designs, a "Main Street" brimming with shops and restaurants, tree-lined streets, garages accessible from private rear lanes, and wide front porches that enhance the pedestrian-friendly character of the neighborhoods. Adding to Avalon Park's self-contained appeal are two schools on-site, neighborhood parks, swimming pools, picnic areas, and 234 acres of ponds for fishing, canoeing, and bird watching.

Avalon Park's line-up of award-winning builders has referenced styles from a wide range of historical home designs such as Neo-Classical, Florida Cracker, and Mediterranean. With town-homes priced from $160,000 and the single-family homes now start in the low $200,000s. Avalon Park has a strong appeal to the middle income market.

The social and commercial epicenter for Avalon Park is The Town Center, a "downtown" area lined with services residents use everyday such as restaurants, legal offices, a bank, a hair salon, and more.

A Business Hub

Avalon Park is well on its way to becoming a dynamic business hub. Its Phase One office and retail development has more than 125,000 square feet of commercial space, including a Publix supermarket, and 51 apartment units. Phase Two, scheduled for completion late 2005 features Town Center II highlighted by an additional 30,000 square feet of commercial space and eighty-four apartment units. Future plans call for two large office buildings with 200,000 square feet of office space and six smaller office buildings with 15,000 to 18,000 square feet of space each.

Enhancing the commercial opportunities at Avalon Park is its centralized location near major employers like Lockheed Martin, Siemens/Westinghouse, and the University of Central Florida in addition to increased accessibility. A developing road network that will include a direct north/south route from Colonial Drive (S.R. 50), one of Orlando's busiest thoroughfares, to Orlando International Airport is in the works. At completion, it's expected that Avalon Park Boulevard, the main road feeding in and out of The Town Center, will carry upwards of 35,000 vehicle trips per day. Currently more than 48 percent of the population living within a 5-mile radius of The Town Center is between the age of twenty-five and fifty-four with incomes between $50,000 and $149,999.

Upon build out in eight to ten years, Avalon Park's half million square feet of commercial space, 3,400 single-family, and 1,431 multi-family units will be home to more than 15,000 residents and dozens of businesses and professional practices.

Park Avenue, Winter Park, Florida.
Photo by Randa Bishop

Florida Extruders

Windows may be considered the "eyes" of a home, so quality in craftsmanship is a key factor in determining the right product for the job. Since 1989, Florida Extruders International has made this choice a lot easier for builders and homeowners by providing high-quality extrusion and fenestration products at a fraction of the cost.

When Joel Lehman established Florida Extruders International in Sanford in 1989, the company's mission was to provide top-notch products and service at a competitive price. As a producer of vertically integrated aluminum billet, aluminum extrusions, and powder coat finishing, as well as aluminum windows and doors, Florida Extruders has fulfilled that mission, quickly becoming a company that builders and contractors turn to for their extrusion and fenestration needs.

A Company's Beginnings

Florida Extruders International was established with a staff of eighteen, a number of whom were members of the Lehman family, and a facility of about 140,000 square feet. Products were originally acquired from outside distributors for resale. Lehman sought a niche for his company in an already established market by having his highly-trained staff supervise every phase of production at the plant, making the process not only more convenient, but cost-effective as well.

The young company grew from a small firm to a large, successful corporation over the next decade, adding major equipment and service capabilities with each passing year. Multi-ton extrusion presses and a powder coating facility, as well a remelt facility capable of casting 40 million pounds of aluminum billet were all part of the company's development. In 1997, $12 million was invested in the physical expansion of the facility to a total of 385,000 square feet. In 1997, the company covered 650,000 square feet. Currently, Florida Extruders has plans for further expansion, having purchased thirty-six acres in Sanford for future facilities.

Florida Extruders is known for its long list of stellar products, including patio and pool enclosure extrusions, blank and prehung patio screen doors, and patented aluminum framing components; all treated with a highly durable powder coated finish. The company is able to deliver and export its products with a truck fleet and distributions throughout Florida, demonstrating its commitment to excellent customer service.

A Milestone® in development

In 1995, Florida Extruders expanded its line of service and products with the introduction of Milestone® window and door designs. The company oversees the entire process of production, from manipulation of the raw materials to the completed window or door, enabling beautiful results for a modest price. Advanced designs

coupled with only the most durable of materials are what make Milestone® windows and doors such an incredible value.

In business, however, a product, no matter how beautifully made, is only as successful as its popularity with customers. And the enormous response to the Milestone® product line speaks volumes on behalf of the customers. Since its inception, Milestone® windows and doors have been hailed as one of the state's most prominent window and sliding glass door manufacturers. It has been honored by *Window & Door* magazine with a ranking among the top 100 North American window and door manufacturers. The Milestone® not only makes an impression aesthetically, but also competitively as a young brand that has already experienced phenomenal success.

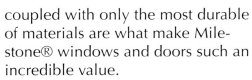

Florida Extruders International is a company that has made its mark in the industry. Joel Lehman saw an entrance into a competitive market, and with hard work and a dedicated staff, he was able to carve a niche. 2003 was a banner year for the company, with several awards and honors bestowed on Lehman and his company. Florida Extruders made Florida Trend magazine's list of the Top 200 Florida-based private companies. Lehman himself was the recipient of the first Dynetech Distinguished Entrepreneur Award, instituted by the Crummer Graduate School of Business at Rollins College, as well as the 2003 Ernst & Young Entrepreneur of the Year

Award in the Manufacturing/Distribution Category in the state of Florida.

Truly, the vision of Florida Extruder's successful future is as clear as if one looked through a Milestone® window. By maintaining excellent products and outstanding service, Lehman and his loyal staff can expect many more important milestones to come.

By guaranteeing the lowest rates of any major rental car company and providing a fleet of new vehicles, superb customer service, state-of-the-art reservation processes, and an efficient check in and check out experience, E-Z Rent-A-Car strongly lives up to it's motto to be "The Best Value in Car Rental."

"With a clear vision on being The Best Value in Car Rental, E-Z Rent-A-Car continues to grow"

If you haven't already heard of E-Z Rent-A-Car, you will. The ten year-old car rental business is one of Orlando's fastest growing companies. It started with a fleet of nine cars and one location in Orlando and has grown to a fleet of 5,000 vehicles and thirteen locations in three states (Florida, Georgia, and Texas) with 250 employees. E-Z Rent-A-Car has in-terminal locations in Orlando and Fort Lauderdale, FL as well as Dallas, Texas. Additional off-airport locations include West Palm Beach, Clearwater, Miami, Kissimmee, Sanford, International Drive, and Orlando in Florida, Dallas/Fort Worth and Dallas Love Field in Texas and Main Street in College Park, Georgia in the Atlanta area.

E-Z Rent-A-Car has an aggressive expansion plan to transform from a regional to a national company with a goal to become the 7th largest rental car company in four years. Plans for 2004 call for airport locations in Houston, Texas and Jacksonville, Florida.

Technology Leverage and Service

E-Z Rent-A-Car is the successful dream of three long-time friends and Orlando residents who capitalized on a unique opportunity in the world's largest rental car market. At its inception, E-Z Rent-A-Car concentrated its efforts on customers under twenty-five years of age and cash rentals, markets that weren't being adequately served by major car rental companies in the mid-1990s. The company quickly evolved to accommodate a wider range of markets by growing its presence on the Internet.

By maintaining an informative, creative, and efficient Web site, E-Z Rent-A-Car competes successfully with all other major rental car companies. The Web site generates thousands of visits each day through search engine optimization, exterior links, and affiliate programs. Major links include Priceline.com, Orbitz.com and Sidestep.com as well as links with major hotels and resorts. Most important for customers, E-Z Rent-A-Car adjusts its Web site rates frequently, typically several times a day and provides an uncomplicated, fluid reservation process. An informative travel guide is also provided.

Above and beyond receiving a low rate, E-Z Rent-A-Car customers are treated to a speedy and efficient check-in and check-out process at counters well-staffed by courteous

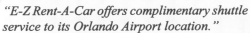

and knowledgeable employees. Vehicle selection is also a strong feature for E-Z Rent-A-Car, which has up to twelve car classes ranging from compact, economy automobiles to 15-passenger vans. In addition, they offer a wide variety of specialty vehicles such as SUVs, convertibles, mini-vans and sports cars.

Special Programs

Innovation, especially in the corporate meeting and convention markets, has contributed greatly to E-Z Rent-A-Car's mercurial growth pattern. Its CASH Back Rewards program for frequent renters, the first of its kind in the industry, rewards E-Z's most loyal customers with a 3 precent cash rebate. To assist CASH Back Rewards members, E-Z Rent-A-Car offers an individualized information landing page on its Web site for each company/group that tracks reservations, contracts, earnings, payouts and drivers. CASH Back Reward members can make reservations on the page and edit any of their information.

Through its relationships with convention and visitor's bureaus in its major markets, E-Z Rent-A-Car

communicates directly with meeting planners to set up convention accounts and address specific desires and needs. Convention and Special Event accounts have access to special rates and privileges such as no additional driver fees and a lower underage fee. Meeting planners and other event representatives have the opportunity to earn complimentary car rentals or commission from the contracts which their accounts generate.

Rest assured, with E-Z Rent-A-Car's innovative and aggressive expansion plans, you'll be hearing a lot about the company in the coming years. Its cornerstones of best value, technology leverage, and a service level to deliver the product will, no doubt, accelerate E-Z Rent-A-Car's presence as a major, national car rental company.

Knight Images

*A*t Knight Images (KI), a marketing and advertising agency located in the heart of downtown Orlando, business is personal. From traditional agency services to specialties including publishing, multi-media, and web development, the agency serves its clients in many areas.

Its strength, however, lies in the agency's ability to develop and grow meaningful relationships. It is for this very reason that the people at Knight Images continuously find themselves working with clients that believe in the power of relationships, partnerships, and community.

Community Ties

A homegrown Orlando business, Knight Images has focused a great deal of its efforts on work that affects the Orlando community. The company has found itself working for important Central Florida entities like Hughes Supply, UCF, the Orlando Regional Chamber of Commerce, Fairwinds Credit Union, the Downtown Development Board, and Orlando's Cultural Audience Development Initiative. Working with these as well as many other community-minded partners, Knight Images has developed a tradition of bringing groups together for a common good. In fact, very few KI clients and partners have not worked or teamed up with others.

"It is a natural fit for a lot of the people we work with," says Mike Hinn, Knight Images' president and CEO. "We have close ties with a number of groups that have common goals, which often include ways to enhance our community. When we show them how much more effective they can be by working together, relationships are formed and great things happen." The people at Knight Images see their constantly developing company and partnerships as proof that Orlando is a great place to do busi-

ness, where new ideas and thinking are embraced. As active and involved members of the community, they're excited about the growth and development of the downtown area they call home and the region as a whole.

The Work

The Knight Images team consists of a mix of talented, creative individuals that bring various skills and personalities together to create a unique environment, great chemistry, and some extremely original work. Winners of countless industry awards, the Knight Images team continuously strives to bring the quality and creativity of KI's work to a new level.

From a strategic perspective, Mike Foristall, creative director, views this as a key priority. "If we're going to be able to focus on relationships and help our clients work better, great service and creative work have to be a given," says Foristall. "We work hard to ensure the quality of our work never comes into question so that we can keep our clients focused on strategy."

People First

Perhaps the reason Knight Images is so successful in developing relationships and partnerships in the community has to do with how they approach business-people first. Whether dealing with employees, vendors, clients, or partners, Knight Images employs the belief that no matter what the business relationship is, it is important to

Knight Images team members work hard, but they also take time to let loose, as evidenced by company Attitude Adjustment Days.

remember the human element. It is this philosophy that has resulted in company policies such as Attitude Adjustment Day, when the office shuts down on a quarterly basis and spurs employees to "play" as a team. Past Attitude Adjustment Day activities have included visiting theme parks, playing sports, go-carting, and other excursions brainstormed by the team. In addition to scheduled fun time, Knight Images promotes a casual environment where employees are encouraged to express themselves and share their outside lives.

"We like to think that your workplace should enhance your life," says Hinn. "If we can include things we care about in our lives outside of work, it will only add passion and energy to what goes on inside our walls."

Year after year, KI is noted among Central Florida's Top 100 Companies for Working Families and has repeatedly won the Small Wonder Award for its attention to quality of life and work balance.

An active and involved community member, Knight Images is located in the heart of downtown Orlando.

Looking Ahead

As Knight Images barrels toward the future, the company strives to keep its people-first attitude and innovative, entrepreneurial spirit. As markets change, the team expects that they will need to adapt, just as they have in the past. However, they believe their ability to solve problems creatively and approach situations with unique perspective will give them the edge they need to stay ahead of the game.

A people-first business philosophy makes the team at Knight Images a tightly knit group.

Orlando Marriott Downtown

*A*n unmatched location is high atop the list of numerous assets for the Orlando Marriott Downtown Hotel. Situated alongside Interstate 4, directly across the street from the Bob Carr Performing Arts Centre and the T.D. Waterhouse Centre, the Orlando Marriott Downtown Hotel allows guests the opportunity to enjoy everything downtown has to offer with easy access to major theme parks and attractions.

Guests at the Orlando Marriott Downtown can walk across the street for a plethora of events including Orlando Magic basketball games, major concerts, and Broadway plays to name a few.

Amazing Amenities

The smartly appointed 290 guest rooms and 9 suites at Orlando Marriott Downtown are designed to accommodate all the needs and desires of the discerning business traveler or conference delegate as well as the vacationer. All rooms feature high-speed internet access, 2-line speaker phones, modem-hook-ups, 27-inch color TVs, HBO, in-room movies, irons/ironing boards, hairdryers, and in-room coffee makers.

The amenities continue outside the guest rooms as well. For health conscious guests, the newly renovated Fitness Center, with state-of-the-art equipment featuring the Cardio Theater is open 24 hours a day. A one mile jogging/fitness trail and outdoor heated swimming pool and Jacuzzi are other options for the active traveler. Tennis enthusiasts enjoy access to a multi-court tennis complex two blocks away and golfers are afforded priority tee time access to MetroWest Country Club, Alaqua Lakes Golf Club, and Cypress Creek Country Club courses.

Dining Pleasure

For a hotel its size, the Orlando Marriott Downtown has an impressive line-up of dining options. Livingston Street Cafe is a convenient, casual eatery open for breakfast and lunch with an All-American menu selection. The upscale Zinfandels offers Contemporary/American cuisine with seasonal foods, an excellent wine list, and comfortable ambiance. For sports fans, Spectators Sports Bar, known as the headquarters for Orlando Magic fans, is a good time haven where big screen televisions show the biggest games.

Successful Meetings

For conference meetings, social events, and weddings, Orlando Marriott Downtown offers Marriott's renowned meeting expertise and a flexible venue in a superb location, easily accessible to meeting attendees and special event guests. There are 12,000 square feet of meeting space within the hotel. Plus an additional 25,000 square feet of meeting and banquet space in the adjoining University of Central Florida Centre. The largest meeting room is Hall 300 Ivanhoe with maximum meeting space of 25,000 square feet and maximum seating capacity of 2,000.

Amenities include high-speed Internet access, a business center, express check-in/check-out, and concierge services.

THE ART CENTER at maitland

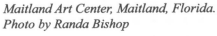
Maitland Art Center, Maitland, Florida.
Photo by Randa Bishop

Priority Healthcare

Thanks to cutting edge technologies and research, today's patients with severe illnesses and conditions often have a much brighter prognosis than their predecessors did ten years ago.

Unfortunately, many of these new therapies are accompanied by complicated instructions, painful injections and challenging side effects. Patients find themselves unable to cope with the overwhelming prospect of treating their conditions: local pharmacies often do not keep their medication and supplies in stock, and those that do may not be able to answer patients' questions with complete information specific to their disease state. For a patient living with a debilitating illness or the rollercoaster ride of infertility treatments, this lack of support can be the straw that breaks the camel's back. Customers living with chronic illnesses and conditions have enough to worry about … Priority Healthcare makes sure the right patient gets the right drug at the right time.

Filling Prescriptions with Compassion

A world apart from traditional pharmacies, Priority Healthcare is a national specialty pharmacy and distribution company committed to serving patients with chronic diseases and genetic disorders that require complex therapies. Headquartered in Lake Mary, Florida, Priority Healthcare has worked since 1994 to serve thousands of patients and healthcare providers in all fifty states. In addition to always having specialty therapeutics in stock, Priority

Healthcare ensures that they will arrive intact by monitoring every step of their shipping process, from climate control to custom designed packaging. By routinely shipping test batches from each of their distribution facilities, Priority Healthcare works to maintain strict quality control standards. When dealing with life-changing therapeutics, nothing short of perfection will do.

Priority Healthcare's commitment to its customers extends beyond simply delivering medication. Upon referral, patients are assigned a team of staff to support them for the duration of their treatment. Patient care coordinators set up deliveries and facilitate orders while specialized pharmacists and nurses are available twenty-four hours a day to answer detailed questions regarding their medications, ranging from dosing to side effects. The final key to Priority Healthcare's seamless customer care is their staff of dedicated registered nurses. Trained to support the unique medical needs of Priority Healthcare customers, nurses are on-call around the clock for easy patient access. Together, they work passionately to provide specialized medications and support for specialized conditions.

Managing the care of so many customers is a daunting task. To serve their customers better, Priority Healthcare carefully trains its administrative staff to provide compassionate customer service. Patient advocates coordinate payment plans, facilitate financial aid programs, and assist customers with reimbursement issues, while call center managers provide a strong front line to get customers the answers they need quickly. Priority Healthcare also prides itself

on its innovative information technology professional staff. In addition to managing inventory, reimbursement, and incoming orders, the IT team has also developed an extremely customer-friendly Web site. Boasting secure condition-specific online communities, Priority Healthcare gives patients, caregivers, and healthcare professionals access to online support chats and message boards, as well as comprehensive diagnosis and treatment information, current clinical trials, and available financial support programs. IT also strives to provide the vital online link between clinicians, patients, and payors while maintaining HIPAA privacy standards.

Aside from the wide spectrum of support that Priority Healthcare offers, part of what makes it unique is its breadth of service. Offering more centers of excellence than any other pharmacy and distribution company, Priority Healthcare supports patients including those living with cancer, hepatitis, hemophilia, multiple sclerosis, rheumatoid arthritis, age related macular degeneration, human growth hormone insufficiency, Crohn's disease, chronic sinusitis, and infertility. Priority Healthcare is also committed to managing customers' pain management needs for a variety of diagnoses.

Meeting Physicians' Needs

In addition to patient-direct delivery, Priority Healthcare offers a specialty distribution service tailored to the individual needs of physicians. By providing competitively priced pharmaceuticals and medical supplies for office or clinic administration, Priority Healthcare helps physicians better manage the health and wellbeing of their patients. As well as having access to online purchasing and account management, physicians working with Priority Healthcare are able to order small packages of only the medications they need, when they need it. Twenty-four hour expert clinical support acts as an extension of the physician's practice, even providing clinical updates on patients when requested.

Clinical Programs

Finally, Priority Healthcare works closely with biopharmaceutical companies to coordinate clinical trial and new product rollouts. By assigning highly trained nurses and pharmacists to facilitate these projects, Priority Healthcare assures both vendors and physicians that they will have support every step of the way.

Like the life-giving tree central to their logo, Priority Healthcare continually reaches toward innovative progress and focuses on remaining a deeply rooted, steadfast company. Priority Healthcare is committed to achieving the highest possible levels of customer service and patient care, while providing growth for their associates and shareholders.

Bill Darden

The first Red Lobster in Lakeland, FL.

When Bill Darden, Joe Lee and a team that included Wally Buckley, Charlie Woodsby, Al Woods, Darden's brother Denham and later Gus Gornto, opened the first Red Lobster seafood restaurant in Lakeland, Florida, in 1968, they were two innovative entrepreneurs who had no idea they were about to change the dining-out habits of an entire nation. By finding a niche between quick service restaurants and fine dining and using a simple concept of uncommon quality, service and affordable prices, Red Lobster and its parent company, Orlando-based Darden Restaurants Inc., has ascended to unprecedented heights.

Darden and Lee's timing was perfect. In the late 1960s fast food restaurants were starting to flourish, but many consumers were also seeking full-service restaurants that were affordable, unpretentious and had high service levels. Enter Red Lobster, which has been at the forefront of casual dining trends ever since.

From the small, casual restaurant in Lakeland, Darden Restaurants has evolved to become the world's largest casual dining restaurant company (based on market share, sales and number of company-owned and operated restaurants). The company operates more than 1,300 Red Lobster, Olive Garden, Bahama Breeze, Smokey Bones Barbeque & Grill and Seasons 52 restaurants in North America, employing more than 140,000 people who serve 300 million meals annually.

Astounding Growth

In its 2004 fiscal year, Darden Restaurants' sales totaled a whopping $5 billion–plus. When you pause to think where the company started, Darden is truly the quintessential great American corporate success story.

The first Red Lobster in Lakeland was inspired by two of Bill Darden's other restaurant ventures, Jacksonville's Thunderbird Inn and onetime Orlando landmark Gary's Duck Inn. At the time, Darden and his team sensed that the Red Lobster concept would catch on, but their initial goal was just to grow into a good-sized regional chain with 30 or 40 restaurants.

Red Lobster's mass appeal took hold rather quickly. In 1970, just 24 months after opening the Lakeland restaurant, Darden sold his growing chain of five restaurants (two of which were under construction) to Minneapolis-based General Mills, joining the company as president of the restaurant division. Suddenly, Darden Restaurants was on a fast track to bringing its affordable, service-oriented, casual seafood restaurant concept to the rest of America. One immediate challenge to this growth was finding enough high-quality, competitively priced seafood to support it. So, in 1971 the company formed an in-house department for worldwide seafood purchasing. Just three

Bill Darden and Joe Lee.

years later, General Mills opened its 100th Red Lobster restaurant in Omaha, Nebraska.

In 1975 Joe Lee was named president of Red Lobster and by 1981 General Mills had opened the 300th Red Lobster in Dallas, with chain-wide sales exceeding $500 million. A year later, using Red Lobster's recipe for success in the casual dining market, General Mills introduced the first Olive Garden in Orlando, which today is the largest casual dining Italian restaurant chain in the United States.

In 1995, General Mills spun off its restaurant division, and an independent company called Darden Restaurants, Inc. was formed, named for its late founder, who died in 1994. Since then the company has introduced two other successful casual dining concepts, Bahama Breeze and Smokey Bones Barbeque & Grill, and a new test restaurant, Seasons 52.

The future certainly looks bright, as Darden has embarked on an aggressive plan to grow sales to more than $10 billion in the next 10 years, led by new CEO Clarence Otis, who assumed the role in November 2004 when Joe Lee retired from the position, and new Darden President and Chief Operating Officer Drew Madsen. Lee is still Chairman of Darden's Board of Directors, until his full retirement in December 2005.

Core Values

Lee explains the company's growth this way: "We take great pride in providing a terrific dining experience to every guest, every time, in every one of our restaurants. That is how we will be the best company in casual dining, now and for generations."

Otis adds that Darden's core purpose is "to nourish and delight everyone we serve," and credits the company's success to a set of core values that Bill Darden established and the company has adhered to since its inception. They include: integrity and fairness, respect and caring, diversity, always learning - always teaching, being "of service," teamwork, and excellence.

Otis says if you walk into any of Darden's more than 1,300 restaurants you'll see employees who live these core values, as evidenced by their unabashed enthusiasm, spirit and dedication to their jobs.

Lee—a farm boy from Waycross, Georgia, who often picked cotton to help his family—traces

his caring corporate value system to his disciplined upbringing, the traditional values he learned as a youngster and the success principles he learned from Bill Darden.

Before starting Darden Restaurants, Bill Darden once owned several Howard Johnson's restaurants and a collection of lesser-known restaurants and inns. His uncompromising philosophy, passed on to Lee, focused on teamwork, quality food, fair play and customer service.

Darden lived long enough to see the company he started break the $1 billion sales mark before he died in 1994 at age 75.

Bahama Breeze puts guests in an island state of mind.

Seafood Success

For more than 36 years, Red Lobster has continually proven you don't have to be located next to an ocean to provide a great seafood dining experience. With nearly 700 restaurants and total sales of $2.4 billion in fiscal 2004, Red Lobster is the market leader in the seafood casual dining segment.

One of the keys to Red Lobster's success story has been its ability to change and evolve with its customers' wants and needs. For instance, ongoing menu innovations are constantly being added to well-loved, longtime favorite entrées like the Ultimate Feast and Walt's Favorite Fried Shrimp. Red Lobster's menu also puts a large emphasis on fresh fish, harvested from the Gulf of Mexico to the Caspian Sea and shipped directly to the restaurants. The company is also responding to the dining public's desire for new, more exotic tastes with dishes like basil-infused fish with mixed greens salad and farm-raised tilapia in a bag.

Red Lobster also recently introduced its LightHouse Selections Menu, highlighting healthy entrées, including nutrition information, and a new Kids' Menu that includes healthy options and was named Best Kids Menu in America by *Restaurant Hospitality* magazine.

Italian Inspiration

One of the top-performing brands in casual dining, Olive Garden has grown even faster than Red Lobster. Only five years after Darden started expanding the full-service casual Italian chain nationally, it exceeded $500 million in sales, and three years after that sales had doubled to more than $1 billion. Today, Olive Garden serves about three million guests a week in more than 540 restaurants throughout North America, and had total sales of $2.2 billion in fiscal 2004.

In its early years, Olive Garden was perhaps best known for its unlimited soup, salad and breadsticks and hearty entrées. Those are still on the menu, but the company has changed with its guests' tastes, offering increasingly authentic but still approachable Italian food, some of it developed at Olive

Garden's own Culinary Institute of Tuscany in Italy, where its managers also go for inspiration and an immersion in Italian cuisine and culture. Italian inspiration also led to Olive Garden developing one of the best wine lists in casual dining.

The essence of the Olive Garden brand is to delight guests with a genuine Italian dining experience featuring fresh, simple, delicious Italian food, complemented by a great glass of wine in a comfortable home-like Italian setting, where you're welcomed by people who treat you like family.

A Relaxing Island Escape

Since its debut in 1996 on International Drive in Orlando, Bahama Breeze has proven to be a big hit with diners who love the Caribbean-inspired menu, tropical drinks, live music and relaxing atmosphere. The company has grown to more than 30 restaurants and generated sales of $176 million in fiscal 2004.

At the heart of Bahama Breeze's appeal is a "kitchen forward" philosophy. All lunch and dinner items are made-from-scratch by chefs, and the tropical drinks are hand-crafted too. From the wood-burning oven and open flame grill to the sauté chefs in the large, brightly-colored display kitchen, Bahama Breeze offers an extensive selection of fresh seafood, chicken, beef, pork, salads, sandwiches, wood-fired pizzas and pastas.

Take a glance at the Bahama Breeze menu and you'll find familiar fare with an enticing island twist, like the coconut prawns appetizer, served with a citrus-spiked mustard sauce; West Indies Ribs, slow-roasted with caramelized sweet guava glaze; Jumbo Sea Scallops with Chimichurri, a fresh lemon-cilantro pesto; and Jerk Chicken Pasta, Jamaican-style marinated chicken with fresh asparagus and bowtie pasta. Even the desserts are island-inspired, featuring items like Piña Colada Bread Pudding, Chocolate Island and Key Lime Pie made fresh daily in the restaurant.

It's easy to imagine you've escaped to the islands at Bahama Breeze—the restaurant itself doesn't look or feel like any other casual dining establishment. A soaring tin roof, tropical wood architecture, bright colors, Caribbean appointments and artwork and lush landscaping help put guests in an island state of mind. Adding to the good-time island ambience is a covered outdoor deck, featuring live island-style music and a festive atmosphere. In colder climates, the decks are glassed in and heated during the winter months.

The Real Flavor of Barbeque

Make no mistake—Americans are passionate about their barbeque. With Smokey Bones Barbeque & Grill, Darden Restaurants has successfully tapped into that passion. Featuring a combination of genuine slow-smoked barbeque and other American favorites, served in a lively, comfortable mountain lodge setting, complemented by 40 televisions and plasma screens showing nearly all professional and college sports events and other televised entertainment, Smokey Bones is scoring big with consumers across the United States.

Since the first Smokey Bones opened in September 1999 near

Smokey Bones is feeding America's passion for genuine barbeque.

Fashion Square Mall in Orlando, the brand has quickly grown to over 100 restaurants in 18 states… and counting.

Using an 11-hour slow-smoking process that creates moist, succulent meats that are flavorful and tender, Smokey Bones' menu includes platters of full- and half-racks of baby back and St. Louis-style ribs, hand-pulled pork, brisket and choice steaks, as well as grilled chicken, fish, buffalo burgers, salads and veggie burgers. Some side offerings include Brunswick stew, barbeque baked beans and coleslaw. The restaurant's signature dessert is a bag of freshly-baked hot cinnamon-sugar doughnuts.

Enhancing Smokey Bones' appeal is the restaurant's Rocky Mountain lodge décor, 30-seat center bar and individual table-top sound controls that let guests choose which of the multitude of televisions they want to listen to. The brand's unique combination of great barbeque, mountain lodge comfort, televised sports viewing and warm, friendly service is helping Smokey Bones grow into Darden's next major national brand.

What's Cookin'?

Darden Restaurants' "guest first" philosophy is more than a slogan. It helps guide the company in developing new casual dining concepts, from restaurant design, ambience and décor to recipe and menu development. Using exhaustive market research, competitive analyses and well-honed business models, Darden has managed to stay at the forefront of the highly competitive and constantly changing casual dining industry.

The company's newest test concept, Seasons 52, is a perfect example. A casually sophisticated fresh grill and wine bar on Sand Lake Road in Orlando, by Altamonte Mall in Altamonte Springs, Florida, and in Ft. Lauderdale in South Florida, Seasons 52 features seasonally inspired, nutritionally balanced menus and an extensive international wine list, and is strategically positioned to appeal to baby boomers looking for more sophisticated fare with high nutritional value.

Designed to explore popular culinary trends such as grilled foods, fresher ingredients, bolder flavors and lighter preparations, the Seasons 52 concept, as the name suggests, offers guests a constantly changing array of the freshest seasonal vegetables, fruits, fish and meats. Menu items include Cedar Plank Salmon, Mesquite Roasted Pork Tenderloin with herb polenta, and Grilled Deep Water Sea Scallops with toasted pearl pasta and grilled fresh asparagus. And the restaurant doesn't rely on added fat or high-calorie sauces to enhance the flavor of items like these—in fact, Seasons 52 doesn't use butter and you won't find any fryers in the restaurant. Instead, they use an assortment of natural cooking methods, such as open-fire oak and mesquite grilling and stone hearth roasting, to prepare deliciously satisfying, full-flavored meals, none of which are more than 475 calories!

To complement the seasonally fresh cuisine, Seasons 52 also features an extensive international wine list of more than 100 different wines, 65 of them available by the glass. With its warm contemporary design and artwork, as well as a piano bar, Seasons 52's ambience is upscale and elegant, yet casual and unpretentious.

A Legacy of Community Involvement

Long before corporate responsibility became a staple of business school curricula, Bill Darden lived the principles of good corporate citizenship. He fostered a spirit of volunteerism, ethical business practices and philanthropy that still define Darden Restaurants today.

By combining the hands-on efforts of thousands of Darden volunteers across North America with the financial resources of the philanthropic Darden Restaurants Foundation, the company is helping create thriving, vibrant communities that offer a high quality of life for all citizens.

"As we see it, our success is directly related to the community's success," says Joe Lee. "That's why we believe we have a responsibility to enhance the quality of life in communities where we do business."

When Darden employees see a problem or need in the community, they jump in and go to work. On almost any day of the year, you'll find Darden volunteers working to better their communities by serving on boards of charitable organizations, working in the schools, raising funds to fight disease, collecting toys for underprivileged children, mentoring students… or any of thousands of other acts of community service.

In Central Florida, Darden is a trusted and respected corporate citizen that has donated millions of dollars and hundreds of thousands of volunteer hours to programs like United Arts, the Orlando Science Center, Orange County Regional History Center, the University of Central Florida, and Boys & Girls Clubs, to name a few.

That passion for community service is a thread that ties together Darden's diverse community of employees. In fact, volunteerism "runs in the family" at Darden. Red Lobster, Olive Garden, Bahama Breeze, Smokey Bones and Seasons 52 and their employees are all involved in a variety of regional and national community events and programs to find cures for disease, fight hunger, benefit education and

create better communities.

For example, after the devastating hurricanes in the summer of 2004, all 140 of Darden's Florida restaurants participated in Dine Out for Disaster Relief. Every restaurant donated 100 percent of its profits on October 14, 2004, to the Florida Hurricane Relief Fund—a total of $203,000. That was on top of a $1 million grant to the fund from the Darden Restaurants Foundation, to help Floridians most affected by the storms rebuild their lives.

Darden is also committed to promoting and celebrating diversity, not just because it's the right thing to do, but also because the company sees it as critical to future growth. "We respect and cherish the different perspectives and experiences our diverse employees bring to the workplace and believe they make us a stronger company," says new Darden COO Drew Madsen. "In the same way, we also believe supporting and fostering diversity across the nation makes our communities stronger."

That commitment has placed Darden among the top U.S. companies recognized for diversity. In October 2003, the Executive Leadership Council – the nation's largest association of African American officers in Fortune 100 companies – gave Darden its Corporate Best Practices Award for diversity excellence; *Fortune* magazine has ranked Darden among the top 50 companies for diversity since 1999; and *Diversity, Inc.* magazine named the company one of 20 noteworthy organizations for diversity.

In many ways, Darden Restaurants' remarkable growth as a giant in the casual dining industry mirrors the dynamism of Orlando itself. No doubt, both the company and the city are destined for even more success in the future.

Fantasy Of Flight

*F*antasy of Flight founder and creator Kermit Weeks believes that, "flight, more than anything, symbolizes mankind's desire to push our boundaries and reach beyond ourselves," and "while not everyone likes airplanes, everyone has a fascination for flight."

Kermit Weeks, Founder

The Fantasy of Flight Facility

Right: Early Flight Emersion Experience in the Attraction

For those seeking to immerse themselves in a time when mankind was pushing its boundaries in the air, there is no better place than Fantasy of Flight, a one-of-a-kind, aviation-themed attraction located midway between Tampa and Orlando, twenty miles west of the Walt Disney World Resort.

Enjoy the Flight

Guests at Fantasy of Flight can enjoy themed immersion experiences detailing memorable moments in aviation history. Stroll through the 1930s period facility and see part of the largest private collection of vintage aircraft in the world. Fly the flight simulators and capture the sensation of participating in a WWII aerial battle over the Pacific. Tour the back lots of the collection storage areas, the restoration shops, and watch a historic Aircraft-of-the-Day demonstration.

The multi-sensory, self-guided tour begins with the sights and sounds of important eras in aviation and immerses you in Early Flight, which chronicles man's early attempts to fly; World War I, where guests witness the drama of an aerial dogfight; and World War II, which is highlighted by guests boarding a REAL B-17 Flying Fortress and re-enacting a bombing mission at 25,000 feet over enemy territory.

Next, walk through the hangars and see many rare and historic aircraft from the world's largest private collection. Some are famous movie stars like the WWI Standard trainer used in "The Great Waldo Pepper" or the Ford Tri-motor used in the Indiana Jones film "Temple of Doom." You'll find rare aircraft like the P-51C Mustang fighter and the B-24 Liberator bomber as well as replica aircraft of the "Spirit of St. Louis" and Gee Bee Racers.

Once guests view the aircraft up close and personal they may want to climb into a cockpit and take off. Fortunately Fantasy of Flight affords them the opportunity with seasonal vintage open-cockpit biplane rides and hot air balloon flights.

One of Kermit's passions is the restoration process and guests are allowed a behind-the-scene's glimpse of expert craftsman restoring vintage aircraft. In the Back Lot area, guests view an eclectic collection of aircraft parts, movie props, and a warehouse filled with hundreds of vintage aircraft engines. Kermit doesn't collect anything he does not intend to fly, so many of the aircraft are kept flyable. One is flown daily during the aircraft of the day talk and demonstration.

Compass Rose Restaurant

Enhancing the overall experience at Fantasy of Flight are the Compass Rose Diner, a full service, Art Deco style restaurant and a gift shop with a mix of hard-to-find, aviation-themed merchandise, aviation antiques, books, videos, and apparel.

Extraordinary Events

For meetings, incentive groups, and corporate parties, Fantasy of Flight provides an intriguing ready-made venue for special events. The complex, which can host parties of 50 to 5,000, has 85,000 square feet of function space. Where else could you find a better environment to inspire you employees to "Soar to the Sky" or "Fly to New Heights"? One event possibility may include a lavish, sit-down dinner in USO style, surrounded by famous aircraft and servers in period uniforms and costumes. How about a laid back approach and throw your corporate picnic for your employees and families with aircraft rides and a barbeque?

To assure an event is truly memorable; guests can get behind the controls of a Corsair Fighter flight game and engage in a mock air battle over the Pacific Ocean by diving, barrel rolling, and dog fighting their way to victory. Groups and individuals can play for score, making the experience a superb activity.

The Grand Vision

A world-renowned aerobatics competitor, aircraft designer and builder, Kermit Weeks is also a respected entrepreneur with big dreams. Immediate plans call for a series of expansive hangars that will feature each important period of aviation in its own period environment including a turn of the century exposition hall, WWI airfield, Golden Age period area, WWII airfield, and Clipper Seaplane Base.

Kermit's long-term vision sees Fantasy of Flight as part of a bigger project to create an area known for unleashing human potential. In many ways the future Fantasy of Flight will look like a theme park on the surface, but Weeks says, "We will be a park with a purpose!" By using the entertainment industry and man's fascination for flight, we hope to get people to reflect on their experience of life, discover their purpose and still have lots of fun!

Weeks says, "We are very proud of what we have created so far but are very excited about the future," and reflects that, "this is not just my vision, but everyone's—to discover and realize their full potential." Fantasy of Flight will continue to develop and grow, as it becomes all it can be as "An Attraction on a Higher Plane."

Corsair Flight Game in Fightertown

North Hanger: Private party in the North Hangar with the Sunderland Flying Boat

It may come as a surprise to many, but the largest private accredited institution in the United States is University of Phoenix. Founded in 1976 to address the needs of working professionals in a knowledge-based economy, the University of Phoenix's innovative learning model allows students to attend classes at the times and places that best fit their schedules.

Offering on-line classes, weekly face-to-face classes with instructors or a combination of both, University of Phoenix offers undergraduate and graduate degrees in an efficient and convenient program for working professionals.

There are more than 150 University of Phoenix campuses and learning centers in the United States, Puerto Rico, and Canada. Online courses are available around the world. University of Phoenix opened its first Florida campus in Orlando eight years ago and now has three locations in the Orlando metropolitan area—Maitland (2290 Lucien Way), South Orlando (5750 North Major Boulevard) and East Orlando (1900 Alafaya Trail). Future plans call for expansion outside the Orlando metro area.

Curriculum That Counts

One of the key elements to the University of Phoenix's astounding success is time-saving flexibility for its busy students whose average age is 34 with eleven years of work experience. Students have three options to take classes: exclusively online, in a structured on-site environment one night a week with an instructor or FlexNet®, which offers a combination of online and in-class instruction. In addition, learning teams, a collaboration of three to five students, are organized to replicate the typical work environment. Students can conduct virtually all administrative business via the Internet, including ordering books, and can address research needs with access to the University of Phoenix Online Library.

At various University of Phoenix campuses, the curriculum emphasis is on degree programs and professional certificates in many high demand fields, including Business, e-Business, Technology Management, Information Systems, Criminal Justice, Education, Counseling and Nursing. Enhancing the curriculum are customized training and onsite programs to many of the world's largest corporations.

University of Phoenix programs are designed to leverage an adult student's experience to cover more ground in less time. The programs emphasize the immediate application of all learning to the workplace and are continually updated to include the skills and expertise that are in high demand. Faculty at the University of Phoenix are industry leaders with graduate degrees who average 16 years of practical experience and hold high-level positions within their fields.

Competitive tuition is a strong appeal at the University of Phoenix, which offers cash paying plans allowing students to pay for one course at a time, as well as several low-interest financial aid options for those who qualify. Major corporations are firm believers in the University of Phoenix mission as nearly 60 percent of all University of Phoenix students receive all or part of their tuition from their employer.

Park Avenue, Winter Park, Florida.
Photo by Randa Bishop

Central Florida News 13

*F*rom minute-by-minute tracking of hurricanes and other severe weather developments to covering important local stories in-depth, Central Florida News 13 prides itself on an ability to bring immediate local television coverage to a wide variety of news concerns. Living by the slogan "All Local, All the Time," Central Florida News 13 offers 24-hour access to local, national, and international news, as well as weather and sports stories that impact the entire Central Florida area.

Seen exclusively on Bright House Networks, Central Florida News 13 has a staff of reporters and news professionals who work around the clock to provide the latest local news and weather. In addition, the news channel offers special segments on a wide variety of topics relevant to daily life, including Your Health, featuring the latest information from the world of medicine; Your Fitness, with advice on exercise and nutrition; Your Home, providing helpful advice for the do-it-yourself enthusiast; Smart Woman, a daily report addressing health, money, family, career, and other issues; Florida on a Tankful, a travel segment detailing interesting and fun locations around Central Florida; Generation to Generation, a look at our aging population's relationships with family, friends, and our community; Your Kids, which focuses on issues related to the younger generation; Building Community, spotlighting businesses in the community that are making a difference in people's lives; Your Technology, a review of what's new in technology; Lawn and Garden, featuring tips on gardening in Florida's unique environment and Focus on Finance, aimed at higher-end investors looking for long-term financial planning.

Enhancing Central Florida News 13's comprehensive local coverage is a content-sharing partnership with CNN, Tribune and other 24-hour news channels across the country. Other major news partners include, Orlando Sentinel, Orlando Business Journal and El Nuevo Dia.

The Future is Bright

Central Florida News 13 made its debut in October 1997 as a joint venture, the first ever partnership of its kind joining a newspaper and technology/entertainment company together for a station featuring local news 24-hours a day, 7 days a week. In 2004, Bright House Networks assumed full ownership of Central Florida News 13 from Orlando Sentinel Communications and now operates the news channel exclusively.

"Bright House Networks brought a phenomenal new dimension to our product," says Robin Smythe, Central Florida News 13 general manager. "It's one of the premier providers of technology in the market and one of the most innovative technology companies in the nation."

Bright House Networks provides cable television entertainment and high-speed Internet access to more than 750,000 customers in a nine-county area of Central Florida. Owned by Advance/Newhouse, Bright House Networks serves over 2 million customers in cable television systems in and around Tampa Bay, Central Florida, Indianapolis, Indiana; Birmingham, Alabama; Bakersfield, California; and Detroit, Michigan along with several smaller systems in Alabama and the Florida Panhandle. The company also exclusively provides Bay News 9, a 24-hour local news station in the Tampa Bay Area. Advance/Newhouse is a privately

held company with headquarters in Syracuse, New York. The Advance/Newhouse partners' other interests include Conde Nast and Fairchild magazines, PARADE magazine, daily newspapers serving twenty-six cities, American City Business Journals, which publishes business journals in over forty-five cities, Advance Internet and CondeNet, producers of online services, and significant interests in Discovery Communications, Inc. and Time Warner Telecom, Inc.

Inside Look

"Central Florida News 13 is a much different product for the viewer than local broadcast news programming," says Smythe. "We're only in the news business and we don't have to work within the constraints of entertainment programming commitments. We have the sufficient air-time and resources to provide comprehensive coverage especially in times of weather emergencies and late breaking local, national, and international news that affects Central Floridians."

Smythe says producers at Central Florida News 13 work diligently to provide concise, informative reports that are not sensationalized. "That's one of the reasons our channel is constantly on at fire stations, hospitals, restaurants, and other businesses," says Smythe. "They know they can trust News 13 to provide accurate, up-to-the-minute information that is useful."

Weather Coverage

Smythe is particularly proud of Central Florida News 13's weather coverage. Weather reporting in Florida is never taken lightly, especially by viewers who constantly seek up-to-date information about rapidly changing weather patterns ranging from massive hurricanes

and summer thunderstorms to occasional freeze warnings and windswept wildfires. Central Florida News 13 puts a strong emphasis on the immediacy and accuracy of its weather reporting. Staffed by highly trained, experienced meteorologists and reporters, Central Florida News 13 offers more in-depth coverage more often than anyone else in the Central Florida viewing area.

Weather reporters known as "Stormchasers," are constantly on the road monitoring weather developments. They provide immediate updates on changing weather patterns. Featuring state-of-the-art radar and forecasting technology, Central Florida News 13 features "Weather on the 1's" every ten minutes to keep viewers abreast of weather conditions.

Helping Central Florida

Central Florida News 13's focus on localism is an integral part of the daily fabric of life in Central Florida in ways that transcend its position as a 24-hour news source. In 2001, the news channel was the first recipient of National Philanthropy Day Outstanding Media Award of the Central Florida Chapter of the Association of Fundraising Professionals. News 13 health reporter Carolyn Scofield won two separate awards from the American Heart Association for Excellence in Cardiovascular Communications in 2003 for stories on heart disease. The Orange County Child Abuse Prevention Task Force, which is involved in child abuse and neglect prevention projects, awarded Central Florida News 13 its "2004 Superstar Prevention" award citing that station's efforts to inform residents of local nonprofit resources and improving access to services for many struggling families.

Nemours Children's Clinic

*F*or anxious parents with sick children, the Nemours Children's Clinic located in Orlando, Florida is a welcome oasis for hope and healing. Inside its doors on West Columbia Street near Orlando Regional Medical Center, the atmosphere and attitude at Nemours is positive, uplifting, professional, and patient-centered to afford every sick child access to the best possible care for their health problems.

Since its founding in 1996, the combination of high quality care in a child and family focused environment at Nemours has served thousands of infants, children, and adolescents from the greater Orlando area.

By offering a long list of pediatric specialty medical services with a staff of more than fifty pediatric physicians, Nemours can serve most children with acute health problems and needs. Among the specialties provided are Anesthesiology, Audiology, Behavioral Pediatrics, Critical Care, Endocrinology, Gastroenterology, Genetics Me-

tabolism, Hematology/Oncology, Hospitalist Program, Infectious Disease, Nephrology, Orthopedics, Otolaryngology, Pulmonology, Surgery and Urology.

"With so many services available in a multi-specialty group practice, it saves parents and kids a lot of time and, just as important, helps alleviate stress," said Dr. Mark Swanson, Medical Director of the Nemours Children's Clinic in Orlando. "We believe children do much better when they have access to the type of care and environment available at Nemours."

"Our goal at Nemours is a simple and direct one," said Swanson. "We want to address the specialty healthcare needs of all the children in our region." The vast majority of Nemours' patients come from Orlando and the twenty counties nearest the city.

Nemours cared for more than 227,000 children with complex or chronic medical conditions during 2003, making them one of the nation's largest pediatric sub-specialty group practices. More than 400 pediatric physicians, subspecialists and surgeons serve at sites in Delaware and Florida. Nemours owns and operates the Alfred I. duPont Hospital for Children in Wilmington, Delaware, as well as four major children's specialty centers in Wilmington, Jacksonville, Orlando, and Pensacola. The hospital in Delaware features the nation's largest academic pediatric orthopedic practice, as well as a specialized cancer program for children.

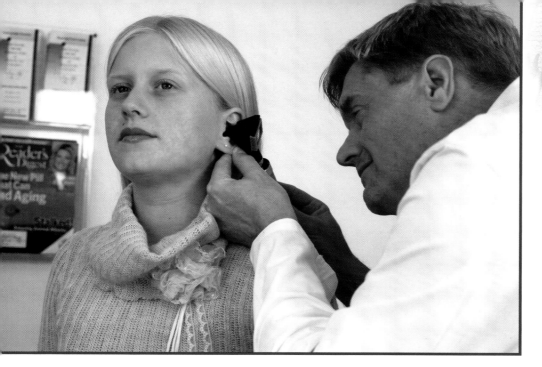

Nemours Legacy

"It has been my firm conviction throughout life that it is the duty of everyone in the world to do what is within his power to alleviate human suffering. It is, therefore, natural that I should desire, after having made provision for the immediate members of my family and others whom I have seen fit to remember, that the remaining portion of my estate be utilized for charitable needs."

These heartfelt words, recorded in the will of philanthropist Alfred I. duPont, provided for the establishment of Nemours. Mr. duPont died in 1935 and Nemours was incorporated the following year. Since 1940, Nemours has operated non-profit health care institutions to carry out its mission: To provide leadership, institutions, and services to restore and improve the health of children through care and programs not readily available, with one high standard of quality and distinction regardless of the recipient's financial status.

Nemours health, prevention and research efforts include more than 300 researchers focused on making a difference in the lives of children by shortening the distance between theory and practice.

Expanding Possibilities

To better serve the children of Central Florida, Nemours will debut a new, comprehensive, state-of-the-art building in late 2006 on a 14-acre site across from the Mall of Millennia. Utilizing the latest high technology and an expanded physician roster, the new center promises to offer a 21st century complex that can address an even wider range of children's health-care issues.

"We're very excited about the possibilities at our new location because it will merge a world class facility, the latest in technological advances and excellent, dedicated physicians in a setting where we can offer the absolute best treatment and care," said Swanson. "The new building will be easily expandable and will allow us the flexibility to grow with Orlando."

While Washington Mutual is the seventh largest bank in the U. S., they really don't view themselves as a bank. Breaking numerous stereotypes of a traditional bank, the company sees itself as a provider of financial services to the general consumer. Unlike most banks which put an overemphasis on large business and wealthy clients, Washington Mutual strives to bring great value and friendly service to middle market consumers and some business owners.

Different and Delightful

Walk into any Washington Mutual store (the company does not call them branches) and you won't see employees wearing mundane dress shirts and ties. Rather, the look is smart casual, typically a stonewash shirt with a Washington Mutual logo and khaki pants. Employees are situated at open work stations with a video screen that allows easy access to financial services and customer balances. Washington Mutual's newest concept store is called "Occasio," which features a friendly concierge who directs first-time customers who might not be familiar with the company's unbank-like design and approach. Appearing more like a welcoming retail environment, Washington Mutual's goal is to break down barriers between customer and employee.

Washington Mutual is also decidedly different than your average fee-happy bank. They were the first national lender to offer free checking to the mass market. Washington Mutual offers free checking with no minimum balance to avoid monthly fees; no charge for using an ATM, doing a debit card transaction or seeing a teller; no requirement that the customer accept check safekeeping; and no requirement to use direct deposit. There isn't even a charge for basic online banking. Better still, it only takes $1 and the price of checks to open an account.

Innovation is the Key

Rapidly expanding, Washington Mutual has 1,800 stores in eleven states, including 53 stores in the Greater Orlando area which have 550 employees and approximately $1.8 billion in deposits. The Seattle, Washington-based company's vision is to become the nation's leading retailer for financial services. Judging from its recent accolades, the company is well on its way to achieving that goal. It has been voted the "Number One trusted retail bank for customer privacy" two years in a row by *American Banking Magazine*. *Fortune Magazine* ranked Washington Mutual number one across all industries in innovation in its "America's Most Admired Companies" issue.

Innovation is the engine that has propelled Washington Mutual to unparalleled success in the highly competitive financial services arena. The company's latest innovation is its Home Loan Center of the Future which features a retail store area stocked with helpful books, and high-speed Internet access to provide online house tours and fast links to loan calculators and research tools.

One of the innovations Washington Mutual is most proud of is its CAN! (Committed Active Neighbors) volunteer program, which last year saw employees donating nearly 200,000 hours of their time at more that 2,200 local events and celebrations throughout the country. In Orlando, volunteers contributed to organizations such as the United Way, March of Dimes, and Habitat for Humanity.

Pottery student at the Crealde School of
Art. Photo by Randa Bishop

Ginn Clubs & Resorts

A Florida vacation can certainly be a luxurious treat for a family, but what if a vacation didn't have to mean returning to ordinary accommodations when the day was over? This is a question that Bobby Ginn pondered when he began his company more than thirty years ago, and it's what keeps him reshaping the idea of what a family vacation should be with each new resort community his company creates.

Reunion Resort & Club of Orlando's Clubhouse overlooks the Arnold Palmer Signature Legacy Course.

Redefining the Florida Vacation

As a private real estate and resort development and management firm, Ginn Clubs & Resorts' reputation for building leisure and resort communities in Florida is unsurpassed. It has gained international distinction as a company dedicated to the creation of world class residential and resort properties, as well as the development of mixed-use properties and golf courses designed by PGA champions. Whether you arrive in Florida ready to hit the links or simply to spend some quality time with your family, you will find what many have already discovered: Once you arrive at one of Ginn Clubs & Resorts' resort communities, you'll leave only to come back again soon.

Location, Location, Location

Florida offers a gorgeous year-round climate that attracts northern vacationers when winter hits. It's easy to simply think of Florida as one of the fifty states, but when you look at Florida from the perspective of world geography, what once was uniquely American has now expanded, with the help of Ginn Clubs & Resorts, to a popular destination for vacationers the world over. The Florida peninsula reaches out into the Atlantic and beckons

to vacationers from South America, Europe, and Australia, among other distant locales. The diversity of the people booking stays in Ginn resorts is remarkable, although all of these visitors choose Florida for the same reasons: beautiful climate, gorgeous accommodations, and the wonderful people who welcome them to their vacations.

A Place Where Memories Come to Life

With the wealth of locations, styles, and amenities offered by Ginn Clubs & Resorts, one would be hard pressed to rank the resort communities in order of preference. Indeed, this task would be like choosing between rubies and diamonds or, as Bobby Ginn, President and CEO of Ginn Clubs & Resorts, suggests the equivalent of asking him to pick a favorite among his own children. Perhaps the easier task, then, would be to choose a property that is the company's true calling card; the one that best proves the mission of Ginn Clubs & Resorts and, better yet, offers a glimpse of the greatness yet to come. The choice would have to be Reunion Resort & Club of Orlando.

The name of this premier property alone is an indicator of the company's vision in creating its design. The look and feel of the resort community is that of a place where vacationing families feel like they are coming home to a friendly community, rather than an impersonal hotel environment.

Do the names Arnold Palmer, Tom Watson and Jack Nicklaus ring any bells? These three PGA champions have designed the resort's three Signature golf courses, including Palmer's Legacy Course, Watson's Independence Course, and Nicklaus' Tradition Course. In addition to premier golfing opportunities, guests will enjoy a multi-million dollar water and swim pavilion, a spa and fitness center, tennis courts, horse stables, and trails for riding, biking, and walking. All told, it is quite possibly the finest backyard in America.

In 2004, Ginn Clubs & Resorts set the bar high when it made a total of $170 million dollars in sales in only six hours when the Reunion's West Side went on the market. The market has given Reunion resounding endorsements, making it one of the most rapid-selling communities in Florida real estate history, and there is little wonder why: With the seemingly endless amenities and opportunities, Reunion is destination living at its finest.

The Guard House at Reunion welcomes owners and guests.

Many of the homesites at Bella Collina overlook the shores of Lake Apopka.

The impressive grand entrance at The Club at Hammock Beach.

Uncompromising Standards and a Love for the Land

Bella Collina, a primary residence club community, evokes a Tuscan spirit to be surpassed only by Italy itself. Nestled on 1,900 acres of picturesque green hills, residents literally have the best of both worlds. Bella Collina homeowners can live only twenty-five minutes from downtown Orlando, yet still enjoy the naturally calm and beautiful setting of orange groves and woodlands of Florida's highlands. With views of Lake Siena and Lake Apopka, it is not surprising that Bella Collina broke Reunion's selling record, this time selling a total of $174 million dol-

The Club at Hammock Beach offers spectacular views of the Atlantic Ocean.

lars' worth of homesites in only four hours, during its initial sales event.

Yet another choice for guests and members is Hammock Beach. The Club at Hammock Beach, which is a 12-story luxury suite tower offering guests majestic views of the Atlantic, is the crown jewel of the entire community. The Club, built on one of the last major tracts of the East Coast's undeveloped oceanfront, presents picturesque views of the ocean, as well as a multi-million dollar water and swim pavilion. A first-class spa and fitness center, golf, sumptuous restaurants, and an array of recreational and social amenities, will certainly maintain a full schedule for members and guests.

Are We There Yet?

Although Ginn Clubs & Resorts has dedicated itself to the development of Florida resort properties, Bobby Ginn states that if and when their clients begin to crave another type of vacation, whether it be a new style of relaxation or even a new geographical location, Ginn Clubs & Resorts will happily oblige. Thousands of acres are un-

The picturesque setting at Bella Collina.

der development in Florida alone for future ventures, but if members and guests should decide they want a different climate or other amenities, Ginn Clubs & Resorts stands ready for the task. Already it has answered the call with Belvidere Resort & Club encompassing Belvidere Cottages, RiverTowne Country Club and Patriots Point, in Mount Pleasant, S.C., just twenty minutes from Charleston.

"Wherever the clients want to go, we'll go, too," says Bobby Ginn, indicating that the Bahamas, Virgin Islands, Colorado and California may be future locations of Ginn Company resorts.

Ginn Clubs & Resorts might be paving the way for future generations of vacationing families, but its method for receiving feedback and suggestions from clients is decidedly traditional. In addition to an interactive Web site through which clients may post suggestions and comments, Ginn Clubs & Resorts contacts resort visitors and primary residence owners via telephone. Bobby Ginn affirms just how valuable the experience of speaking directly to the clients can be for

current and future real estate ventures.

"Our members and guests shape what we do," he says. By the way things are shaping up for Ginn Clubs & Resorts, Florida can expect to be entertaining vacationing families for many generations to come.

Seven Eagles Resort Villas at Reunion Resort & Club of Orlando.

Bank of America has been a leader and pioneer in the Central Florida banking industry for decades.

Since its early beginnings dating back to 1807, Bank of America has always been about higher standards. Throughout history, the bank has been a pioneer in shaping the U.S. banking industry and has helped influence America's landscape and culture.

During the Great Depression, when no other bank would put up the funds, Bank of America helped finance construction of the Golden Gate Bridge. And, as the only bank willing to invest in the fledgling motion picture industry, Bank of America financed hundreds of popular movies like *Gone with the Wind*, *Lawrence of Arabia* and Walt Disney's *Snow White and the Seven Dwarfs*. Mr. Disney's dreams were further fulfilled when Bank of America lent him the money to build Disneyland—and the Disney dream lives on right here in Central Florida. It's the innovative services and high-tech products designed to make life easier for its customers that are at the core of Bank of America's success story. Bank of America introduced the first ATM network and now boasts the largest proprietary ATM network in the nation with 16,500 ATMs and an award winning Web site comprising the largest on-line banking customer base in the world with over 12 million active users.

Central Florida Bank of America customers, like other customers across the nation, have access to the vast resources of one of the world's leading financial services companies while experiencing the local bank's community friendly, service-first attitude that emphasizes individual customer satisfaction. Walk into any Bank of America center in Central Florida—there are over 95 centers and 170 ATMs—and you will quickly notice a welcoming atmosphere where each consumer's needs are important. "Providing a higher standard of service to our customers everyday is our mission," Says Ed Timberlake, President of Central Florida. Moreover, the banking firm meets growing business needs by serving small and middle market businesses and large corporations with a full range of banking, investing, asset management and risk-management products and services. Bank of America is the number one Small Business Administration (SBA) lending company in Florida and has assisted small businesses locally through generous funding of the Hispanic Business Initiative Fund—an organization providing technical assistance and micro loans to the Hispanic business community. The bank's ongoing support has encouraged business development and improved capacity for the Central Florida business community.

Community Development

In 1998, Bank of America made an unprecedented ten year, $350 billion commitment to community development lending and investment. In Orlando and Central Florida, that has meant more than $3.3 billion in community development lending and investments. In 2004, the bank launched a new nation-wide goal to lend and invest $750 billion over ten years with a focus on affordable housing, economic development, consumer lending, and small business lending.

One of the more prominent local results of Bank of America's Community Development Banking program is the City View de-

Community partners join together at the groundbreaking of the City View development. Among those pictured here are Ed Timberlake, Bank of America President, Florida Secretary of State, Glenda Hood and David Hughes, CEO, Hughes Supply Inc.

velopment in downtown Orlando. City View is the largest mixed-use construction project in the history of the city and was built through a strategic alliance between Bank of America, Hughes Supply, Inc., the City of Orlando, and the Orlando Neighborhood Improvement Corporation. This investment and lending partnership resulted in a combined $65 million dollar development, keeping 600 jobs and adding 266 market-rate and affordable apartments in downtown Orlando. City View has served as a catalyst for further investment and ongoing revitalization of the historic Parramore neighborhood.

Community Involvement

Bank of America has always believed its success and that of the community in which it is located is tied closely together. In Central Florida, the company demonstrates its commitment through a variety of ways, most notably through associate volunteerism and board involvement, foundation and volunteer grants, matching gifts and sponsorships. Bank of America has one of the largest philanthropic budgets of any financial institution in the United States. In 2004, they contributed more than $108 million in cash to non-profits and in 2005 the bank will begin its unprecedented $1.5 billion, ten year philanthropic goal. Locally, Bank of America's history of philanthropic contributions exceeds several million dollars and can be seen through the success of many local programs. For instance, through the bank's generous support of educational programs like those offered by Junior Achievement, YMCA Y-Achievers, Boys & Girls Clubs and others, hundreds of thousands of Central Florida students have been positively impacted. Giving back to the community is a Bank of America tradition and

bank associates play an important role in keeping that tradition alive. Associates of the bank—over 1,500 in Central Florida—are committed and caring individuals that exhibit these traits through participation in bank-sponsored programs like "Volunteer Time in Schools." This program allows full-time bank associates to take up to two hours of paid time off from work each week to volunteer in schools. Through the Team Bank of America volunteer network, associates participate in a multitude of community events each year such as the United Way Days of Caring and the March of Dimes Walk-a-Thon, where Bank of America was named the #1 Bank Fundraiser.

In an effort to uniquely recognize the people and non-profits that positively impact our communities, Bank of America launched the "Neighborhood Excellence Initiative"-a program created to reward and nurture specially selected organizations, local heroes and student leaders for their "excellence" in community work. The program awarded $500,000 to its honorees who helped create a positive change in local communities. Recipients included the Second Harvest Food Bank and A Gift for Teaching, who each received $200,000 in unrestricted funding.

Hundreds of bank associates dedicate countless hours of their time to special community events like the United Way Days of Caring.

The Neighborhood Excellence Award recognizes organizations and individuals that make positive changes in their communities. The Second Harvest Food Bank receives the Neighborhood Builders award.

The Team Bank of America volunteer spirit shines at the March of Dimes Walk-a-thon. Philanthropy through generous financial contributions and associate volunteerism is a Bank of America tradition.

Loews Hotels at Universal Orlando

The gorgeous Orlando sunshine is reason enough to plan a vacation, but how can one even begin to choose accommodations in a city known for treating its tourists well? If you are looking for an exciting getaway to a premier resort, then look no further than this top-notch trio of Loews Hotels at Universal Orlando Resort: Portofino Bay Hotel, Hard Rock Hotel, and Royal Pacific Resort.

Guests at Portofino Bay Hotel enjoy the charm and romance of the Mediterranean and can travel aboard complimentary water taxis that connect the entire Universal Orlando Resort.

The music never dies at the Hard Rock Hotel at Universal Orlando. Guests can even enjoy tunes under the water at the hotel's 12,000 square foot pool, complete with an underwater sound system, sand beach, interactive fountains and a 260-foot water slide.

"It has always been our belief at Loews Hotels that the hotel business mirrors the entertainment industry—people want an experience they can remember, that exceeds their expectations, and makes them go 'Wow, this is cool!'" says Jonathan Tisch, chairman and CEO of Loews Hotels.

The range of hotel options at Universal Orlando Resort is further proof of a new wave in vacations. The three on-site hotels provide guests with a world-class resort experience, as well as place them in close proximity to both Universal Studios and Universal's Islands of Adventure theme parks, in addition to CityWalk, Orlando's premier entertainment complex.

Portofino Bay Hotel, which opened in 1999, was the first of the three Loews properties at Universal Orlando Resort. Although Florida is the locale for the 750-room resort, guests feel that they have instead arrived at the real Italian village of Portofino. Every inch of the 49 acres has a Mediterranean mood, from the olive tree-lined cobblestone streets and sidewalk cafes to the Vespas and Italian sports cars parked in the piazza. This premier luxury resort offers the utmost in European style and elegance, with authentic Italian furnishings, marble accents and luxury extras. But the decor and scenery are not the only aspects that have gotten Portofino ranked among the top hotels in the world according to *Travel and Leisure* and *Conde Nast Traveler*. The award-winning Italian cuisine served up at Mama Della's Ristorante and Trattoria del Porto as well as indulgent treatments at Mandara Spa allow each guest to experience la dolce vita - the sweet life.

Loews' second hotel offering lets its guests party like rock stars - literally. The 650-room Hard Rock Hotel gets its inspiration from the original Hard Rock Cafe restaurant, as well as many of the great personalities that make rock n' roll what it is. Guests can stay in the Graceland Suite and receive wake-up calls form the likes of James Brown, Dee Snider, and N'Sync. The mission-style property is reminiscent of the lavish estate of a rock star, complete with a 260-foot water slide, poolside cocktails, and a private beach. The hotel also boasts an extensive collection of rock memorabilia, with each room

A tropical lagoon, swaying palm trees and warm sands tempt guests to shed their shoes and their cares forever at Royal Pacific Resort at Universal Orlando®, A Loews Hotel.

containing art from the Hard Rock Cafe's private archives. Guests can dine in The Kitchen, where they might catch a legendary rock star whipping up a favorite recipe.

If you want to get away to a tropical paradise, Loews Hotels at Universal can take you there . . . without traveling halfway around the world. Royal Pacific Resort is the newest of the three Loews Hotels and opened in 2002. A massive bamboo forest leads guests to the 1,000 luxury rooms and suites. The authentic Kul-Kul tower, which is a structure used by the Balinese to celebrate special events, sets the mood of an island oasis. A bamboo bridge connects to the hotel lobby, encompassing the Orchid Court, an open-air space containing hundreds of colorful orchids and

exotic trees, as well as stone statues and painted panels that are hand-made in remote island villages. The impressive scenery continues with the enormous, 12,000 square foot lagoon pool, which features its own island. When not soaking up the scenery, guests can dine in Islands Dining Room, Jake's American Bar or at Emeril's Tchoup Chop, a fine restaurant offering South Pacific cuisine from celebrity chef Emeril Lagasse.

On-site accommodations certainly make vacation planning much easier, although the wealth of amenities may make choosing a Universal Orlando resort a difficult task! Regardless of which resort makes the top of their lists, guests can definitely expect a vacation experience that is truly extraordinary.

Lush tropical landscaping accentuates the South Seas mood of the luxurious Royal Pacific Resort at Universal Orlando, A Loews Hotel.

Marriott ExecuStay

In the fast-paced, corporate world of today, long-term temporary assignments and relocation have emerged as key components in the overall success plan for many companies. A 2003 survey of meeting planners showed that employees, especially those in a transition phase, are likely to be more happy and productive if they are comfortable in their new environment.

Having the ability to sustain a regular routine and feeling at home while on the road can help employees maintain a positive outlook.

One of the ways to ensure a first-class living environment is by residing with Marriott ExecuStay—a leading provider of corporate and temporary housing—which offers guests fully-furnished, beautifully appointed accommodations in upscale residential communities virtually anywhere in the United States. Plus, guests will relish in the opportunity to earn Marriott Rewards points with every stay—which are redeemable for vacations, hotel stays, airline miles and much more.

While residing in Orlando Marriott ExecuStay can arrange for a home away from home in locations where the guest wants to be, such as near the airport, or close to theme parks, business corridors, or technology campuses.

Just Pack Your Clothes

The Marriott ExecuStay difference starts with a full-sized apartment, which offers ample living space and privacy. Better yet, guests just need to pack their clothes and toiletries. Every ExecuStay apartment features a fully equipped kitchen, including a microwave, full-size refrigerator, conventional oven, dishwasher, toaster, coffee maker, pots, pans, dishware and glassware. Each apartment also includes a washer and dryer. There are one, two, or three bedroom units available that come with standard queen-size beds. Details like artwork and silk plants give the living and dining

rooms a feeling of home and Marriott ExecuStay can customize its furnishings package to meet the individual needs of each guest. Moreover, Marriott ExecuStay apartments can be customized to meet the unique needs of the traveler with add-ons such as an office in the second bedroom or a nursery for a new baby. Most of the apartment communities accept pets.

When the day planner has been set aside and the computer turned off, there are many options for relaxation. Since Marriott ExecuStay-Orlando's apartments are situated in actual residential apartment communities, amenities typically include fitness centers, spas, swimming pools, and tennis courts.

Marriott ExecuStay also helps alleviate stress and anxiety by addressing time-consuming logistical issues. Pressing items such as the hook-up of utilities (including cable, phone, electric, gas, and water), paying deposits, and arranging for the delivery of furnishings and housewares are coordinated by Marriott ExecuStay. Record keeping/expense reporting is made easy because Marriott ExecuStay provides one monthly invoice detailing all expenses.

It would seem that the gorgeous Florida sunshine makes Orlando skies friendlier than most, but it's really Showalter Flying Service that makes flying a pure joy.

A true love for aviation is the initial reason for a successful flying service—and three Orlando aviation pioneers who shared that love changed the face of aviation in Central Florida. In 1945, just after the end of World War II, Howard and Sandy Showalter, along with Ford "Buck" Rogers, moved to Florida, where they built Showalter Airpark on one hundred acres of land in Winter Park. Their dream was to provide a haven for private pilots and their passengers. Spurred on by the G.I. Bill, the company expanded to include flight training schools at Sanford and Herndon, which was then the Orlando Municipal Airport. A new terminal was built at the airport in 1951, and the team won the bid to start the first Fixed Base Operation there.

The terminal at Herndon saw an increase in business as a general aviation airport in 1968 when the airlines moved to McCoy Jetport (now Orlando International Airport). Herndon later became the Orlando Executive Airport, which today is listed among the ten busiest general aviation airports in the United States.

One of the goals of the Showalter team was to set the standard for aircraft service and support in Orlando. That goal was achieved with excellent customer service coupled with desirable accommodations, and a nationwide reputation for excellence which stands today.

After Howard's death in 1965, Buck single-handedly ran the operation until 1973, when Howard's son, Bob, signed on as partner and Vice President/Sales Manager. This was a true union of good business sense and a love of flying that kept the Showalter dream alive.

In 1994, Bob's wife, Kim, was named President of Showalter Flying Service Inc. after a two-year tenure as chair of the Business Management Committee of the National Air Transportation Association (NATA). Bob and Kim's children assured a third generation of the flying service when they joined the team. Daughter, Jenny Showalter Harwood, has worked as Customer Service Manager since 1996 and son, Sandy, as marketing director and aircraft sales assistant since 2002.

The entire Showalter family has high hopes for a fourth generation in flight with the recent arrival of Evan Lane Harwood, born to proud parents Jenny and Brent. Since Brent is himself a professional pilot, there is little doubt that Evan will share a love for aviation, just like his parents, grandparents, and uncle. It looks like Showalter Flying Service can look forward to many more years of success.

Homewood Suites

Business travelers, vacationers, and visiting relatives all need a place to stay when they are away from home. In the Orlando area, Homewood Suites Orlando-North in Maitland is an excellent choice. Homewood Suites hotels offer more than a box-like room with a bed and a shower. Accommodations include a full kitchen and a living room, separate bedroom and bathroom. Homewood Suites Orlando-North goes beyond even these extras, and it is the extras that make this hotel special.

A complimentary hot breakfast buffet is served every morning. The menu appeals to every appetite, from the coffee-only person to the one who starts the day with eggs, sausages, pancakes, fruit, and muffins, and everyone in between. In the evenings, Monday through Thursday, guests are offered a complimentary "Welcome Home" Dinner, a light evening meal, or if guests have plans for dinner, a chance to relax with complimentary beer, wine, soft drinks and munchies. A warm feeling of home pervades the atmosphere of the hotel. For the guests who want to retreat to their suite and eat in, room service is available from two local well known restaurants.

For the business traveler who must turn out a proposal or keep connected with a home office, the hotel offers a complimentary twenty-four hour, fully equipped business center, and each room is wired for high-speed Internet connection. Complimentary wireless connection is also available. When the time comes to work off stress, there is an exercise room, which is open round the clock.

Amenities for families who are traveling include a pull-out sofa-bed that can sleep two children and a privacy door to the bedroom for parents. "Fun Corners" include games, blocks, toys, crayons, and coloring books, which children can take back to the rooms. A well-stocked video center offers movies and video games, for each room is equipped with a video cassette player and Nintendo.

Homewood Suites was developed by Hilton to compete against Residence Inn by Marriott. In the upper range of upscale extended stay category of hotel chains, Homewood Suites edged out Residence Inn for first place by survey takers. It is not difficult to understand why, since Homewood Suites offers more than just a corporate apartment. This hotel offers all the conveniences of home, whether you are traveling with family or traveling alone. Upon entering, a welcoming lobby with a huge fish

aquarium greets the visitor. Each Suite comes complete with a fully equipped kitchen and contains a full-size refrigerator with icemaker, microwave oven, dishwasher, range, and toaster. There are two televisions with VCR's, two phones, and two phone lines, along with extra space in the closet. Instead of the usual, small, hotel-size chairs, each suite also contains a recliner chair for those kick-off-your-shoes-and-relax times. An outdoor heated pool is available, also. Guest are also provided complimentary transportation to local restaurants, theaters, shopping or anywhere within a 5-mile radius of the hotel. And as a proud member of the Hilton family of brands, Homewood Suites offers Hilton Hhonors points & miles, one of our nations leading frequent guest award programs. Despite all these extras, the rates are comparable to any other hotel in the same class and perhaps even a bit less when the complimentary meals are factored in. A value proposition hard to beat!

The amenities of the hotel are exceptional, but the staff makes all the difference. Staff members are chosen because each fits a niche in the "family", and they are trained with the utmost care. Several of the staff are bilingual and fluent in either Spanish or French, so the international visitor is made to feel comfortable. A 100 percent guarantee comes with every night's stay. Simply stated, if the visitor is not satisfied, the room is free. Guests have rated the hotel in the top ten for the past three years, and Homewood Suites has won the J.D. Power Award for the past two years and just this year the Triple Crown award.

With such exceptional service, it is not surprising that when Hurricanes Charley and Jeanne roared through the area, the hotel was ready to offer any help it could. Although it was forced to turn away many displaced homeowners because all its rooms were already booked, it donated blankets and sheets to a local disaster shelter and ice to anyone who came by looking for a place to stay. A meeting room was set up with games and goodies to help hurricane victims pass the time.
Located on Lake Lucerne, central to businesses and not far from tourist attractions, Homewood Suites Orlando - North is a comfortable, welcoming place to stay for travelers. Whether traveling for business or vacation, guests will find that this hotel is truly a "Home away from Home."

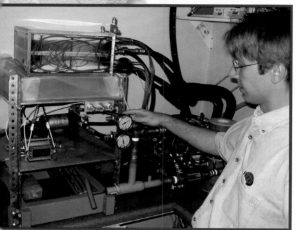

RTI engineer David Van EE Monitors a Prototype Cooling System under development for a High Energy Laser.

*M*ost entrepreneurs start their businesses in living rooms or spare bedrooms, and for most situations, this is entirely appropriate. But if you are someone like Dan Rini, president of Rini Technologies Inc., you'll soon find that you'll need a much bigger space.

Though he earned a PhD in mechanical engineering, Dan Rini has always thought of himself as an entrepreneur. Rini was able to successfully combine his two interests when his work in thermal management caught the attention of the Department of Defense. It was this combination of business intuition and engineering education that gave Rini the tools needed to successfully launch his company.

Going into Business with the Military

As Rini worked on his PhD, he began developing a technology that would work to cool military lasers. A few months before defending his dissertation, Rini presented his ideas to the Missile Defense Agency. Unlike other recent graduates who might find themselves pounding the pavement for employment, Rini's research and development won him a six-month contract with the military for $100,000 in June of 2000 and Rini Technologies Inc. (RTI) was born.

This six-month contract enabled Rini and his firm to further the research and development of the cooling system in order to provide the military with conclusive results of the technology. After a successful six month period, the military then awarded Rini Technologies with a second contract, this time for close to a million dollars.

Rini had begun a very mutually beneficial relationship with the military, receiving contracts over the next few years from the Air Force Research Lab, the Army and DARPA, as well as other military agencies to develop RTI's unique

cooling technologies into prototype systems the military could use. Rini Technologies was started during the time of the telecomm and dot.com bust, so receiving money from venture capitalists was difficult in such uncertain economic times. This made Rini's partnership with the military that much more fortunate, and so his success story continued.

The Nuts and Bolts of Technology

The lasers in question are the ones that the military uses to shoot down missiles; many of the laser technologies funded back in the *Star Wars* days are now becoming a reality, and RTI's advanced cooling technologies are helping to make this possible. Spray cooling is the method used to regulate the temperature of the lasers, which utilizes unique fluids that are sprayed onto the laser elements, and cools them in a more efficient way than can be done with conventional cooling technologies.

Just how hot does a laser get? Despite the fact that these lasers consume as much energy as it takes to power an entire neighborhood, the answer to this seemingly trick question is not very hot at all. That's because RTI's technology is proactive, rather than reactive. The cooling system keeps the laser at room temperature from the start. Without this aggressive cooling, a laser would burn up due to its own heat.

Lasers are not only found in military operations; there are many other commercial ways in which lasers can be used, and Rini Technologies is seeking ways to help

RTI engineers conduct a spray cooling experiment for using in the design of a military laser cooling system.

them all. Lasers are used in factories for cutting and welding metals and other raw materials. Automobile factories would certainly be interested in the results to be gained by Rini's techniques. RTI is also applying this cooling technology to high power electronics used to power electric cars, trains, and Navel ships. Rini currently has a contract with the Office of Navel Research to provide his technology for electric-powered boats and ships.

High Tech Applications for Soldiers and Civilians Alike

When not working on cooling lasers, Rini Technologies is researching and developing personal cooling systems to be used by soldiers, as well as first responders on a local level, such as firefighters, haz-mat teams, and the police. When working in elevated outdoor temperatures while wearing protective clothing, these men and women can become incredibly overheated—that is, until Rini Technologies steps in.

Rini and his team of engineers have developed a personal cooling system so small that it can be worn inside a person's uniform to provide a much cooler and more comfortable environment. The miniature refrigeration system is roughly the size of a water bottle, yet it has enough cooling capacity to regulate an individual's body temperature. The cooler will be worn on the hip, making the individual more comfortable in his or her protective clothing, and therefore better able to respond in tense situations.

RTI currently has contracts from the Army, Homeland Security, and NASA to develop this system and sees a large government market in this area, however a number of more commercial applications of

his technology also exist. Many other people need to keep cool and comfortable on the job and could benefit from this product, including miners, racecar drivers, and even costumed personnel at theme parks!

Research and Development for Products of the Future

With each new contract that comes rolling in for Rini Technologies, it is important to note that the firm does not work for immediate results, but rather a concentrated process of research and development which will culminate in the best possible product. Other high tech firms may have been in business much longer, but Rini Technologies has built its reputation early on simply because it employs better and more effective ways of technology.

Although no business owner is able to predict the future of his or her firm, Rini has a better glimpse than most, because so much of Rini Technologies deals with the development of technology that will be used several years from now.

"In five years from now, we want to have transitioned things out of the laboratory into the user's hands," says Rini. Rini Technologies has secured numerous patents, and is currently undergoing the process for several more, that will enable them to do just that. To expedite the process of getting the product to the user more quickly, Rini will consider outsourced production, or licensing his technology to companies who will then create the product.

RTI engineer Brad Carman and company president, Dr Rini monitor the performance of an experimental cooling technique.

RTI's Miniature refrigeration unit used for personal cooling, along side a water cooled jacket.

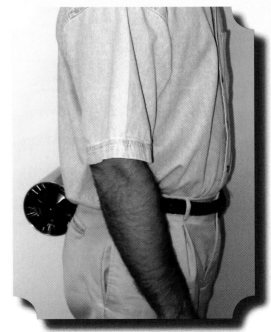

RTI personal cooling unit is worn on the waist line for unrestricted mobility

Frontgate Realty

Imagine a picture-perfect community, one that is the ideal of small-town America, with tree-lined streets, houses with front porches, and early twentieth-century architecture.

Imagine neighbors strolling along the sidewalks, waving hello, and maybe stopping for a chat. Now imagine all this with hidden twenty-first century technology and a long-range blueprint for maintenance and growth. This is Celebration, Florida, a planned community developed by the Walt Disney Company. If this community appeals to you and you would like to live there, the realtor who will guide you is Keith Kropp, President of Frontgate Realty, along with his business partner and Vice President, Kit Zayas, and their staff of fifteen fellow real estate agents.

Frontgate Realty is a relatively new agency, but Kropp has worked for many years in the realty business. When Disney's Michael Eisner decided to take Walt Disney's vision of the community of the future and turn it into a reality, Kropp was chosen to work with the Imagineers to develop this gem within the 33,000 acres upon which Disney World is built. (If you lived in Celebration, you could drive to the entrance of Disney World in minutes without ever having to travel on a highway.) He became the broker of record for the Celebration Company, and helped to generate a plan of housing development and sales. Once the land was divided into house lots, recreational areas, space for a town center, conservation land, and a site for a school campus, he oversaw the lottery for the first three hundred and fifty house lots. He then decided that he wanted to become more per-

sonally involved in helping people through the labyrinth of buying or selling a house; he had a dream of starting his own agency. Finally, Frontgate Realty became a reality, where, he says, he and Zayas have worked hard to develop a good team. The office thrives on teamwork and camaraderie, and each of the nineteen brokers and staff trusts the people with whom he or she works.

However, Frontgate Realty recognizes that it also has a responsibility to the community. The business is involved with the future generation by providing the salary of a part-time technology support position for the faculty who teach at the high school. It also supports the Celebration Foundation, which funds community activities and organizations, such as the Boy Scouts, Girl Scouts, a barber shop quartet, and other non-profit groups.

The community of Celebration is growing, and house values have doubled and tripled since its inception. Frontgate Realty had $60 million in sales in 2003 and expects to do more than that in the coming years. "People recognize that we have a good name and a good reputation," says Kropp. What more could anyone ask?

A cursory glance at Health Central's angled modern building, with its signature red element flanked by yellow trim accented with purple neon, and there is little doubt this is not your typical, mundane hospital. Once inside, Health Central's stunning five-story atrium lobby with trees, waterfalls and grand piano further enhance the hospital's well-earned reputation for innovation and patient comfort.

A Medical Mall

Unlike many hospitals which offer a sprawling campus approach, Health Central features a "medical mall" concept that provides one-stop shopping for healthcare. The 171-bed acute care hospital, medical office building with over 60 physicians, state-of-the-art emergency center, cardiac unit with diagnostic catheterization lab, pediatric unit, and maternity suites are all in one building. Adding to Health Central's self-contained environment is a long list of special features such as a retail pharmacy, vision center, catering services, helipad, and wellness program.

Health Central completed a multi-million dollar expansion in 2001 that included an expanded emergency room and waiting area, thirty new inpatient beds, new observation and recovery units and an advanced cardiac care department. One of the hospital's newest innovations is a Women's Center which offers a menu of advanced services and treatments targeted to women's health issues. The Center includes a day spa with traditional spa services such as manicures, pedicures, and facials as well as massage therapy both in the Wom-

en's Center and at bedside. Health Central also maintains Express Care, a walk-in medical treatment center with diagnostic services.

Off-campus, Health Central's Park is a 228-bed skilled nursing facility housing a state-accredited Alzheimer's and Dementia Special Care Wing.

Caring for the Community

An independent, not-for-profit, community owned hospital, Health Central bills itself as a place where patients can find "advanced medicine in your own back yard." From its inception in 1993, Health Central has been dedicated to pursuing the highest level of technology for its patients.

Health Central's legacy of providing outstanding healthcare and innovation dates back more than fifty years to the West Orange Healthcare District when the 40-bed West Orange Memorial Hospital opened in 1952 as the first fully air-conditioned hospital in Florida. With its wide-ranging community assistance efforts and a strong commitment to providing the highest level of technology, innovation, and patient care, Health Central remains one of Central Florida's most valued healthcare facilities.

Westin Grand Bohemian

*T*he multiple award-winning Westin Grand Bohemian sits in the heart of downtown Orlando; however, the hotel has the unique ambience of a sophisticated, upscale hotel in a European capital like Paris, Milan or Vienna. Step into the exquisitely appointed lobby with its vaulted ceiling, red and gold Italian mosaic tiles, stunning artwork and Imperial Grand Bösendorfer piano and you're instantly engulfed by a motif evoking an early 20th century European/Bohemian theme with a contemporary flair.

The rooms and suites are appointed with custom designed furniture combining dark java wood tones with brushed silver accents and soft velvets of purple and red. Upholstered 6'6" tall headboards are covered with rich, colorful fabrics. Amenities abound in the rooms which feature high-speed Internet and e-mail access, three telephones (two of which contain lines with data ports), interactive television with pay-per-view channels and Nintendo, a large work space, a C/D stereo radio, refreshment center, Starbucks® coffee, Jacuzzi tubs and a safe that is large enough to store a laptop computer. On the Concierge floor, guestrooms include Bose® Wave CD/stereo radios and a private lounge.

First and foremost, The Westin Grand Bohemian specializes in providing guests with a wonderful night's sleep. All guestrooms and suites feature Westin's Heavenly Bed, which consists of a custom designed, pillow-top mattress set, down blanket, high quality, high thread count linens, crisp white duvet coverlet and five queen-size and king-size pillows. Some of the guestrooms also offer the Heavenly Bath, a custom-designed shower with a dual showerhead to provide more power and wider water coverage and a specially-designed curved shower rod allowing eight more inches of elbowroom.

Beyond the luxurious guestrooms and suites, The Westin Grand Bohemian has an impressive amenity list that includes a heated

A Distinctive Guest Experience

Billed as "an experience in art, music, cuisine and hospitality which will forever be remembered," The Westin Grand Bohemian has 214 boutique style guestrooms and 36 signature suites. Rare artwork dominates the hotel's elegant personality with more than 150 pieces on display from internationally and locally renowned artists such as Gustav Klimt, Egon Schiele, Larry Young, and David Wu-Ject Key. The extremely rare, $250,000 Imperial Grand Bösendorfer piano, one of only two in the world, was designed by Hans Hollein and it took nearly nine years to build.

outdoor pool and whirlpool spa, an on-site fitness center and spa services, 24-hour room service, Grand Bohemian Gallery, a Starbucks® Coffee Store located on the lobby level and valet parking. Hotel guests also have access, for a nominal fee, to the private Citrus Athletic Club, which is located across the street. For business groups, the hotel has a business center and 9,600 square feet of flexible meeting space, including a 2,800 square foot ballroom and 1,500 square feet of pre-function space.

Whether for a high-profile business dinner or leisurely, romantic evening, The Westin Grand Bohemian has an impressive dining and entertainment menu. The Boheme Restaurant, with its dark wood floors, metallic walls and sheers along with bright purple and green fabrics that cover the seating in the custom designed booths, offers classic, exotic cuisine with a European flair and a modern fresh attitude as well as an extensive wine list collection from vineyards around the world. The Bosendorfer Lounge is popular with many local movers and shakers and hotel guests who relish the hip, yet elegant, cozy setting dominated by a round bar decorated in black marble, red stones and mirror pieces mounted with table lamps with soft, sensual lighting. To hear the wondrous sounds from the Imperial Grand Bösendorfer Piano, the Klimt Rotunda, located at the entrance of the Boheme Restaurant, is great place to soak up the elegant ambience of the hotel.

Awards Abound

The Westin Grand Bohemian is one of Orlando's most celebrated hotels. Since its opening in 2001, it has received numerous accolades such as the AAA Four-Diamond designation, a selection as one of the "Top 500 Greatest Hotels in the World" by Travel & Leisure Magazine, a member of Conde Nast Traveler's 2003 Gold List and a selection as the "Best Power Lunch" by the Orlando Sentinel. Enhancing The Westin Grand Bohemian's reputation as a world-class property was its selection in 2003 as the "Best in Brand" award winner for Westin Hotels & Resorts in North America. The award is given to the one hotel within the Westin brand that receives the highest scores for guest satisfaction involving every aspect of the guest experience.

The Westin Grand Bohemian is a part of innovative hotel developer Richard C. Kessler's hotel collection, a group of properties that integrate distinctive architecture, interiors, art, music, dining and gracious service. The Kessler Collection includes the AAA four-diamond Casa Monica Hotel in historic, St. Augustine, Florida; the AAA four-diamond Celebration Hotel in Celebration near Orlando; the Doubletree Castle Hotel, Sheraton Studio City Hotel, Sheraton Safari Hotel (an affiliated property) and Red Horse Inn in Orlando; the Historic Kehoe House Bed and Breakfast Inn, Mansion on Forsyth Park and Beaver Creek Lodge, Beaver Creek, Colorado and the Kessler Canyon in Grand Junction, Colorado.

Disney/SBA National Entrepreneur Center

*T*he mission for the Disney/SBA National Entrepreneur Center (NEC) in Orlando is bold and ambitious. It strives "to be a leading catalyst for entrepreneurial growth and success." Backed by leading public sector, private industry, and nonprofit organizations, the center features a single location where entrepreneurs may go for assistance. It is only the second entrepreneur center of its type in the nation, the first being the successful SBA-Cisco Systems-San Jose Entrepreneur Center which opened in California in 2000.

The Disney/SBA National Entrepreneur Center is a partnership between the Walt Disney World Company, Orange County, the University of Central Florida, and the Small Business Administration. Each partner has pledged at least $1 million in support.

One-Stop Shopping

Before the Disney/SBA National Entrepreneur Center debuted one year ago, Central Florida entrepreneurs had to search multiple sources to locate the many and varied organizations that offer counseling and other assistance. The NEC consolidates all of the organizations in one location, a spacious, 22,000 square foot office at the Landmark Center in downtown Orlando overlooking picturesque Lake Eola. Decorated in welcoming soft tan and light blue colors, Orlando's Disney/SBA National Entrepreneur Center encompasses two training facilities, conference rooms, numerous office spaces, and a Business Information Center.

The ten service providers who have offices at the center are as follows: The University of Central Florida Small Business Development Center provides a wide range of economic development services to small businesses. The University of Central Florida Technology Incubator offers advice from an Entrepreneur-in-Residence team, individual consultations, and networking opportunities with professionals who have expertise in strategic and technical support, accounting, finance, banking, capital acquisition, law, real estate, human resource management, insurance and risk management, sales, marketing, public relations, and intellectual property. The U.S. Small Business Administration is an organization whose focus is to empower entrepreneurs through access to capital and credit, procurement opportunities, and business development assistance. The Black Business Investment Fund provides loan guarantees and technical assistance to minority-owned businesses. The Florida Black Business Investment Board assists entrepreneurs through a variety of services such as direct loans, loan mobilization funding, cash flow analysis, procurement

assistance, and franchise financing. The Hispanic Business Initiative Fund offers bilingual technical assistance to Hispanic entrepreneurs who are U.S. citizens or legal permanent residents who intend to open or expand a business in Central Florida. SCORE, Counselors to America's Small Business, has volunteer counselors, successful active and retired business people, who offer free counseling and monthly workshops. The Florida First Capital Finance Corporation is a not-for-profit lender that provides low down payments, long-term, below-market rate real estate acquisition loans to entrepreneurs and other small businesses. The Minority/Women Business Enterprise Alliance supports minority, women, and small businesses through educational seminars and workshops, micro-loans, counseling and strategic alliances with Central Florida community partners. And lastly Orange County Government provides a monthly training workshop on how to do business with Orange County, as well as on the County's minority and women owned business certification programs to enhance small business participation in the County's procurement process.

Dreamers & Doers

Whether it's locating venture capital and other financing, developing a business plan, learning about new business technologies, or acquiring business skills training, the Disney/SBA National Entrepreneur Center assists a wide range of clients. It consulted and trained more than 11,500 clients in its first year. Client profiles run the gamut from dreamers who want to turn a personal idea into a successful, thriving business to company owners that need assistance to bring their company to the next level.

The Disney/SBA National Entrepreneur Center eases the anxiety and trepidation felt by would-be entrepreneurs by providing a professional, inviting environment that is solution oriented. Anytime between 8 a.m. and 5 p.m. Monday through Friday, future or practicing entrepreneurs seeking answers and advice can walk into the NEC. Currently about five people walk in without an appointment every day and services are provided to more than 200 people per week.

One of the more appealing aspects of the Disney/SBA National Entrepreneur Center, especially for entrepreneurs with many ideas but limited monetary resources, is that most of the counseling services are free of charge and the series of training workshops and seminars require nominal fees, typically $20 to $30 per session. Among the offerings are how to write a business plan, organizing cash flow accounting, sales basics, insurance basics, and patents, trademarks and copyrights.

A key component of any entrepreneurial venture is research and the NEC's on-site Business Information Center provides a free of charge, well-organized venue for clients to address a wide variety of information concerns. The stand-alone, self-service lab has computers, high-tech software, online research, library materials, and other support services. In addition, sample business plans and market research models are available for review.

Photographer Biographies

Bill Bachmann:

A native of Pittsburgh, Bill Bachmann travels the world shooting advertising and editorial assignments for a wide variety of clients. Bill has photographed over 900 magazine covers, traveled to well over 150 countries on all seven continents, and authored five books & many magazine articles. His work is represented in stock agencies in most of the developed nations on earth, and his gallery work is displayed worldwide. A frequent guest lecturer, while also appearing on TV talk shows in many countries, Bill is proud to call Lake Mary - and Orlando - home.

Randa Bishop:

From Australia to Zimbabwe, Randa Bishop has photographed in over 60 countries and 50 islands, throughout the world. She has particularly large colorslide archives of Canada, Greece, Las, Vegas, Mexico, and the Caribbean.

Her travel images appear regularly in leading American and International magazines, and newspapers—publications such as *National Geographic, Travel & Leisure, Geo, Stern, Los Angeles Times, Junior Scholastic, Geo Mundo,* and many, many others. Her feature stories cover a wide variety of subjects from solar-powered airplanes to young children learning how to be astronauts.

Eric Breitenbach:

Eric Breitenbach is a documentary photographer and filmmaker who has exhibited his work in both media widely throughout Florida and the southeast. Since 1991 he has had films shown on public and cable television, and more recently has produced documentaries for The Sundance Channel, Fox Television, Lifetime Television, and National Geographic Explorer.

His photographs have been published in such magazines as *Newsweek, Details, The New York Times Magazine, Essence, DoubleTake,* and *Information Week.* He is one of ten photographers represented in *A New Life - Photographs From The Suburban South,* published by DoubleTake Books and W.W.Norton.

He is a senior professor in the Visual Arts Department at Daytona Beach Community College where he has been employed since 1981. He has also taught at the University of Central Florida and at Rollins College. He lives in Sanford with his wife Phyllis, stepdaughter Natalie, and an array of four-legged companions.

Eric Dusenbery:

Eric Dusenbery has been a commercial/documentary photographer in Orlando, Florida for over 20 years. His work has appeared in numerous publications and he has been the recipient of several national awards for commercial/editorial photography. Once known for his strong color photographs, Dusenbery now increasingly works in black and white and avoids slick imagery, instead focusing on being unpretentious and straightforward in his photography.

He recently broadened his scope by developing CINDERIC DOCUMENTARIES, INC.,a documentary photography organization, promoting projects of social, cultural, and industrial diversity and striving to explore the preservation of traditional ideas and beliefs that are important to the community, neighborhood, organization, and family.

Phil Eschbach:

Phil Eschbach is a freelance commercial photographer based in Winter Park, Florida. He has over 30 years specializing in Architecture and travel using both film and digital imaging.

Lee Foster:

Lee Foster is a veteran travel writer/photographer with coverages on over 200 worldwide destinations. Over the years, Foster's travel photography and writing have won seven Lowell Thomas Awards, the highest awards in travel journalism. His most recent book is *Northern California History Weekends* (Globe Pequot). Foster lives in Berkeley, California, but considers Florida one of his favorite subjects, and returns once a year to develop new photos and new articles about the state.

Nancy Granger:

Nancy Granger has been a professional photographer for 20 years working in many venues and handling formats from Polaroid 8x10 and now digital. One of Nancy's loves has been historic architecture. In Orlando, Nancy has been a part of the book Treasures for OLD Inc., a historic preservation group. Nancy has also been a participate in the city's Historic Preservation Calendar on a yearly basis. Manipulating and experimenting to bring out the artistic side of the image only enhances the photographic process, and pleasure. Nancy has been nationally and internationally published.

Tom Hurst:

Tom Hurst is owner of Tom Hurst Photography and is one of Central Florida's most sought-after commercial photographers. For more than 14 years, Hurst has served many of the region's leading businesses and organizations in a wide array of industries, from theme parks and attractions to retail and manufacturing.

Shooting exclusively with the very latest digital equipment, Hurst's photographs are used for a variety of advertising, editorial, and corporate communications applications. He also specializes in architectural imagery and still photography for film and television production.

Hurst's photograph's have received awards from the Florida Public Relations Association and have appeared in publications such as *New York Times, Saturday Evening Post, USA Today* and *People Magazine.*

An Ohio native and graduate of Ohio University, Hurst resides in downtown Orlando, where he enjoys experiencing the city's growth, rich diversity and cultural renaissance – often through the lens of his ubiquitous camera.

Michael Lowry:

Michael Lowry specializes in architectural, restaurant, resort, and lifestyle photography. Michael created U-turn Productions, which brings together photography, video, and web design to serve his clients in all their speciality needs.

Ann Purcell:

Ann Purcell has co-authored several syndicated travel photography and travel destination columns, and three travel photography books: The Traveling Photographer, A Guide to Travel Writing and Photography and Stock Photography: The Complete Guide. Ann is a former president of the Society of American Travel Writers. She has contributed illustrations for multiple guide books and has accumulated an impressive collection of captioned color slides from 69 countries.

Carl Purcell:

Carl Purcell's assignments have taken him over three million miles and to 99 countries. He was Director of Photography for the Peace Corps and has authored five books about photography and travel writing. He is a Marco Polo member of the Society of American Travel Writers. Carl produced documentary films and videos for the Department of State for which he received five Cine Golden Eagle Awards.

Philip G. Schwamberger:

Philip G. Schwamberger has been a professional architectural photographer for 20 years, with a background in architectural design. In Orlando, Philip has been a part of the book Treasures for OLD Inc., a historic preservation group. Philip has also been a participate in the city's Historic Preservation Calendar on a yearly basis. Philip has been nationally and internationally published.

Profile Index